»→ PRAISE FOR *BREW B*

"Jereme Zimmerman challenges homebrewer and craft brewer alike to explore the marvelous brewing world of our ancestors, full of every kind of herbal, full-bodied concoction imaginable. The ancient palette of flavors and aromas went far beyond the hopped, dark malted, or sour beers of today's brewing renaissance, which has only just begun and has much to gain by a close reading of this book and its practical application."

— PATRICK E. McGOVERN, author of *Ancient Brews* and *Uncorking the Past*

"Empowering and refreshing, this book throws aside conventional assumptions about brewing dos and don'ts to embrace adventure and intuition. It's all here: flavor, fearlessness, and, most importantly, *fun*. Jereme is an incredibly informed and totally hang-worthy guide, and after journeying with him through oft-overlooked annals of brewing history, I know you'll come away eager to brew beer like a yeti."

— SARA BIR, author of *The Fruit Forager's Companion*

"Gruits and ales and beers, oh my! This book is a must-have for any ferment adventurer. Jereme Zimmerman, in his enjoyable writing style, takes the reader and brewer through the history of these venerable brews and how they played a role in shaping what we now think of as beer. Guiding the reader through ingredients and techniques to make traditional brews, beyond conventional styles, Jereme builds one's confidence to create their own unique draughts."

— KIRSTEN K. SHOCKEY, author of *Fermented Vegetables* and *Fiery Ferments*

"In *Brew Beer Like a Yeti*, Jereme Zimmerman shares his laid-back yet informed brewing style. Exploring ancient brewing techniques and unique ingredients, he presents the reader with a range of interesting recipes as well as the tools to create distinctive brews of one's own. In a beer landscape often dominated by what is new or novel (and often hoppy), *Brew Beer Like a Yeti* is a refreshing and unique addition to the library of any brewer or beer-lover."

— MIKE SMITH, professional brewer; coauthor of *The Comic Book Story of Beer*

"Get your grain buckets and put on your folklore-thinking caps, because *yeti* brewing is about to get real. Jereme Zimmerman takes an unconventional approach to both the historical presentation and brewing methods of ale to deliver this brilliant beer tome. But rest assured, Big Beer won't want you to read *Brew Beer Like a Yeti*. You'll know too much and stop drinking their swill."

— FRED MINNICK, author of *Mead* and *Bourbon*

"*Brew Beer Like a Yeti* is an essential companion for any beer enthusiast. Both well-researched and informed by the author's personal experience, Jereme Zimmerman's latest book guides you through the joys of beer, from its ancient origins and the rise of regional styles to the delight of brewing with foraged ingredients from your own backyard. Whether you're a novice fermenter or an established brewer, Zimmerman's approachable recipes, paired with his fresh perspective, will encourage you to experiment and embrace the funky, wild side of beer."

— ANDREW MOORE, author of *Pawpaw*

"Jereme Zimmerman has captured the mystique and magic of fermentation in this paean to beer's vital role in human culture and history. The stories are fascinating and blended with the right amount of technique, so that regardless of brewing experience, anyone can dive headfirst into their own experiments. The essence of fermentation is creativity; this book provides the guidelines for infinite variety."

— HANNAH CRUM, coauthor of *The Big Book of Kombucha*

"If you ever thought you didn't care about the history of brewing, think again! Jereme Zimmerman's new book reminds us that the entire beer industry was built on the traditions and lore passed down from many generations of home brewers like us. In *Brew Beer Like a Yeti*, Jereme effortlessly brings beer, mead, and other fascinating fermented drinks into our home kitchens, while weaving in legends and tales of home brewers from many different cultures around the world. Brewing fermented beverages isn't just an interesting hobby; it's a useful skill to be proud of and a tradition worthy of being passed on. *Brew Beer Like a Yeti* gives you even more reasons to look forward to brewing day, and you will be as excited as I am to share these amazing handcrafted drinks, and the stories that go with them."

— VICTORIA REDHED MILLER, author of *Craft Distilling* and *From No-Knead to Sourdough*

"Jereme's newest book gives readers access to both the folklore and history of brewing ales and gruits, as well as the technical background and modern advances of fermenting beer. I firmly believe that this merging of both old and new in *Brew Beer Like a Yeti* is where the most delicious and innovative ferments live, without the intimidating learning curve."

— PETE HALUPKA, Harvest Roots Ferments

"Jereme Zimmerman's curiosity about beer is contagious, and his explanations of ingredients and processes could make even a wine drinker want to brew beer. This book is a great resource."

— AMY HALLORAN, author of *The New Bread Basket*

BREW BEER

BEER
LIKE A YETI

Also by Jereme Zimmerman

Make Mead Like a Viking

BREW BEER

LIKE A YETI

Traditional Techniques and Recipes for Unconventional Ales, Gruits, and Other Ferments Using Minimal Hops

JEREME ZIMMERMAN

Chelsea Green Publishing
White River Junction, Vermont | London, UK

Project Manager: Alexander Bullett
Editor: Michael Metivier
Copy Editor: Laura Jorstad
Proofreader: Nanette Bendyna
Indexer: Nancy Crompton
Designer: Melissa Jacobson

Printed in the United States of America.
First printing August, 2018.
10 9 8 7 6 5 4 3 2 1   18 19 20 21 22

OUR COMMITMENT TO GREEN PUBLISHING
Chelsea Green sees publishing as a tool for cultural change and ecological stewardship. We strive to align our
book manufacturing practices with our editorial mission and to reduce the impact of our business enterprise
in the environment. We print our books and catalogs on chlorine-free recycled paper, using vegetable-based
inks whenever possible. This book may cost slightly more because it was printed on paper that contains
recycled fiber, and we hope you'll agree that it's worth it. Chelsea Green is a member of the Green Press
Initiative (www.greenpressinitiative.org), a nonprofit coalition of publishers, manufacturers, and authors
working to protect the world's endangered forests and conserve natural resources. Brew Beer Like a Yeti was
printed on paper supplied by LSC Communications that contains at least 10% postconsumer recycled fiber.

LIBRARY OF CONGRESS CATALOGING-IN-PUBLICATION DATA
Names: Zimmerman, Jereme, 1976– author.
Title: Brew beer like a yeti : traditional techniques and recipes for unconventional ales, gruits, and other
    ferments using minimal hops / Jereme Zimmerman.
Description: White River Junction, Vermont : Chelsea Green Publishing, [2018]
    | Includes bibliographical references.
Identifiers: LCCN 2018018905| ISBN 9781603587655 (paperback) | ISBN 9781603587662 (ebook)
Subjects: LCSH: Beer. | Brewing—Amateurs' manuals. | BISAC: COOKING / Beverages / Beer.
    | COOKING / Beverages / Wine & Spirits. | COOKING / History.
Classification: LCC TP577 .Z56 2018 | DDC 641.6/23—dc23
LC record available at https://lccn.loc.gov/2018018905

Chelsea Green Publishing
85 North Main Street, Suite 120
White River Junction, VT 05001
(802) 295-6300
www.chelseagreen.com

For the leading ladies in my life:
Jenna, Sadie, Maisie, and Miss Piggy the dog.

And I dare not forget Mom and Dad;
the rest of you know who you are.

CONTENTS

RECIPE LIST

→ PREFACE ←

Although it took me a year to write, this book was many years in the making. From my first sip of beer, the geek in me has wanted to learn more about this mysterious substance that has since refreshed, intoxicated, enlivened, and yes, sometimes sickened me. I found myself wanting to know its history, how to make it, and why it's referenced in so many of the myths, fantasies, and ancient tales I liked to read.

Once I graduated past Budweiser (which, alas, was my first beer), I began to explore the world of craft beer. While I was a poor student at Berea College in eastern Kentucky, craft brewing was barely a blip on the radar in my area of the country; my options were limited, but I was hooked. Upon graduating from college I wanted to try living somewhere completely different and headed to Seattle, where my love affair with beer really took off. You couldn't throw a stone without hitting a microbrewery or brewpub. A stranger in a strange land, I decided to pick up a hobby while I got acclimated. Brewing beer had been in the back of my mind for a while. My dad made wine for years, so I decided to carry on the tradition in my own way: I picked up a basic homebrewing kit and got to work.

Over time I made a number of very tasty beers using kits, which I often customized with additional ingredients, but after a while it all began to feel . . . canned. Where was the creativity in buying a prepackaged set of ingredients, modifying the recipe a bit, and churning out a batch of brew that wasn't much different from what I could get at the corner brewpub? I know many brewers who are perfectly happy brewing this way, but having grown up "poor" on a Kentucky farm, I was accustomed to making do with what little I could afford and what the land around me offered. Plus, I was homeschooled and slow

An advertisement for a malt tonic produced by the Seattle Brewing & Malting Company, makers of Rainier Beer, circa 1909. Courtesy of Seattle Public Library, Wikimedia Commons.

to make friends, so I learned to be creative and think independently as a necessity. As I grew older I returned to my self-sufficient roots and began to think on how people made beer, wine, and other ferments before the days of homebrew stores, supermarkets, and other modern conveniences.

My earliest experiments were primarily with mead and wine, as these were the easiest to make with rudimentary equipment, easily obtainable ingredients, and wild yeast. This led to several articles for magazines such as *New Pioneer* and *Backwoods Home*, and writing online under the pen name RedHeadedYeti. Eventually I began speaking about natural fermentation, specifically mead making, at events such as the Mother Earth News Fair, and wrote my first book, *Make Mead Like a Viking*.

As I was researching and writing that book, I came across a lot of information about beer, and the book you're reading began to take place both in notes and in sections of text that I set aside when I realized I was going too far off topic. It turns out that references to mead in history and myth are dwarfed by mentions of beer and ale. I thought that would make it easier to write this book, but quickly found that was far from the truth. Not only were there vast amounts of information to pore through—in books old and new, magazine articles, scientific and archaeological journals, websites, blogs, and online forums—but a great deal was conjecture and oft-repeated myth. I may have perpetuated some of this myth to a degree in *Make Mead Like a Viking*, but as I've learned with this book, it's difficult not to. Even the most ardent researchers and respected beer writers repeat "facts" they've come across in book after book, article after article, journal after journal. Many have an element of truth to them, or are just too good to pass up because they make for a good story. As writers we do our best (at least I hope most of us do) to wade through all of the information and seek out original sources, but sometimes fact and conjecture are hard to separate. In this book I have done my utmost to back up every "fact" with as reliable a source as possible, to debunk myths, and to acknowledge when a story, idea, or recipe may not have the origins it is often touted to have. I want to provide an enjoyable, useful read, and leave you with some good stories, but in the end I want to provide edification for future writers and hobby researchers on similar subjects. If I've fallen short in accomplishing this to the degree that I would like, I hope that you'll take up the mantle and keep up the good fight. Beer is not going away. Let's make sure we do our part to help future generations understand where it came from.

ZEN AND THE ART OF YETI BREWING

Brewing beer is easy. There, I said it. I let the secret out. It can't be taken back now.

But first allow me to back up and help you understand the mind-set you need to recognize just how easy brewing beer, ale, and the many variations thereof *can* be. As we will learn, from approximately the 15th through the 18th centuries, the production of alcohol went through a multitude of changes that laid the groundwork for the intricate web of regulations, politics, religion, and just plain pigheaded, opinionated, trollish, how-dare-anyone-think-my-opinion-isn't-irrefutable-truth behavior that we find today. Even a century ago the world was much more entrenched in the traditions of our ancestors. Since then, however, we've found a way to make many things—particularly with regard to food and drink production—exponentially more convoluted than necessary.

In short, brewing beer at home used to be as common as bread making, a fairly simple process that didn't necessarily take a lot of time, as people had a lot of other things to concern themselves with to keep their households in order. Of course there were some time-consuming (but not necessarily complicated) brewing recipes people indulged in when they could, but brewing—and fermentation in general—was just a part of what they did to survive.

I fear I'm already making this seem complicated. Here's how my old friend (he was long dead before I met him) John Bickerdyke approached the matter in his book *The Curiosities of Ale & Beer*, first published in 1889:

> In order to give a proper understanding of our subject, and at the risk of ruining the brewing trade, let us then, in ten lines or so, inform the world at large how, with no other utensils than a tea-kettle and a saucepan, a quart or two of ale be brewed, and the revenue defrauded.
>
> Into your tea-kettle, amateur brewer, cast a quart of malt, and on it pour water, hot, but not boiling; let it stand awhile and stir it. Then pour off the sweet tea into the saucepan, and add to the tea-leaves boiling water again, and even a third time, until possibly a husband would rebel at the weak liquid which issues from the spout. The saucepan is now nearly full, thanks to the frequent additions from the tea-kettle, so on to the fire with it, and boil up its contents for an hour or two, not forgetting to add of hops half-an-ounce, or a little more. This process over, let the seething liquor cool, and, when at a little below blood-heat, throw into it a small particle of brewer's yeast. The liquor now ferments; at the end of a [sic] hour skim it, and lo! beneath [sic] the scum is bitter beer—in quantity, a quart or more. After awhile [sic] bottle the results of your brew, place it in a remote corner of your cellar, and order in a barrel of XXX. [sic] from the nearest brewer.[1]

Brewing can be even easier than this if you're still not feeling quite up to par. The reference to *malt* is to malted grains, which are grains that have been partially germinated to enable fermentable simple sugars and starches to be drawn out by pouring hot water over them to create a *mash*. The water drained from this mash is *wort*, which can then be boiled and brewed into beer. However, you don't even have to go this far. Instead of malt, you can use malt extract (a thick and syrupy or powdered and dry substance that can be purchased in modern homebrewing kits), molasses, sorghum, brown sugar, cane sugar, or any combination thereof. Even yeast can be produced without going to the homebrewing store.

Now that we've recognized that brewing can be easy, it's time to adjust our definitions for beer and ale. Ask any beer geek about the difference between beer and ale and you may end up embroiled in a long, convoluted discussion. While there is a fairly straightforward answer as far as a *modern* definition goes, there is a solid historical reason for the confusion. Reading any text on beer or brewing that precedes the 20th century, it quickly becomes evident that there never was a clear answer—or, more likely, such distinctions were less of a concern in olden days. People fermented booze from whatever they could get their hands on, and their names for what they were drinking changed multiple times both between and within different cultures. As far as you should be concerned, if it tastes like beer, looks like beer, *feels* like beer, then it is beer, ingredients be damned!

In the annals of brewing history, there is an astounding array of information, misinformation, and just plain hyperbole regarding beer. Many recipes and techniques that were very common in olden days are strange or just plain dangerous sounding to modern ears. Some old recipes call for raw eggs or even meat gravy to be added to beer—not necessarily unsafe, unless you're using hormone-infused meat or eggs that don't come from your own backyard (or a trustworthy local farm). Ingredients that were very common in ancient, sacred brews—such as henbane and wild rosemary—are considered dangerous or even poisonous, albeit in large amounts, today. Most people today cringe at the thought of these types of ingredients in their beer but, again, the people who wrote down these recipes lived in a very different world than we do today.

Bruce Lee once said, "Empty your cup so that it may be filled; become devoid to gain totality." Lee, in the tradition of great martial arts and Zen masters throughout history, understood that while both filling one's mind with learning and knowledge and practicing incessantly have great benefits, at some point one must realize that the most important knowing is *not knowing*. This is a crucial piece of wisdom that few fully understand and even fewer practice. The first time I felt truly free to brew and ferment with utter abandon and true passion was when I learned to brew with this mentality.

Modern brewing manuals and the stringent practices I once employed worked well for me—I created a fair share of excellent brews. But something was missing. Brewing day was always a chore and a hassle.

I would run around like the proverbial chicken with its head cut off, trying to make sure everything was just right. I cleaned and sanitized incessantly, making sure my temperatures and times were as accurate as possible, and generally wore myself thin just to make a "perfect" batch of beer. Don't get me wrong—stress is a part of learning—but I encourage you to strive for making your brewing day into a relaxing meditative experience. If you're anything like me, eventually you will have various ferments burbling on countertops and pantries and aging in the cellar or some dark corner of your house or apartment. Visit with these ferments often. Get to know them. Sample as appropriate. Some will not turn out to your tastes. Give those to your friends and significant others; you never know, they may like them (unless your instincts tell you there's something just plain *wrong* about them, in which case toss them).

You can start brewing even with the most rudimentary knowledge and equipment. Over time you will inevitably procure all manner of crocks, jars, bottles, siphons, airlocks, et cetera. But before you begin your new fermentation journey, it's important to stop for a moment, empty your mind, and thank the Ancients for the gifts they imparted. Breathe deep, relax, do some tai chi or yoga, or commune with nature for a while. Then smile, turn on some inspiring music, grab a beer, and get to "work." Call this Yeti Brewing Zen if you will. Begin as your ancestors did, but with the knowledge you have gained from your journey through modern life and the wisdom of the Ancients embedded within. Many aspects of food and drink production and preservation are already a part of our inner consciousness. We just need to put ourselves in the right mind-set to unlock that ancestral knowledge. A good place to start is to go back to what ancient cultures meant when they used their respective words for *beer*. Let's explore, shall we?

PART ONE

HISTORY, MYTH, AND FUN

CHAPTER ONE

A History of Ale and Beer

Ale is made of malte and water
and they the which do put any other thynge to ale
then is rehersed, except yest, barme or godesgood*
doth sofystical theyr ale

Bere is made of malte, of hoppes, and water:
it is the natural drynke for a Dutche man,
and nowe of late days it is moche vsed [used] in Englande
to the detryment of many Englysshe men . . .

—Andrew Boorde, 1547[1]

Beer. It's so ubiquitous that most of us assume we know exactly what it is. But the meaning of the English word *beer* has changed throughout history, where you'll find that *beer* isn't as cut-and-dried as it has come to be in modern times. First, let's look at the modern definition. *The Encyclopedia of Beer* defines beer as:

---

* "God's good": fermentation magic.

Any alcoholic beverage made by fermenting grains and usually incorporating hops. In general (in the United States), the term refers to a beverage that has been fermented to an alcohol level of less than 5 percent alcohol by volume (4 percent alcohol by weight). Most Americans think of lager beer when they hear the word beer, but other types of ferment also are correctly called beer. In England, the word beer is usually used to indicate an ale with a lower alcohol content. The English word beer is from the Latin word bibere, "to drink." Originally, the English word beer referred to a beverage that had been brewed with hops, as opposed to ale, which had been brewed without hops.[2]

This definition shows just how difficult it is to explain exactly what beer is. According to this source, beer is fermented from grain and *usually* with hops; contains no more than 4 to 5 percent ABV; and is distinct from ale (one is brewed with hops and one without) depending on the part of the world you're in. A pretty broad definition, right? Since the two words are often used interchangeably, at least in modern times, let's move on to *The Encyclopedia of Beer*'s definition of *ale*:

A top-fermented beer that is the oldest of all brews. From the Old English alu. Ales tend to be stronger than bottom-fermented beers, and come in a variety of colors. Throughout much of history, ale was an unhopped brew. Primitive, spontaneously fermented ales, still found in remote places, are made from diverse materials such as corn, manioc, rice, and grasses.[3]

Again we see that ale didn't traditionally contain hops. But now we learn that, in a way, ale is a subcategory of beer. Finally, the editors admit that ale can be made from various materials that can't be classified as grain. So beer isn't *necessarily* made from grain, although it generally is. Now let's go a little further back to understand what the various words that came to be our descriptors *ale* and *beer* today meant to historical peoples. In *The Curiosities of Ale & Beer*, John Bickerdyke explains thus:

A word or two now as to the distinctions between the beverages known as ale and beer. Going back to the time of the Conquest, or earlier, we find that both words were applied to the same liquor, a fermented drink made usually from malt and water, without hops. The Danes called it ale, the Anglo-Saxons beer. Later on the word beer dropped almost out of use. Meanwhile, in Germany and the Netherlands, the use of hops in brewing had been discovered; and in the fifteenth and sixteenth centuries, the Flemings having introduced their bier into England, the word "beer" came to have in this country a distinct meaning—viz., hopped ale . . . The distinction between ale and beer . . . lasted for a hundred years or more. As hops came into general use, though malt liquors generally were now beer, the word ale was still retained, and was used whether the liquor it was intended to designate was hopped or not. At the present day beer is the generic word, which includes all malt liquors; while the word ale includes all but the black or brown beers—porter and stout. The meanings of the words are, however, subject to local interpretations.[4]

Confused yet? Let's go even further back. During the Anglo-Saxon period (approximately 410 to 1066) beer was as much a synonym for strong drink as it was a specific type of strong drink. In *A Second Handbook of Anglo-Saxon Food and Drink*, scholar Ann Hager references an earlier historian who believed *Beor* "to be a cereal-derived drink, as he saw *Beor* as etymologically derived from *bere* (barley)."[5] So while some sources, like *The Encyclopedia of Beer*, claim that *beer* is derived from *bibere* ("to drink"), others believe it comes from *bere* (barley).

Another possible Anglo-Saxon source of the word comes from Scandinavia (the Anglo-Saxons resided primarily in the areas we know as England and Denmark today). "*Beor*," Hagen notes, "would seem to have continental parallels, though having had evidence of false etymology in the *beor*/beer derivation, we have to be cautious about assuming that words have similar meanings because they sound similar. *Bjorr*, recorded in Denmark during the Viking period [was] a sweet, strong drink, drunk in the halls of the great, and Valhalla. . . . Unfortunately the possible ety-mology of *bjorr*, deriving from the Latin *biber*, a drink, does not give any information as to what it was made from."[6] In the end, "strong drink" (which was likely made from all manner of ingredients) is the best defi-nition we have for these various words. Regarding ale, Hagen indicates that it was often (though not always, necessarily) a grain-based drink. "The Anglo-Saxons had a term (*malt/mealt*) for malt, and the technology to malt barley, or other grains. . . . Presumably barley was usually used."[7]

Now that we know (or rather, don't know) where the word *beer* comes from and what it actually means, let's dispense with nitpicking over nomenclature and get to the definition of *beer* for the purpose of the book: "a fermented beverage ranging from around 3 percent to around 8 percent ABV (alcohol by volume), usually made with at least some portion of grain but also with varying ratios of alcohol-producing and flavoring adjuncts such as molasses, sorghum, honey, or sugar." For the sake of our modern understanding of what beer is, most recipes and techniques outlined in this book will focus on grain as the primary source of fermentable sugars, but—like brewers of the past—we won't get too concerned if some recipes stray a bit.

Ancient Origins

Nearly all histories of beer start with the ancient Egyptians and Sumeri-ans.* This is for a good reason. These cultures were the first to document their beer-making practices in some form, whether through Egyptian hieroglyphs or the Sumerian "Hymn to Ninkasi," the earliest written description of the brewing process, dated circa 1800 BC. However, beer- and ale-like drinks are referenced much earlier through oral myth and storytelling across many cultures, not to mention traditional brewing practices that likely have been passed down for thousands of years.

Despite our knowledge that the history of brewing goes back much further than the ancient Sumerians and Egyptians, the written evidence

---

* For you historical geography buffs, ancient Egyptians settled near the Nile River in what is now northeastern Africa; the Sumerians were a now extinct civilization in southern Mesopotamia, currently southeastern Iraq.

these cultures left behind is important in that it gives us an idea as to how they brewed beer—and by extension, a likely case for how other cultures discovered and pursued the process of brewing. Most interpretations of the information left behind by the Sumerians and Egyptians suggest the following as the basic process for brewing beer:

1. Barley was harvested (stalk and all), moistened, and left to dry for a day or so.
2. The barley was then moistened again, placed in a perforated vessel, and left until the seeds separated from the stalk.
3. The vessel was shaken to separate the chaff from the grain (in other words, winnowing).
4. The grain was ground and made into bread, which was baked (akin to modern techniques for kilning and drying grains to release starch and sugar for fermentation).
5. Water, possibly sweetened with additional sugars such as honey, was poured over the bread and strained through a sieve.
6. Finally, what was now wort (unfermented beer) was then fermented. It may or may not have been heated first.

This wooden model located at the Rosicrucian Egyptian Museum in San Jose, California, depicts beer being brewed in ancient Egypt. Courtesy of E. Michael Smith, Wikimedia Commons.

The Sumerians and Egyptians didn't just fool around with brewing beer as a hobby; rather, they produced it on a scale nearly akin to today's modern industrialized breweries, and regulated its drinking through formal drinking sessions and designated drinking places. We know that the Sumerians produced several different types of beer, including eight barley styles, eight wheat styles, and three mixed-grain styles. The remains of the world's oldest known brewery—dating to circa 3400 BC—are located in Hierakonpolis (modern-day Al Kawm al Ahmar), Egypt, which was able to produce up to 300 gallons per day of a Sumerian-style beer.[8]

We know, though, thanks to modern archaeological research, that brewing traditions predate the Sumerians and Egyptians by as much as several thousand years. Two researchers in particular, Dr. Patrick McGovern (aka "Dr. Beer"), a biomolecular archaeologist and the scientific director of the Biomolecular Archaeology Laboratory for Cuisine, Fermented Beverages, and Health at the University of Pennsylvania, and Merryn Dineley, an experimental archaeologist specializing in British prehistory, have come up with several interesting finds that shed light on how people brewed beer and other alcoholic beverages before the process was recorded through writing or imagery. As a matter of fact, it very well may be the desire to brew beer that led people to settle into communities and begin domesticating and growing grain.

As for what types of beer they brewed, evidence of a barley and emmer-wheat beer (sometimes also brewed with honey or ground acorns) was discovered by University of Barcelona researchers in the early 2000s. This highly herb-infused beer was stored in jars, which the researchers found in caves throughout Barcelona and in central Spain and determined to date back as far as 5000 BC. Some researchers have also theorized that long horseshoe-shaped troughs found throughout Ireland, known as *fulacht fiadh* (wild pits), could have been the floors of the earliest malt houses. It is suspected that they were filled with malted grains and water and then heated, to draw out the starches and sugars needed to ferment the resultant mash via hot stones, a primitive method that is still used today for *Steinbier*, or "stone beer."[9]

Scholars have long theorized that the dawn of agriculture and the settling down of former hunter-gatherers into communities were precursors to the malting and fermentation of grains into beer. Researchers have been challenging this assumption, however. As Solomon H. Katz and Mary M. Voigt noted in *Expedition* magazine in 1986:

> Our own explanation for the beginnings of cereal cultivation is consistent with the biocultural model for the evolution of cuisine. The key element in this explanation, the event that 'primed the pump' and led people to choose to invest energy in the collection and propagation of wild wheat and barley, was the discovery of new food processing techniques—the sprouting and fermentation of these grains.[10]

The proponents of this "fermentation-first" theory go on to note that it could very well be the altered state of awareness—with no noticeable toxic side effects—brought on by drinking the by-product of fermented grain, along with the "substantial improvement in nutritional value over unprocessed cereal grains," that led people to begin domesticating cereal grains. They theorize that this decision came about due to the following factors: People got a high from drinking beer; they felt better nourished over time when partaking in fermented grains on a regular basis; and they found cereals to be a valuable resource due to the relative ease of harvest and transportation and the extended storage time.[11]

Likely, gruel preceded both bread and beer, as people would have first found that grains were more easily digested when coarsely ground and blended with water. When heated and left to cool, wild yeast would have caused the mixture to begin fermenting, which eventually resulted in the purposeful baking of leavened bread and the fermentation of excess liquid into beer. From there, the process was likely quickly fine-tuned. After all, what sounds more appetizing: an inert, dense, bland gruel, or fresh-baked bread and freshly brewed beer?

Fermentation happens, plain and simple. In every part of the world, it has always been one of the primary ways of preserving food and drink. Before we had refrigerators and pasteurization, it was pretty much impossible to fully stop fermentation. And when it comes to fermenting things with high sugar content, alcohol happens. Even cider, which we have in modern times taken to calling "hard" when it is turned into alcohol, was always at least somewhat alcoholic (depending on the stage of fermentation) in pre-industrialized cultures. So it goes without saying that any fruit or vegetables with high sugar or starch content that indigenous cultures would have had access to would have naturally been turned into booze with or without human intervention.

Indigenous cultures of North and South America have long-standing fermentation traditions, including types of beer. Some of the many drinks we know of are *balché,* mead made from tree bark and honey; *paiwari,* made from chewed cassava or from *manihot esculenta,* a woody shrub native to South America; *pulque,* fermented agave juice; and *chicha,* made from chewed corn. Corn, once it became domesticated enough to produce soft, chewable grains, was *the* grain for producing a wide range of fermented drinks throughout the Americas. Corn was made fermentable for chicha and other corn beers through mastication. Chewing grain kernels is, in a way, another form of malting. The saliva produced from chewing provides the needed enzymes for converting starches into fermentable sugars, while also breaking apart the hard outer kernel, allowing wild yeasts to have their way with the spat-out corn.[12] The primary catalyst for this process is the diastase enzyme (*ptyalin*), which causes carbohydrates to break down into sugars.

When we chew starchy foods and swallow them, the gut finishes the job, with myriad microorganisms processing the starches and passing them along to our cells to fortify our bodies.[13] While our ancestors were whiling away the hours in caves, trying various plants for edibility, they chewed all kinds of stuff, spitting out anything that didn't break down enough to swallow. Among the many dried and preserved organic remains left behind in caves in the Americas from the Neolithic hunter-gatherers who occupied them thousands of years ago was maize (*Zea mays*)—a *lot* of it. Remains of almost the entirety of the plant have been found by archaeologists in these caves. As Dr. Patrick McGovern notes, "Many of the maize remains were congealed together, apparently as the result of assiduous chewing. Quids (chewed wads) of husks, leaves, or stalks were even separated from one another. . . . It turns out that sugar is found not only in the maize kernels. As the plant matures, a lusciously sweet sap flows up through the main stalk and is concentrated in the kernels over time. This liquid can be sucked out of the stem like a mother's milk from her breast. To get even more sugar, you can follow up your sucking by chewing the stem and other parts of the plant. Thanks to the enzymes in our saliva, some of the tough carbohydrates will be converted to the sweet stuff in liquid form, ready to be fermented."[14] One can imagine that it didn't take long for people to notice that the sugary liquids that resulted from all of this masticating fermented over just a couple of days, producing a fizzy, flavorful, and soul-lifting drink.

As with theories about making other types of grain-based beer, archaeologists think that early peoples began to settle in fixed communities in

Traditional chicha should be enjoyed young, while still fermenting. It loses its luster quickly with aging and bottling. More modern brewing methods can be applied when brewing it for long-term consumption.

the Americas once they discovered how to ferment corn into beer- and wine-like beverages, after domesticating the wild grass *teosinte*. Through the research of archaeologists and ethnobotanists we know that early forms of domesticated corn propagated in the Americas around 8700 BC in what is now the Balsas River Valley in southeastern Mexico, with domestication really taking off around 1100 BC.[15] Corn was such an integral part of ancient Central American cultures that it even played a large role in their creation myth. In the *Popol Vuh*, an ancient text that is an invaluable source of information on Mayan mythology and culture, man is created from yellow and white maize dough. There were also various maize gods in Mayan and Incan culture, of which statues were made that still survive today. One more recent example, from AD 715, is stylized with a large headdress in the shape of a corncob, with hair that appears to be made of corn silk. It appears to have been decapitated at some point, which makes sense, as the maize god, like the corn plant, was said to be decapitated at harvesttime and reborn in time for the growing season.[16]

Beer in Early Europe

Although wine was the preferred drink of ancient Greeks and Romans, at least among the elite, there is evidence that a type of beer was drunk by the less fortunate, laying the foundation for beer's reputation as the drink of the working class. As the historian and Stoic philosopher Posidonius noted, "The liquor drank in the houses of the rich is wine brought from Italy. . . . But among the needier inhabitants a beer is drunk made from wheat, with honey added; the masses drink it plain."[17] It was also beer that eventually brought down the Roman Empire. Greek historian and teacher of rhetoric Dionysius of Halicarnassus referred to the drink of the Celts (who were the epitome of barbarism to the Romans) as "rotted barley water."[18] It was this rotted barley water that helped fortify the "barbarians" who attacked the walls of Rome in hordes. It's worth noting that the Celts of the first century drank a brew that differed little from that of the original Neolithic inhabitants of the Orkney Islands, and likely contained psychoactive ingredients. No wonder they fought with such impunity!

But before the Fall of Rome, the Romans expanded their territory west to the British Isles, declining to venture north into the thick, dark forests of Bavaria after encountering a number of ferocious, beer-drinking Germanic tribes. By AD 96, upon conquering most of what became England and Wales, they imported much of their culture, including their wine. However, they also developed a taste for British ale, even commissioning the first officially named brewer in British history, Arrectus, to supply their garrisoned troops with liquid bread.

Although the Roman Empire still preferred wine as the drink of the sophisticated, and spread vineyards and wineries throughout Europe, beer began to take over large swaths of Europe along with the barbarians who drank it in vast quantities.[19] Starting with the Vandals in the third and fourth centuries, who devastated Roman Gaul in AD 406, other Germanic tribes, including the Ostrogoths and the Visigoths, brought the Roman Empire to its knees. By AD 412 Rome began pulling its garrisons from Britain, leaving it wide open to conquest by its original inhabitants, the Picts and the Celts, who vied for control with the Angles and Saxons (hailing from Germany and Denmark).[20]

The Anglo-Saxons brought with them a new drinking culture, along with a designated place for drinking and socialization—the mead hall. Mead wasn't the only beverage drunk in the mead hall, though; ale and wine were also imbibed, and sometimes all three together in a type of grog.[21] The Anglo-Saxons shared similar drinking customs and even gods—with myths that venerated excess both in drink and in battle— with a group of people that resided in northern Scandinavia and would soon take Europe by storm: the Vikings.

We don't know for sure what the ale drunk by the Vikings was like, but judging from archaeologists' (including Patrick McGovern) analysis of residue on pottery shards and from ancient Scandinavian recipes passed down to modern times, it was likely a dark, malty, sweet and smoky beverage of around 6 to 8 percent ABV. It would have been flavored with various herbs, notably meadowsweet and yarrow, and sometimes berries such as lingonberry or cranberry. It may have also had a hint of spruce and an earthy, woody juniper flavor, as the brew would have likely been filtered with spruce or juniper branches. There would certainly have been many variations on this recipe, but most would have had at least some of these elements. As bottling hadn't been perfected yet by Viking times, these ales would have been drunk young and sweet, and sometimes blended with older ales that had started to go sour.

Gruit and the Transition to Hopped Beer

By the 1500s the types of beerlike beverages consumed in Europe and Britain were vast and diverse, and they varied significantly in quality. Industrialization and the development of dynastic states with legal codices (and by extension the laws set forth by the church) brought beer from the home and mead hall to the inn, alehouse, and tavern. The commercialization of brewing brought with it what commercialization usually brings—the desire to produce as much as possible for the lowest cost possible. Because of this, competition was fierce. Rather than compete by producing the highest-quality beverage possible, many brewers cut corners and produced low-grade swill with questionable ingredients.

The one thing most brews had in common was high sugar content, as higher-alcohol brews took longer to spoil. Beyond that, all manner of edible (and some not-so-edible) ingredients were added. London in particular saw a massive growth in breweries starting around the 12th century. Because of its dense population, sewage was literally running

Peasants Eating and Drinking in an Interior by Abraham Teniers (1629–70) is an idealized representation of an early alehouse. Courtesy of Christie's, Wikimedia Commons.

through the streets, polluting the rivers and poisoning sources of drinking water. Until the underground sewage system was put into place after the Great Stink of 1858, fermented beverages were the drink of choice for man, woman, and child. A drink made from water that had been boiled and then preserved via fermentation into alcohol was much less likely to make one sick than what was essentially sewer water.

This naturally led to a population that was constantly buzzed (the buzz of a healthy, lightly fermented, herb-laden drink of 1 to 2 percent alcohol), or just plain drunk, which caused no shortness of concern among the authorities. It also offered them an opportunity. If people couldn't live without drink, then why not tax them? Governments presented this as being for the good of the people, of course. They were helping keep drunkenness under control while simultaneously raising money for infrastructure and services. The people of course saw this, one of history's first sin taxes, as an attempt to take away their hard-earned money, and found ways around the new laws.

One method of taxation was based on the type of establishment. Inns, alehouses, and taverns were all taxed differently. Although these establishments had similarities, each was considered a separate entity by the authorities. Real life made the distinction more difficult, though. The boon to historians is that impeccable records of the number of drinking establishments were kept, though not all businesses registered appropriately, if at all. By the 14th century there was approximately one drinking establishment per 21 London inhabitants. With more than 35,000 residents in city limits alone, there must have been a lot of drinking![22]

To ensure brewers were producing brews of the appropriate quality level, some auspicious individual was given the position of royal ale taster and was officially referred to as the Assize of Bread and Ale. His (or her) job was to visit as many breweries as possible to sample the brews provided and report to the king if the brew had any unsavory elements or was too weak.[23]

Recipes—which tended to vary a lot—began to change due to these new laws and the need to homogenize brewing for easier sales and distribution. Up until around the 15th century, most breweries used a recipe consisting of malted grain and various herbs known as gruit. The Dutch word *gruit* itself had multiple definitions; its initial, singular meaning has grown murky over time. It could refer to a specific drink (a sort of herbed ale), a mixture of herbs and grains cooked down into an extract and dried, or a tax pertaining to its production. Think of it as the precursor to *beer* becoming the generic name for the wide range of fermented grain drinks available today.

But while herbed ales were indeed the norm before hops took over, an herbed ale does not necessarily make a gruit. Herbed ales were popular throughout Europe, and were veritable cocktails of herbs and other flavoring agents, including honey, tree bark, bog myrtle, wormwood, heather, alehoof, meadowsweet, yarrow, mugwort, wild rosemary, and much more. Even plants that are known today to be toxic in large amounts were used for their hallucinogenic properties, including henbane and deadly nightshade. Actual gruit, though, was specific to the Low Countries (Belgium, the Netherlands, and Luxembourg), although it did begin to spread across Europe before being stopped dead in its tracks by hopped beer. The only herbs we know for sure to have been used in gruit were bog myrtle (*Myrica gale*), wild rosemary (*Ledum palustre*), and yarrow (*Achillea millefolium*).

Gruit production was big business, and wherever there is big business, there is government regulation. The earliest documented gruit laws were instituted in AD 974 by Emperor Otto II through a charter that transferred gruit rights from Fosses (Belgium) to the church at Liège. Gruit law was made official at some point (it's unclear when or by whom) as the *gruitrecht* in the Low Countries, which granted the right to make beer with gruit recipes to a limited number of monasteries and towns. While these laws did lead to higher levels of quality and consistent flavoring, their true aim was to ensure that gruit brewers paid the appropriate taxes, which directly benefited nobility and the church. So tightly controlled was the gruit production process that a monopoly developed—in essence a precursor to today's macrobreweries.

The proprietary techniques and ingredients of commercial gruit producers (homebrewers could produce whatever the heck they wanted with little government intrusion) were controlled and protected by an official government representative, the *gruiter*, who operated from a *gruithuis*.[24] The exact nature of gruit is yet another matter of debate among historians. Much of what we know (or think we know) about gruit has been passed down by various writers as fact; however, the original sources of this information are elusive and potentially unreliable. Hence historians are starting to rethink the nature of gruit. One brewing historian, Roel Mulder, posits that one of these original sources, while it pulled from sources of its own, was heavily opinionated:

> What exactly was gruit? The sources are quite vague on this subject, not helped by the fact that gruit disappeared from the Low Countries during the fourteenth and fifteenth century, precisely because brewers started to use hops. Everywhere the gruit monopoly was somehow converted into a general tax on beer, which included the hopped beer. Confusingly enough, this tax was then sometimes called 'gruit' as well, without the act of actually supplying a substance of the same name. As a consequence, in later centuries, people didn't have a clue what sort of thing gruit had actually been. One of the most significant contributors to the debate, and at the same time a cause of more confusion, was the engineer Gerard Doorman (1878–1967). In 1955 he published De Middeleeuwse brouwerij en de gruit ('The Medieval brewery and the gruit'), in which he pulled together a wealth of source material. In his opinion, there was no room for doubt: gruit had been a mixture of herbs.[25]

Others have postulated that gruit may have actually been boiled-down mash that acted as a fermentation enhancer for future batches of wort, as the sugars and nutrients were much more effective in their concentrated form. Pharmacists and physicians often employed this practice to enhance the effects of their herbs and help preserve them, so this is a likely theory.[26] One of the first modern scholars to push for the concentrated yeast-accelerant theory was the Dutch historian Hans Ebbing, who in 1994 contradicted Doorman's findings in his thesis Gruytgeld Ende Hoppenbier. After examining Doorman's work closely, he theorized that Doorman had his own theory in mind at the start and took liberty with the facts. Ebbing determined that gruit was more likely a porridge or thick syrup that could be purchased and transported easily and kept well until being rehydrated, which lends well to the idea of it being a popular substance that was created using closely guarded secrets.[27]

Another source of confusion regarding the actual meaning of the word *gruit* likely stems from its correlation with *fermentum*, its Latin counterpart. *Fermentum*, which stems from the Latin *fervere* (to boil), was often used to describe the entire process of fermentation, or to refer to the final product (that is, beer), but its original meaning was that of a fermentation enhancer, or catalyst (yeast, or possibly yeast with a nutrient blend). *Fermentum* was sometimes used as a synonym for *gruit*, as was *levarentur cerevisiae* (levitating the beer).[28] It's worth considering that in medieval times there was no straightforward definition of *yeast* since it hadn't yet been discovered as a substance of its own, meaning that anything that helped cause a fermentation could be referred to as a *fermentum* or *gruit*.

Gruit, like *beer*, is a word that could have various meanings and spellings depending on the time period and context. One meaning of the word *gruit* (or *grut*) is "small fragments of things." Being that the gruithuis (essentially a facility that had many brewing-related functions) was known to contain a grain-crushing machine, gruit could have been a porridge made from crushed malted grains that may or may not have been flavored with herbs from which wort was extracted and boiled down.[29] So essentially what we have is a word that started out as a description of a process (*fermentum*), became a description of the substance that resulted from the fermentation, then transitioned to a word to reference the legal right to purchase a fermentation starter, and finally made its way into the law books as a term for taxation. Through this strange set of circumstances, what happened—in a way—was that a simple microorganism (yeast) eventually became a legal entity unbeknownst to itself.

Whatever the word *gruit* means, the drink (not the legal entity, yeast starter, or whatever else it could have been) was likely a sweet, sometimes sour, highly inebriating drink with varying degrees of bitterness, herbal flavor, and fruitiness depending on the ingredients. But as it became clear that beer made with hops was more beneficial for industry, brewing laws began to focus more on hopped beers, making it a requirement that beer be made with hops and that gruit be retired. It took several centuries for hopped beers to be accepted by the masses. Many reviled this new substance and held tightly to their precious gruit and herbed ales.

The English in particular clung to their sweet, high-alcohol ales. As hops had spread from the Low Countries, the English were particularly displeased with the Dutch. One 16th-century English source states that hopped beer made men fat, which explained why the Dutch had fat faces and bellies.[30] The fat faces and bellies won the day, as over barely 100 years hopped beer took over England, save for a few alehouses.[31] A popular adage of the time was

> Hops, Reformation, Bays and Beer
> Came to England in one Bad Year

But in a short time, attitudes changed so much that unhopped ale was referred to by William Harrison in 1577 as "an old and sick man's drink."[32] There were several reasons for its rapid adoption, but the biggest was hops' preservative power, giving beer the ability to endure long trips, making it possible for breweries to make large batches of beer and transport it by wagon and boat without worry of spoilage. Not only did this lead to greater consistency, but beer could now be kept long enough to age, resulting in a crisper, more clarified product with an appealing taste (once acquired).

The last nail in the coffin for gruit, at least for commercial breweries, was that beer required less malt—traditionally ale and gruit were made with significant amounts of malt to improve their chances of keeping. With hops, brewers could now cut their grain bills (the portion of a recipe that outlines the types and amounts of grains to use) nearly in half. In the first book written on the cultivation of hop plants and their use in brewing, *A Perfite platforme of a Hoppe Garden* (1576), Reynolde Scot wrote, "And in the favour of the Hoppe thus much more I say that wheras you cannot make above eyght (8) or nyne (9) gallons of indifferent Ale out of one bushell of Mault, you may draw XVIII (18) or XX (20) gallons of very good Beere."[33]

Enter the Reinheitsgebot

To show that they meant business, Germany took the codification of beer a step further, instituting the *Reinheitsgebot* in place of the gruitrecht in 1516 (based on a 1487 law instituted by Duke Albert IV in 1487). The elector of Bavaria, William VI, established the law, which stated that only three ingredients could be used in beer: barley, hops, and water.[34] It's commonly believed that yeast was later added to the law once it was fully understood as a separate substance, but since yeast was saved and intentionally introduced to start new batches, it's more likely that it was a given that beer contained yeast. After all, you can't have fermentation without yeast.

The Reinheitsgebot had an inestimable effect on brewing history, not just in Europe but throughout the world. Rarely do you come across a "traditional" beer marketed and sold anywhere today that doesn't consist of these core ingredients and little to nothing else (take the ubiquitous Corona, Dos Equis, and other "Mexican" beers as an example—all are based on recipes from Germans who settled in Mexico and are by no means traditional Mexican beers). By 1516 Germans had become highly efficient, quality-focused brewers and felt the need to formalize the process that worked so well for them. However, the Reinheitsgebot wasn't just about limiting the number of beer ingredients. German brewers also insisted on using the purest, freshest ingredients available, kept meticulous records, and maintained scrupulous standards. Even today, to become qualified to run an authentic Hofbräuhaus in America, brewers must undergo background checks and inspections from German beer authorities and send samples back to Germany regularly for testing.[35] This is certainly a model worth following, and is in large part responsible for the consistency and quality of German beer, but it is possible to maintain high-quality standards without adhering to such strict guidelines for ingredients, particularly now that we don't live in an era when it is considered acceptable to toss sewage in the streets.

As the transition from household brewing to commercial brewing moved into full swing, men began taking over the brewing world. Up through the Middle Ages, brewing, grain production, and malting were domestic tasks alongside food preparation and crop maintenance. For the most part women ran these operations. These "brewsters" or "alewives" brewed primarily for their own households, but would also sell excess to friends and neighbors.[36] It wasn't the most profitable work, paying much less than what most men made in their trades, but it did help pay the bills, and some industrious brewsters managed to make a thriving business, hanging brooms above their doors to indicate when a fresh batch was ready.

Alewives were often also their community's herbalists. Since many of their ales were made with herbal combinations with specific medicinal qualities, townspeople would come to these women for help with health

ELINOVR RVMMIN,
The famous Ale-wife of *England.*

When Skelton *wore the Lawrell Crowne;*
My Ale put all the Ale-wiues downe.

This image of Elinour Rummin, a famous alehouse landlady, demonstrates the typical derogatory stereotype of alewives as questionable, unsightly characters. Courtesy of Wellcome Images, Wikimedia Commons.

Amber "Pixie" Shehan

My friend Amber Shehan is a fellow brewer, mead maker, plant lover, and overall mischievous miscreant, who for a long time I only knew as "Pixie," as I first learned of her through her website and blog, pixiespocket.com. As we began interacting in social media circles and by email (and eventually met in person for a drink at an Asheville, North Carolina pub), I began to understand why she refers to herself as a "tipsy fae creature." Along with her partner, Eric, she spends her free time as a performance artist—attending fairy festivals, performing in burlesque shows, and just being fae folke in general. As part of that lifestyle, Amber brews up all manner of concoctions and blogs about them on her website.

Although she told me she doesn't often think of herself as a brewer, she does like to concoct all manner of "beers, wines, meads, and things that defy classification." When I asked for her thoughts on the historical place of women in brewing, her response was, "My love of history and the knowledge and skills of our ancestors has made me very aware of the role of women in brewing, from the priestesses of Ninkasi to the household brews that used to be so ubiquitous to every home or inn." Although Asheville experienced a boom in craft brewing starting around the early 2000s, Amber said she has never been made to feel unwelcome and encourages other female brewers to "test the waters."

problems. But the paternalistic society that dominated the Middle Ages could only tolerate giving women this much sway for so long. Disgruntled men who ran the power establishments and superstitious peasants began associating the brewing cauldrons and brooms with witchcraft, not to mention the tall, wide-brimmed hats alewives wore to stand out while selling their wares in the marketplace.[37] All of these factors combined to cement the image of the conniving, cackling witch with a wide-brimmed hat and broomstick indelibly into popular culture.

In sharing her recipes online and viewing her website statistics, she has noticed a strong following of women passionate about brewing, but has also noticed male followers with similar reactions. "I think the love of brewing transcends our perceived differences!"

As for her brewing technique, she told me, "I am a mad scientist, a witch with a cauldron! I love to explore my yard and wild places to see what is blooming and make brews based on whatever is in abundance." Rather than focusing on technicalities and precise measuring, she admitted, "I throw the idea of consistency out of the window—most of my brews are a one of a kind. . . . My technique is 60 percent intuition, 20 percent personal technique, and 20 percent pure luck and magic." Her preference is to mix whatever sugars and flavoring ingredients sound good (or are seasonally available) at the time, throw in whatever yeast strikes her fancy, taste the brew once it's most of the way through primary fermentation, and either bottle or rack onto some additional sugars or flavoring ingredients if she feels it needs a bit more of something. If all else fails, she adjusts the flavor with one of her homemade syrups when she opens a bottle. Like me, she doesn't worry too much about what to call each brew. "I don't enjoy the current trend of making hyper-specific brewing techniques the feature of the experience," she told me, "but I do like knowing what to expect if I order an ale from a brewpub!"

As brewing transitioned from "just" a household task to a profitable commercial venture, the role of women was diminished. Women never stopped brewing entirely; they often kept up with the low-paying, low-skill aspects of brewing—or continued to run much of the business—while men were the faces of the business and eventually took over the trade entirely. So remember this, fellas, we have women—many of whom were publicly reviled and privately relied upon—to thank for the beer we drink today.

Lager Crosses the Pond

The Netherlands was one of the first parts of Europe to become heavily urbanized in the Middle Ages. Consequently, brewing practices were highly efficient; the Dutch consistently produced high-quality brews, in particular due to their use of hops. As did ale in England, hopped beers quickly replaced gruit as the beer of choice for Dutch commercial brewers. Over time, the people acquiesced (begrudgingly at first) and gruit fell by the wayside. In addition to building some of the first industrial-sized breweries by the 1500s and surpassing the Germans in both quality and quantity—not a bad feat!—the Dutch also had a sophisticated distribution model and were much more open to trading in foreign markets than most other Europeans. Because of these combined factors, they were leagues ahead of other American colonies when they settled New Amsterdam in 1612—and built New York's (as it would come to be known) first brewery. They also had much more success than other colonists in cultivating the necessary ingredients for beer, growing rye, barley, wheat, oats, and hops with nary a problem.[38]

Germany wasn't far behind, though—in a short time German immigrants were producing beer in America in volumes that rivaled the Dutch. They weren't producing the robust beer (primarily made from oats with wheat and barley as adjuncts) of the Dutch, though. The Germans had become experts in a fairly new style of beer—and one that took over America through much of the 20th century—the lager.

To *lager* means "to store," which is what Bavarians had been doing with their beer for centuries. With access to cool mountain caves, and blocks of ice from rivers and lakes, they were able to store their beer for much longer than other regions of Europe. But it wasn't just long storage that made the lager the king of German beers. Unlike the dark, malty, yeasty, fruity beers they had become accustomed to, some Bavarian beers started coming out of lagering clear, crisp, evenly carbonated, and refreshing. Through some new magic, German brewers accidentally invented a brand-new style of beer. Unbeknownst to them, the yeast strain *Saccharomyces eubayanus*, which had previously existed only in Patagonia, had begun propagating in Bavarian beers, with the only plausible explanation for its arrival in Europe being that it stowed away on a ship coming back from the New World. *Saccharomyces eubayanus* didn't work on its own, though; it actually fused with *S. cerevisiae*—a yeast strain that had been used (albeit unknowingly by brewers until modern microbiology) to ferment alcohol and leaven bread for centuries to create a hybrid, *S. pastorianus*.[39] In sum, a wild South American yeast strain became a crucial player in a style of beer that is now associated with both German brewing and 20th-century American macrobreweries.

Schlitz, "the beer that made Milwaukee famous," was one of the earliest German American breweries. Courtesy of Daderot, Wikimedia Commons.

The lagering process, combined with modern refrigeration and transportation methods and the Germans' obsession with quality control and pure ingredients, opened the floodgates for the glut of large German American breweries that popped up as Germans began emigrating to America. Although sadly, the rich, malty, smoky brews of the past were largely forgotten, a variety of new styles were made possible by *S. pastorianus*, including bocks, doppelbocks, *Märzens, Helles*, and the almighty pilsner, the workhorse of 20th-century mega-brewing. By 1873 America had 4,131 breweries producing more than 9 million barrels of beer a year—primarily lager.[40]

Prohibition, Macrobreweries, Homebrewing, and the Craft-Beer Revolution

America was on the way to becoming the world's largest producer of beer, but one bump in the road altered the course of beer history forever—Prohibition.

America's Prohibition era had its seeds in Britain's early-19th-century Temperance movement, when a number of people began preaching the unthinkable—too much booze is bad for you! This was already understood (but largely ignored) when it came to spirits, but beer and wine had been regarded as healthful beverages for so long that hardly anyone suggested drinking of all types of booze should be curtailed. In fact, it was considered a necessity for workingmen in particular to have several drinks throughout the day to stay fortified (what else were they supposed to drink, water?). This changed when social reformer and politician Joseph Livesey began to campaign on the benefits of sobriety for factory workers, pointing out that workers who were constantly buzzed were more prone to accidents, were often tardy, and lacked the required precision for increasingly monotonous and detail-oriented factory work.[41] Temperance groups began to spring up all over England, and the movement had its proponents in America as well, though it was largely ignored by the drinking class until its explosive rise in the late 18th and early 19th centuries.

America's Temperance movement was largely related to the campaign for women's suffrage. Not only had men taken the historic role of brewer away from women, but they increasingly did their drinking outside of the home with the rise of saloons, wide-open rooms with long bars behind which barkeeps attended to impressive stocks of whiskey, lager, and other booze. When the industrial revolution began to pace itself, many workers were given breaks at lunch and dinner rather than being forced to work through the day. Saloons capitalized on this by offering a free lunch.[42] Who could resist having a couple of beers when lunch is being paid for? Workingmen began spending lunch and dinner at the saloon while their wives toiled at home. So women took the fight to the men. If they were to be abused and impoverished in large part due to a beverage they no longer played a part in producing, they felt they should have the right to take this beverage away from its abusers.

Emboldened, women took to the streets, invading saloons or setting up near the entrance if they weren't allowed in, giving speeches on the evils of drink, singing hymns, and dropping to their knees in prayer while men drank and jeered. It started to work, at least for a time. Men began spending more time at home and giving up or limiting drink after coming to the realization that if Momma ain't happy, ain't nobody happy.

Over time more and more state-level anti-alcohol laws began passing, and work was being done to bring them to the federal level, often fueled by anti-immigrant as much as anti-alcohol sentiment. The ingenuity, work ethic, and resultant success of immigrant groups that ran successful breweries and distilleries meant that they were integrating their traditions into American society. Notwithstanding the fact that America from the very beginning was built by immigrants from many cultures, immigrants were often blamed for American society's drinking problem.

The American Temperance movement eventually led to the ratification of the 18th Amendment and the implementation of the Volstead Act, which established parameters for the ruthless enforcement of Prohibition in 1919. Prohibition lasted just shy of 14 years and by no means curtailed drinking. Rather, it gave rise to a criminal underground that thrived by selling and distributing alcohol, and to a society that increasingly drank more for the pleasure of getting smashed than for fortification or the slow savoring of a fine beverage. To its credit, it also unleashed an underground homebrew movement, but much of what was being produced was of inferior quality, sometimes to the point of being toxic.

After repealing Prohibition in December 1933, and in the midst of the Great Depression, America slowly began returning to its roots of making alcohol based on long-standing traditions, though now it relied heavily on industrialization and an increasingly efficient transportation industry. Thousands of small breweries that existed before Prohibition had been wiped out, but breweries such as Anheuser-Busch, Miller, Schlitz, Pabst, and Yuengling held on largely due to their fleets of refrigerated trucks. During their 14-year hiatus from beer, they began producing some of the first commercial soft drinks and ice cream, distributing them nationwide. Coors saw success producing malted milk, primarily for the Mars candy company, and even diversified by manufacturing porcelain.[43] Another way they survived was by creating malt extracts for use in baking, which they claimed had health benefits and could thus be used for medicinal purposes. Conveniently, it was pretty simple to add water and yeast to these extracts and make beer from them. When Prohibition agents caught on to this, they tried to stop the sale of extracts, but were shot down when a court ruled them as legal.

With their competition nearly obliterated by Prohibition, each remaining brewery began aggressively cornering the market. Through savvy marketing, catchy advertising campaigns and labeling, and ruthless cost cutting, the modern American lager was born. Cheap, mildly alcoholic, one-dimensional in flavor, slightly sweet due to the use of more corn than barley, but easy to drink and refreshing, it was the beer of choice for both ball games and the new pastime of cracking one open in front of the television. It took until the 1980s for Americans to rediscover the joys of a well-crafted, flavorful high-malt beer.

The Craft-Beer Revolution took its first faltering steps out on the West Coast, where San Francisco's Anchor Brewing was one of the few smaller breweries that stuck around in some form after Prohibition days. Tracing its origins back to the California Gold Rush, it officially began operations in 1896, when it adopted the name Anchor. It had eked by producing the lighter, corn-based beer that Americans had come to expect from its brewers, but that changed when Frederick "Fritz" Maytag (a direct descendant of the Maytag Washing Machine Company's founder) purchased the company in 1965. A savvy businessman with an eye (and a taste) for quality, Maytag returned to an all-barley recipe and started playing around with hops and other natural preservation methods for the long shelf life the major breweries enjoyed.[44] Maytag is considered by many to be the founding father of the modern craft-beer movement, and was a strong proponent of other DIY fermentation and alcohol-production hobbies, including winemaking, cheese making, and distilling.[45]

Anchor was, and still is, known for its "steam beer." The name has varying origin stories, but it refers to a type of lager that was fermented at ale temperatures by German immigrants who set up shop in California during the Gold Rush. They continued to use lager yeast but lacked the ability to maintain lagering temperature. They were still able to make tasty beer, but it wasn't quite the same as a true lager. Hence, they created a hybrid unique to the West Coast. To cool the wort to yeast-pitching temperature, the breweries used long, shallow metallic "coolships" placed on the roof. As the wort cooled, it produced steam. Many breweries outside of California used this method, though, whose origins trace back to the Middle Ages. Another theory is that the name comes from the hissing sound and explosion of foam upon opening a newly krausened (clarified and carbonated by the addition of sugar or active wort) barrel, which was similar to the sound of the latest transportation innovation: steam power. Regardless, Fritz Maytag started a movement that was to become a behemoth. Once Americans got a taste of rich, flavorful, all-malt beers, they slowly began letting go of their cherished "yellow beer."

Elsewhere in California, another revolution was taking place: Homebrewers were coming out of hiding. The Prohibition-era ban on brewing beer at home was lifted in 1978, and homebrewers Charlie Papazian and Charlie Matzen established the American Homebrewers Association (AHA) and began publishing homebrewing guides, which eventually led to the publication of Papazian's seminal book *The Complete Joy of Homebrewing*, the first book that taught me how to brew beer.

Papazian and Matzen also consulted and partnered with several newly created microbreweries (the term *microbrewery* was coined in the early 1980s by Stuart Harris, a staff writer of Papazian's homebrewing magazine *Zymurgy*, who compared all of the burgeoning small breweries to microcomputers[46]), launching a tradition that is still followed by most craft breweries today: a spirit of collaboration, not competition. One of the collaborators was Sierra Nevada Brewing Co., which gets credit for launching the hop craze, producing some of the first modern-day commercial pale ales and India Pale Ales (IPAs). While their pale ale had its share of hoppy aroma, their IPA was based on the beers made for the British navy, which could withstand the long, hot trip to India. Sierra Nevada's head brewers, Ken Grossman and Paul Camusi, played around with varying amounts of American Cascade hops and experimented with various malts and bottle-conditioning methods. The end result was a highly drinkable beer with a hoppy aroma and a malt bill that kept the beer well balanced. They had created their own unique West Coast style of beer that inspired thousands of emulators over the next couple of decades, as the movement spread to the Pacific Northwest and eventually across the country.

This is where this book comes in. As much as I've enjoyed the innovations of modern-day microbreweries in resurrecting traditional hopped, malty beers, I'm ready for the next revolution in traditional brewing. There are already several breweries resurrecting older styles and methods, from *gose*, to spontaneous and "wild" beers, to sour beers, to even some gruit-like beers (lots of herbs and little to no hops). I'm all for that, and look forward to continuing to sample their products, but I'm much more interested in inspiring homebrewers to experiment with nearly lost techniques and styles. It's great if you can procure locally sourced organic grain. If not, try brewing with molasses or sorghum, or even brown sugar or honey. If you want to use hops, also great. I truly do think hops can make for a great beer, but prefer them for balance and preservation rather than a dominant flavor. Don't be afraid to leave the hops out altogether. There are many more herbs and plants that can be used to flavor and preserve beer. Just be sure to approach these brews with the understanding that many of them won't taste much (or at all) like how you expect a beer to taste. Sometimes this will be a good thing. Sometimes not. Some you will need to develop a taste for. Some may be better for someone with different tastes than you. That's what homebrewing is all about. You can make a great beer pretty easily using a beer kit or someone else's recipe—but why not experiment, have fun, and learn from your mistakes? After all, that's what it's all about.

CHAPTER TWO

STORIES, FOLKLORE, AND FEASTING TRADITIONS

W ho doesn't love a good drinking story or song? Oh, you don't? Why don't you head on over to chapter 3 while the rest of us have some fun?

Der Grossvater erzählt eine Geschichte (The Grandfather Tells a Story). In this 1884 painting by German painter Albert Anker (1831–1910), a grandfather tells a story to a rapt young audience—a tradition that dates back to the beginnings of humankind. Courtesy of Albert Anker, Sandor Kuthy und andere, Orell Füssli Verlag, Zürich, Wikimedia Commons.

Now that the party poopers are gone, let's talk about why the rest of us are here. While we enjoy learning about the history and technicalities of beer, why do we *really* drink it? Yes, it can be nutritious in the appropriate amounts and with the right ingredients. And yes, some of us enjoy slowly sampling a new beer and pontificating over the subtle nuances of its flavor characteristics. Most of us, though, drink to have *fun*! There's no debating the fact that over the thousands of years humans have been drinking beer and other fermented beverages, they've had a lot of fun in the process. After all, who wouldn't want to pursue making a beverage that lightens your load and helps transfer you to other realms? Fermented drinks may have been used for sacred rituals and serious, highly regimented social customs, but once that was out of the way, it was time to have some fun. And as a final disclaimer, we know that excessive alcohol consumption can lead to all kinds of unpleasant things, but one can enjoy a fair amount of drink responsibly (well, mostly . . .) without succumbing to full-blown alcoholism or the other outcomes of excessive indulgence (never drink and joust).

The available material on beer history and drinking stories, songs, and feasting customs is unbelievably rich. But it's important to note that many stories that have been repeated as fact in beer literature all the way up to the present have dubious origins or are just plain false. In passing along stories and historical "facts" about beer and brewing, I will note whenever possible whether there is a strong element of truth to each or if it is just one of those stories that, no matter how enjoyable, is likely not true. Sometimes a good story is simply a good story. Further, many stories, particularly those with strong mythological or cultural/historical elements, can provide insight into what people drank and how they brewed through history. The details in the stories and myths presented in this chapter are backed up by multiple sources. A serious academic discussion would require careful analysis of every reference, which I've done here to the degree I am able. I'll leave the rest to the academics. So, where to start?

Sumerian and Egyptian Myths and Stories

Sumer is as likely a candidate as any for a place settled with the primary purpose of establishing a system of agriculture. It was initially a loose network of city-states (namely, Ur, Eridu, Lagash, and Uruk) that emerged around 3400 BC in the Fertile Crescent. Sumerians developed what are likely the first large-scale organized irrigation systems and plow technologies, as well as the first written language, a type of cuneiform. Over time, as the city-states expanded and developed urban centers, Sumer became part of the Akkadian empire, with the southernmost region known as Babylonia. Its capital was Babylon, around 50 miles (80 km) south of modern-day Baghdad.[1] The Sumerians clearly enjoyed brewing beer, and they were quite proficient at it, as evidenced by the advanced brewing technologies they utilized. They also employed a wide range of flavorings and grain types, due to the various names that have been identified for the beer they brewed, including black beer, barley beer, red beer, spelt beer, and variations such as fine black beer and fine white beer.[2]

Sumer is now known as the cradle of civilization, and the record holder for the oldest known drinking song, "The Hymn to Ninkasi." More accurately, the hymn is a song about the making of beer, describing in detail the process of malting grain; making "beer bread" (*bappir*) flavored with honey, dates, and various herbs from the malt; and then brewing beer from the bappir after mixing it with hulled grain and warming it to create a mash. The mash was then cooled on reed mats, mixed with water in a large vat, and sweetened (likely with honey) to initiate fermentation, after which the beer was filtered into a vat.[3]

Ninkasi was the Sumerian goddess of beer and the chief brewer of the gods, but she also appears to have been the personification of beer itself, as the hymn starts out saying that Ninkasi was "given birth by the flowing water . . . ," indicating that she first came about from water that was turned into beer wort. She was a very popular goddess. Her name can be translated to either "lady who fills the mouth (with beer)" or "she who sates the desires."[4] The gods and goddesses of Sumerian mythology took part in much beer drinking, sometimes to their detriment. One example comes from the poem "Inanna and Enki," in which Enki, the Lord of Wisdom, sits down to drink and dine with Inanna, the Queen of Heaven, and after "their hearts had become happy with drink," he unwittingly gives the goddess "the over one hundred divine decrees which . . . control the culture pattern of civilization itself."[5]

Enki clearly loved a good party. In another poem, "Enki's Journey to Nibru," Enki journeys by barge to the shrine of Nibru to visit Enlil

Excerpt from "The Hymn to Ninkasi"*

Ninkasi, you are the one who handles dough [and] . . . with a big shovel,
Mixing, in a pit, the bappir with sweet aromatics.
Ninkasi, you are the one who bakes the bappir in the big oven,
Puts in order the piles of hulled grain.
Ninkasi, you are the one who waters the earth-covered malt (munu),
The noble dogs guard [it even] from the potentates.
Ninkasi, you are the one who soaks the malt (sun) in a jar,
The waves rise, the waves fall.
Ninkasi, you are the one who spreads the cooked mash (titab)
    on large reed mats,
Coolness overcomes . . .
Ninkasi, you are the one who holds with both hands the great
    sweetwort (dida),
Brewing [it] with honey [and] wine.
Ninkasi, [. . .]
[You . . .] the sweetwort (dida) to the vessel.
The fermenting vat, which makes a pleasant sound,
You place appropriately on [top of] a large collector vat (lahtan).
Ninkasi, you are the one who pours out the filtered beer of the
    collector vat,
It is [like] the onrush of the Tigris and the Euphrates.[6]

---

* Sumerian terms in parentheses.

(the father of all gods) and celebrate along with several other gods the construction of Enki's temple Eridug, an "artfully built mountain which floats on the water." The gods indulge in plenty of beer and liquor. It is unclear what is meant by liquor, but the beer is described as emmer-wheat beer to which date syrup is added for flavor. They are also portrayed playing drinking games: "They filled the bronze *aga* vessels to the brim and started a competition, drinking from the bronze vessels

This ancient writing tablet is the earliest known form of writing (cuneiform) and depicts the allocation of beer. It is likely from southern Iraq, Late Prehistoric period, 3100–3000 BC. Courtesy of BabelStone, Wikimedia Commons.

of Uraš." (Uraš, or Urash, was the goddess of earth.) Once much "beer and liquor had been libated and enjoyed . . . Enlil was made happy in Nibru."[7] It seems there are scant few mythological traditions in which the gods at some point don't enjoy a good drinking party.

Much has been written about the love ancient Egyptians had for beer and how it helped satiate the workers who built the pyramids. This is primarily due to the discovery of hieroglyphs that depict beer brewing and bread making (as part of the same process) along with beer drinking. The Egyptians perfected the process the Sumerians originated, turning the thick, sweet porridge that had to be drunk through straws into a more refined beverage that was strained into containers and drunk more like a modern beer. As in other cultures, women were the primary brewers and, also as with other cultures, men took over when brewing transitioned from the home to the commercial sector. Like the Sumerians, they at least paid respect to women brewers through their goddess of beer, Tenenet, who was also the goddess of childbirth.

While the ancient Egyptians didn't have a myth for the creation of beer that we know of, beer is prevalent in the stories about their gods. We know that the god Osiris gave people knowledge on how to brew beer, along with agriculture, but this story doesn't exist in a specific myth.[8] There are stories in which beer plays a part, however. In the *Legend of the Destruction of Mankind*, the god Ra—who has been ruling humans for eons—hears that humans have been murmuring against him and talking about him as if he were old news. Furious at their impunity, Ra elects to send his Great Eye (in the guise of the goddess Sekhmet) to obliterate mankind from the earth. She takes to her task with great joy, tearing through human communities, ripping people apart, and drinking their blood. When the other gods become concerned that there will be no one left to worship them and implore that Ra put a stop to Sekhmet's rampage, he agrees, particularly as the lesson he is teaching them will be pointless if no one is alive to pass it along, but Sekhmet's bloodlust can't be sated. Knowing the powers of a well-brewed beer, Ra demands that 7,000 vessels of beer be brewed from wheat and the tataat fruit (possibly pomegranates, or "love apples," the fruit of the mandrake plant), mixed with human blood, and poured into a river at a site where Sekhmet is known to be engaging in slaughter. The ruse works. Sekhmet sees the deluge of red liquid and eagerly laps it up, eventually falling into a happy slumber. When she wakes, she has transformed into Hathor, a peaceful goddess devoted to love, sex, dancing, music, drunkenness, and other good times (doesn't sound much like your last hangover, does it?).

To commemorate Sekhmet's transformation, a popular festival known as The Tekh Festival, or The Festival of Drunkenness, was created. Participants would drink to excess, fall asleep in a great hall, and then be woken by the beating of drums. This allowed them—still drunk and partially asleep—to catch a glimpse of the divine, and to participate in certain shenanigans due to their lessened inhibitions. This wasn't the only festival at which beer was a major player, though. State-supplied beer was provided in vast quantities at festivals such as those for Bast, Sekhmet, and Hathor.⁹ The ancient Egyptians and Sumerians provide multiple examples of why we can't have civilization without beer.

The Legend of Heather Ale

While there are many stories with references to ale and mead in Celtic and Norse mythology, one in particular has fascinated me for some time. It encompasses the mythology and history of not only the Celts but also the Norse and the Picts. It's also much debated by scholars. Because of its many variations and questions as to its authenticity, I've gone into a little more depth than with other stories.

I once, on a quest for books on mythology in my old college library, came across a book called *Viking Ale*. Upon opening it, I realized that it wasn't actually a book on Viking ale, or even on brewing. Rather, it was a series of essays on Scandinavian folklore by folklorist and philologist Bo Almqvist. According to the editor's introduction, Almqvist studied Scandinavian folklore and language in great detail, and had also ventured far into Gaelic folklore. This particular volume was a compilation of essays on the correlation between myths from both Northern and Western European cultures. *Viking Ale* just happened to be the name of one of these essays. What caused me to swoon was this little tale:

> A long time ago the Irish had killed off all the Vikings except for an old man and his son. In the end these two were captured, but the Irish offered to spare their lives on [the] condition that they told them how to make beer out of heather. This beer had a wonderful taste and it was only the Vikings who knew how to make it. "Kill my son first," the old Viking whispered to his guards, "I am ashamed

to speak in his presence." The son was then thrown over a cliff. When the old Viking saw this he laughed. "Now," said he, "I am the only one who knows the secret; you may kill me, I will never tell it to you." So they killed the old Viking, and that is why the Irish never learnt to make heather ale.[10]

As I read further into Almqvist's account of the tale's origins, I realized that there is a great deal of debate among scholars, historians, and folklorists about its origins and, more important, which cultural tradition it could be traced to. Additionally, there has been much debate as to whether or not the ale truly exists, as there are many tales and songs that reference this mythical heather-based concoction, but little in the manner of actual recipes or technique. Almqvist presents a compelling argument that, despite claims of Gaelic or even Germanic origin, it is more likely firmly rooted in the Norse cultural (and brewing) tradition:

> In the summer of 1957, I spent a couple months in Dunquin on the Dingle peninsula in County Kerry, Ireland. There I was fortunate enough to make the acquaintance of an elderly man, Míchaél Ó Gaoithín, locally known as An File (The Poet), and son of the famous storyteller Peig Sayers. He received me with the warm welcome one gets everywhere in this part of Ireland and agreed to help me along in my stumbling attempts to learn Irish. Many were the evenings we sat reading or talking by his peat fire. . . . There was little I could do to express my gratitude to this fine man; however, since he did not object to a beer, I now and then brought him a bottle or two from the local pub. One day he happened to mention that he had once tasted an especially good beer, which had been offered him by some Danes who had visited the parish. As a friend of mine was about to come down from Dublin, I wrote to him and asked him to bring along a few bottles of Carlsberg, as I surmised that that would have been what Míchaél had had. Míchaél was very pleasantly surprised when he got the gift and after tasting it he remarked with

a smile, "That's a true Viking beer" (Fíor-bheoir lochlan-nach is ea é san). I took this to be a pun and thought that Mícheál referred to the beer's being Danish as well as to my own nickname in the parish—I was, as I have to admit for the sake of the story, called An Lochlannach ("The Viking"). And in fact it was a pun, but there was more to it than I had suspected. Mícheál continued by asking me whether I "had" the story about the Viking beer. I told him that I had never heard it and then he proceeded to tell a tale that went somewhat as follows: [Here, he proceeds to tell the story outlined above.] "But perhaps they still know how to make it in Denmark," Mícheál summed up, taking another draught from the bottle.[11]

Like me, Almqvist seems to have felt a bit of a shiver down his spine upon hearing the story and surmising its implications: "It is very hard to describe what I felt upon hearing Mícheál's story. But perhaps it would be most correct to say that I was overawed in spite of the humorous circumstances."[12]

I was aware of this story through the Robert Louis Stevenson poem "Heather Ale, A Galloway Legend," which references the Picts rather than Vikings being the holders of this ancient brew. The first two stanzas read:

> From the bonny bells of heather
>   They brewed a drink long-syne,
> Was sweeter far than honey,
>   Was stronger far than wine.
> They brewed it and they drank it,
>   And lay in a blessed swound
> For days and days together
>   In their dwellings underground.
>
> There rose a king in Scotland,
>   A fell man to his foes,
> He smote the Picts in battle,
>   He hunted them like roes.

Over miles of the red mountain
   He hunted as they fled,
And strewed the dwarfish bodies
   Of the dying and the dead.[13]

The Bullion Stone found in Angus, Scotland, depicts a Pictish warrior drinking from a drinking horn. It is housed in the National Museum of Scotland. Courtesy of Kim Traynor, Wikimedia Commons.

The Picts were a fierce, diminutive people who thwarted the Romans in their attempts to make Britain part of their territory, and also resisted incursions by the Celts, Anglo-Saxons, and Vikings (who were rumored to have respected their prowess in battle, referring to them as the *péttar*, or "the painted," due to their full-body tattoos). Legend goes that the Scots eventually eradicated them. Although the Picts as a people may be lost to time, like the Norse, their culture and their genes were simply integrated with those of other peoples.[14]

Similarly the lost heather ale, which it turns out may never have really vanished after all. In researching Picts and the legendary heather ale further, I encountered an article from 1900 published in *The Scottish Antiquary; or, Northern Notes and Queries* titled "Memories of the Picts," by David MacRitchie, in which he writes:

> Not only [have Picts] existed in Scotland for an unknown period, but this very heather-ale was no more "exterminated" than the Picts were. When the Welsh traveler Pennant was visiting Islay in 1772, he found that "ale is frequently made in this island of the young tops of heath, mixing two-thirds of that plant with one of malt, sometimes adding hops."[15]

As to a full picture of who the Picts were, alas, there seems to be no true consensus. They left no written records, but rather, strange pictures carved into stones that no one has been able to interpret—hence the words *pictograph* and *picture*. What was known of them has passed from oral tradition to highly biased legend and folktales created by those who sought to suppress them. They did, however, seem to have a strong connection with the Norse, who settled the Orkney Islands where the Picts were prevalent in the ninth century, the same century in which the Scots are recorded to have overthrown them.[16] In *Viking Ale*, Almqvist goes even further to draw this connection: "The deeds and final fate of the Vikings—and also, if to a somewhat lesser degree, of the Picts, with whom the Vikings are often confused in folk tradition—have constantly worked upon the popular imagination. There is a quite unbelievable number of stories, ballads and sayings attached to the foreigners from the Northern World."[17]

In discussing the Pict-Viking connection, Almqvist also draws from his readings of *Historia Norvegiæ*, a Latin history of the Norwegian kings "probably written before 1200 with English readers in mind, but in all likelihood by a Norwegian," from which he references a description of the people who lived on the Orkney Islands when the Norse arrived: "The Picts, 'who were hardly bigger than dwarfs in stature, worked wonders in building villages in the morning and evening, but in the middle of the day they lost their strength altogether and hid in terror in small subterranean dwellings.'"[18] These dwellings, essentially underground "earth houses" hand-hewed and lined with stones and wood, were known as *souterrains*. They were more likely used for storage and fortification than actual living quarters, but the parallels between the legends of pixies, fairies, and Tolkien's Dwarves and Hobbits, are clear. In his book *Sacred and Herbal Healing Beers*, Stephen Harrod Buhner notes that the heather ale of the Picts was usually brewed by shamans and known to be highly intoxicating:

> There is considerable evidence that fermented heather was one of the sacred beverages of the Picts and Celts and an integral part of Druidic sacred life and ceremonies. Its use is ancient in fermentation. . . . Considered to be the first fermented beverage in the British Isles, it has enjoyed wide historical use throughout ancient Druidic lands. . . . Both the Greeks and Romans commented on Pictish production of a remarkable fermented beverage brewed from heather and coveted highly. Those among the Picts who brewed the heather ale for ceremonial use were highly revered in Pictish society (some asserting that only the chiefs among them were allowed to make it).[19]

We'll never know what exactly went into this legendary ale, but we do have a clue as to what may have given it its mystical qualities. The heather found in Scotland grows in symbiosis with a naturally occurring fungus known as "the fogg" that has narcotic and mildly hallucinogenic properties that were likely enhanced by the process of fermentation into alcohol. The ale could also have been brewed with heather honey, which is known for its unique, strong flavor and thick, almost gelatinous consistency. When looking for "true" heather honey (which can be difficult to find outside of Great Britain), note that there are two types of single-flower heather honey. One comes from ling heather (*Calluna vulgaris*), which is considered a "true heather." The symbol of Scotland and one of Norway's national flowers, *C. vulgaris* belongs to the Ericaceae family. Ling heather honey—often categorized as Scotch, summer, or autumn honey—is different from what is known as Erica honey, which can be derived from many different Erica species of the same family, including blueberries and rhododendrons. Honey from ling heather is interesting in that it possesses the property of *thixotopism*. While it is gelatinous and firm when inert, it will turn temporarily to liquid if agitated. A good way to know if you have ling heather honey is to place the jar on its side and wait for it to begin flowing. Most other honeys will begin flowing very quickly (provided they are not cold and thus crystallized), but pure ling heather honey will take several minutes to flow. Pure ling heather honey also contains small, yet visible, air bubbles, and won't be clear despite its bright appearance.[20]

Beer and Brewing in Welsh Myth

The *Mabinogion*, a collection of Welsh tales drawn primarily from two medieval Welsh manuscripts, is one of the earliest sources of Arthurian legend, introducing the world to characters such as Arthur and Merlin and containing the oldest known Arthurian romance, *Culhwch and Olwen*. A rollicking example of nearly every motif one would expect in a fairy tale or Arthurian tale, it features a giant king, Ysbaddaden; a hunt for a giant magical boar; and a band of heroes, led by King Arthur, who set out on a quest to accomplish several impossible tasks so that the main hero, Culhwch—Arthur's first cousin—can lift a curse set upon him by his jealous stepmother before he can wed Ysbaddaden's daughter Olwen, which Ysbaddaden prefers not to happen, as he will die if Olwen ever weds. The tasks include acquiring honey "nine times sweeter than the honey of a virgin swarm, without drones and without bees, to make bragget for the [wedding] feast."[21] *Bragot* (honey beer—see chapter 9) was a highly esteemed drink in Wales, although not as esteemed as mead (honey wine). Mead, bragot, and ale were types of currency and often used as payment for land. The medieval Welsh book of law, the *Book of*

Blegywryd, states that court officials should receive as payment "more ale than bragget and more bragget than mead."[22] Mead was clearly king, but bragot came in a close second.

Drinking and Brewing in Norse Mythology

Although much of Norse mythology references mead as the drink of choice for both nobles and the gods, according to the original translations, the drink could just as well have been ale or a type of bragot. More likely—as evidenced by recent biomolecular analysis of Bronze Age pottery shards—it was a combination of ale, mead, and wine, also known as grog. Regardless, there are some great stories in Norse mythology about the gods and their attempts to procure booze.

One of my favorites is "The Lay of Hymir" (aka *Hymiskviða*), which begins when several Norse gods who are in the midst of holding a great feast suddenly realize they're out of booze. Finding it increasingly difficult to enjoy their feast, they seek a divine solution to their problem by using runes, which tell them to seek out Aegir, the god of the sea, who lives with his wife, Rán, in a great golden hall beneath the waves off the island of Hlesey. Upon arriving, Thor loudly bursts into Aegir's hall demanding Aegir brew them ale—lots of ale. This irks Aegir (who is enjoying a quiet dinner with Rán) to no end, but he responds coolly that he would be happy to brew them some ale were it not for the small size of his cauldron. Tyr responds excitedly that his father, the giant Hymir, has a massive cauldron that is a league (about 3½ miles/5.6 km) deep and a league wide and suggests they retrieve it from him. Thor, pleased by this prospect, is ready to head out immediately. Tyr—more of a thinker and a planner than impetuous Thor—agrees, but warns that they must use guile, as Hymir isn't likely to give up his prize easily. Aware that Thor's reputation as a blowhard is well known by the giants, he suggests Thor go instead by the name of Veur.

When they reach Hymir's hall high on a mountain at the far edges of Midgard (the realm of man, literally "middle earth"), they must first deal with Tyr's grandmother—a giant with 900 monstrous heads—who despises Tyr. Fortunately, Tyr's mother (who is much more pleasing to the eye) steps in and tells Grandma to shove off. Well aware of their intent, she warns them of her husband's displeasure at the idea of unexpected guests, and recommends they hide beneath one of the great kettles lying about the hall until she can assuage him. Grumbling, Thor lifts up a kettle and they both climb under. When Hymir finally comes stomping in from a late hunt, eyes glaring and beard clinking with huge icicles, his wife greets him at the door and carefully alerts him that he has dinner guests. Upon seeing Tyr and Thor climb out from under the cauldrons, Hymir (possibly fearing the wrath of his wife) begrudgingly agrees to prepare dinner for them. After Thor promptly devours two of the three oxen Hymir's servants prepare for dinner, Hymir grumbles that they're going to have to go hunting if they want to eat again. Thor, unperturbed, suggests they go fishing instead. Hymir agrees and sends Thor out to his field to slaughter an oxen for bait—not expecting Thor to go straight for his most prized ox, Himinhrjot the Heaven Bellower. His annoyance with Thor growing, Hymir baits his hook with the oxen heads left over from dinner, and Thor his with Himinhrjot's massive head.

Hymir prides himself on pulling in two whales, but Thor's bait attracts something much more monstrous. After he tosses his line into the sea, the waters begin to froth and foam violently. Jormungand, the Great World Serpent who encircles Midgard beneath the oceans with the end of its tail in his mouth—waiting patiently for Ragnarok—had let go of its tail and seized the tempting treat. Thor quickly pulls the great monster's head above the waves and into the boat and begins pounding on it with his hammer, Mjolnir. Roaring and spitting poison, Jormungand manages to wrench the barb from its mouth and sinks back to the bottom of the sea. Mouth agape in awe at the strength and seemingly unending audacity of Thor, Hymir sullenly rows them back to land. When they get back to Hymir's hall (with Thor dragging the boat, whales and all, behind him), Hymir makes it clear that his pride has been wounded and demands that Thor take a goblet and break it. When Thor flings it against a pillar and it just clinks to the floor, Hymir's wife quietly suggests that Thor throw the goblet at Hymir's head (knowing her husband to be a thickheaded lout). Upon striking Hymir's forehead, the supposedly unbreakable goblet splits in two and clatters to the floor.

Defeated, Hymir bids the gods to take his brewing cauldron—if they can. Tyr's attempts at lifting the cauldron are futile, but Thor shoves him aside, gives a mighty heave, and hoists the cauldron to his shoulders, his feet breaking through the hall's wood floor and pressing into the earth below. Upon returning home (after Thor defeats a throng of multiheaded giants sent by Hymir with a single toss of Mjolnir), they find the gods gathered solemnly at the Well of Urd beneath the branches of the World Tree Yggdrasill, contemplating the prospect that they may never drink good ale again. Imagine the looks of utter joy upon their faces as they saw a beaming Thor and a bewildered Tyr on the horizon. Aegir, realizing he has been bested—and genuinely impressed at Thor's feat—happily brews everyone enough ale to warm them through many winters.

Hymir looks aghast as Thor wrestles the Great World Snake from its home at the bottom of the sea. Courtesy of the Árni Magnússon Institute in Iceland. Public Domain.

Beer and Brewing in Finnish Myth

The Kalevala is the national epic of Finland. First published in print in 1835 as *The Old Kalevala*, it was expanded and published again as *The Kalevala* in 1849. Its roots, though, go back much further. *The Kalevala* is essentially Finland's origin story, an epic tale that starts at the creation of the world and contains many heroes and epic quests, as well as a magical talisman, the Sampo. It comprises 50 runes, or songs (designated by Roman numerals), which are organized by "cycles." Rune XX, "The Great Ox, and the Brewing of the Ale," not only is an entertaining story, but provides a fair bit of insight into the way beer was brewed in early Europe.

In the story (part of the "Ilmarinen's Wedding Feast" cycle), the hero Ilmarinen has recently succeeded in a number of extremely challenging and dangerous tasks to win the hand of the Maiden of the North and is now preparing for the massive wedding feast at Pohjola (according to Finnish mythology, a dark and cold place in the far north). Ilmarinen's challenges preparing for a feast of this magnitude are nearly as great as the epic quest to win the Maiden's hand. His first task is to butcher the mighty bull of Suomi, who is so enormous that it takes an ermine an entire week to run from one end of his yoke to the other, an entire day for a bird to fly through the space between his horn tips to find a perch, and a squirrel a month to run from his neck to the end of his tail. Once meat for the feast is secured, a structure large enough to hold the feast party needs to be built. A great hall is erected, so large that if a cock crows at the smoke hole, it cannot be heard by those within.

Next, it is time to brew a batch of beer. Louhi, hostess of the Northland, seeks someone to brew the beer, but Louhi knows nothing of brewing, and the secret of how it is brewed has been lost to time. An old man in the corner tries to help her out, explaining at length how to cultivate and harvest barley (malting isn't mentioned) and hops, combine them with water, and heat it all with fire. The task is given to the brewster Osmotar:

> She, the maid who beer concocted,
> Took, on this, the grains of barley,
> Gathered six grains of barley,
> Seven hop-tassels next she gathered,

And eight ladles took of water,
Then upon the fire she placed it,
And allowed it there to simmer,
And she boiled the ale of barley
Through the fleeting days of summer,
Out upon the cloudy headland,
Cape upon the shady island;
Poured it then into wooden barrels,
And in tubs of birchwood stored it.[23]

She seems to be unaware of one key ingredient, though, for the beer is still and won't ferment.

"What must now be added to it,
What is needful to provide for,
That the ale may be fermented,
And the beer be brought to foaming?"[24]

Larin Paraske by Albert Edelfelt, 1893. Paraske, an oral poet, is considered a key figure in Finnish folk poetry whose interpretations of *The Kalevala* inspired composer Jean Sibelius, among others. Courtesy of Carulmare, Wikimedia Commons.

Several individuals attempt to assist, sending a magic squirrel for ripe pinecones, a magic golden-breasted martin to gather foam from the lips of enraged bears (perhaps they associated the foam with an active ferment?), and finally, a honeybee to gather the "sweetened juices" of herbs and flowers. The pinecone does nothing, the angry-bear drool flops, but lo and behold, upon mixing in the honey, the beer proceeds to rise and foam until it overflows its barrels. This parallels what we know from archaeological finds regarding many ancient beers: Honey was likely used as a yeast source as well as for flavoring. Thus is the beer prepared for the wedding feast and the secret to brewing rediscovered. The beer is a particularly good one, as noted by this song of praise:

> Said to make the feeble hardy,
> Famed to dry the tears of women,
> Famed to cheer the broken-hearted,
> Make the aged young and supple,
> Make the timid brave and mighty,
> Make the brave men ever braver,
> Fill the heart with joy and gladness,
> Fill the mind with wisdom-sayings,
> Fill the tongue with ancient legends,
> Only makes the fool more foolish.[25]

Feasting, Merrymaking, and Seasonal Brewing and Drinking Customs

Regrettably, as with myth and folklore, the customs outlined here are non-inclusive and mostly Eurocentric. This is primarily because I have only limited space for covering a very broad topic, but also because most of the available English-language books on beer history are focused on Europe and the British Isles. My hope is that the topic is someday covered in more detail and spanning multiple cultures.

A good starting point for this subject is Merry Old England. As my friend-whom-I've-never-met John Bickerdyke puts it: "These simple, hearty festivals of old, in which our ancestors so much delighted, served to light up the dull round of the recurring seasons, and to mark with a red letter the day in the calendar appropriate to their celebration. It was these that gained for our country in mediaeval times the name of 'Merrie England.'"[26]

The festivities Bickerdyke refers to had their origins in ancient times. Not just in England, but in every agricultural society, changes in season, growing and harvesting times, weddings, funerals, and other cycles of life were marked with some sort of a celebration or ceremony. Drink was nearly always a part of—and often the reason for—these events. Many celebrations even contained *ale* in their name, due in part to the fact that the drinking of ale was an integral part of the festivities, but also because the word *ale* was synonymous with *festival*. A few examples of these festivals include Scot-Ales, Whitsun-Ales, Easter-Ales, Church-Ales, and Bride-Ales. Some of these were meant as much to bring in money as they were to celebrate. A Church-Ale, for instance, was a festival held by many parishes in the Middle Ages to raise money for upkeep of the church and for charity. Much ale was brewed to lure in revelers and their money, and the festivals themselves could get a little out of hand in their raucousness (although some accounts are doubtless exaggerated by prudish sorts). Easter-Ales and Whitsun-Ales were types of Church-Ales put on during holy days (Whitsun is another word for Pentecost).

A Scot-Ale was much like a Church-Ale, only less fun and attendance was mandatory. For these, the lord of a manor, the officer of a forest, or some other bailiff would require attendance for a fee. Ale was provided but the compulsory attendance at the threat of displeasure from the lord of the land likely put a damper on festivities. A Bride-Ale is just what it sounds like, a wedding celebration, and, you guessed it, the origin of the word *bridal*. The word *bride* even has beer-related connections, stemming from the Old High German *bruta*, or "daughter-in-law," which itself has roots in the Proto-Indo-European *bhreu*, meaning "boil," "bubble," or "effervesce,"[27] obvious references to brewing and cooking, the responsibilities of a daughter-in-law in ancient times. What a Bride-Ale was not was an ale brewed specifically for a wedding feast, though special brews were certainly made for wedding feasts.[28]

Health-Drinking

Health-drinking is another ancient custom that was popular throughout Europe, particularly among the Romans, Anglo-Saxons, and Danes.
Health-drinking could range from informal toasts to elaborate drinking
rituals that could lead to ostracism or worse if not performed properly.
Generally, though, it was simply a way to express pleasure or show
respect to friends present and past while sharing drinks and food at
social gatherings. It was considered impolite in some circles to drink
without drinking to the health of a person, idea, or important event.

Games and contests were often included along with health-drinking. The Danes, in a custom that likely goes back to Viking times,
would empty a horn after each toast. If more than a drop dripped off
the drinker's thumbnail, they would have to immediately down another.
This practice was known as *supernaculum*, or "to the last drop." For the
English and Saxons, taking a drink without toasting someone at the
table was considered rude, and games often accompanied the practice,
such as the person being honored not being permitted to move a muscle
until the drink was downed.[29]

The sheer scope of drinking games, customs, stories, and feasting traditions referenced throughout literary and historical texts would require
many more pages to fully explore. Hopefully this tidbit has encouraged
you to resurrect some of these practices yourself or even come up with
your own.

Wassail

Winter festivities were always a good excuse to drink ale, both for warmth
and to pass the time with food, friends, and family while the land was
hard with frost. One festive health-drinking tradition that is still alive
in some communities today is the wassail. A *wassail* (stemming from the
Old Norse *ves heill*, or "be healthy") is an activity, toast, drink, and the
drink's receptacle all in one. On New Year's Day (although sometimes
during the time between Yule and New Year's Day) revelers would go
through the village and enter their friends' houses unannounced, bear-
ing a wassail-bowl of spiced ale—singing carols and presenting wishes

for a year of good health by exuberantly exclaiming *wassail!* as the bowl was held up, drunk from, and passed along. It was then expected that each household contribute to the festivities by adding its own brew to the bowl and then joining the throng as it moved on to the next house. There are many, many wassail songs celebrating all of the aspects of life for which good health and cheer are offered.

Nearly every household had its own wassail recipe, which could vary quite a bit. In general, the drink was warm and spiced with exotic flavorings. It could range from a mulled wine, to a mulled mead, to a spiced ale or cider, to any combination of these. Often it was a bragot (a spiced honey ale—see chapter 9), although the bragot wasn't always made with fermented honey, or even spiced at brewing. Sometimes the honey and spices were added later, after the ale was warmed. The wassail-bowl didn't always consist of liquid nourishment only; a version known as lambswool was made by sprinkling apples with sugar, grated nutmeg, cinnamon, ginger, and other spices, then roasting them until soft. The skins were removed from the apples, warmed ale was poured

A pot of wassail I made for a wassail tour in Berea, Kentucky.

over them, and everything was blended into a puree. The bowl was then served while still warm, often with spiced sweet cakes or toast floating on it. I have come across claims that to offer a drink as a "toast" came from this tradition but have been unable to verify it. Still, it's a worthy concept to consider.

INGREDIENTS TO SERVE 6–8

6 apples

1 teaspoon each freshly grated nutmeg, cinnamon, cloves, ginger, or any other spices that suit your fancy

½ cup (125 mL) organic cane sugar or brown sugar

1 cup (250 mL) water (or substitute hard cider, ginger beer, red wine, Madeira, port, mead, or what-have-you)

1 small lemon or orange

4 pints low-to-no-hopped ale, preferably British-style ale, spiced dark ale, or bragot

Dark rum, brandy, or other spirits (optional)

Mugs of lambswool wassail.

PROCESS

1. Core the apples and place them in a pot or deep baking dish.
2. Sprinkle the spices and sugar and pour the water or what-have-you over the apples.
3. Squeeze the juice of the lemon or orange (or both) over everything.
4. Place a pot on a medium-high burner, or put a baking dish into the oven at 350°F/180°C.
5. Cook for about 45 minutes or until the apples are soft and mushy.
6. Remove from the heat and allow the apples to warm enough to carefully remove their skins.
7. Once the skins are removed, take a masher, large fork, or blender and blend everything (including the ale) into a puree (for the lambswool option; otherwise, remove the apples and make them into boozy applesauce).
8. Place the lambswool in a bowl with a serving spoon, or ladle it into individual mugs.
9. Optional: Add as much additional dark rum, brandy, or other spirits as you desire; I like to keep this going for several days by continuing to add various drinks and spices to it and rewarming it.
10. *Wassail!*

PART TWO
BEYOND THE
REINHEITSGEBOT

In the next four chapters, I will discuss the ingredients that, according to the Reinheitsgebot, should be all that beer is made of. But why devote so much to these ingredients if the purpose of this book is to teach brewers how to think beyond the Reinheitsgebot? Although I don't feel all of these ingredients need to be included in every brew to call it a beer, they are all important to discuss, from both historical and practical perspectives. Like any beer lover, I enjoy a good grain-based beer or ale. If you want to brew beer that at least has some semblance to the drink you've fallen in love with, it is essential to understand each of these ingredients both independently and in the symphony that is a well-balanced modern beer. Then in chapter 7 I'll tell the Reinheitsgebot to shove off and delve into the many ingredients and techniques that can be employed to make beer however you want.

CHAPTER THREE

GRAIN

lcohol cannot exist without a sugar source, and to produce enough alcohol for human consumption—a batch of beer, say—there needs to be a good amount of sugar, whether from one of the many sources found in nature, or industrially processed sugar. Each sugar, combined with varying flavorings and yeasts, produces a different type of alcohol. The potency of an alcohol also increases with the amount

A field of barley in Oregon. Courtesy of Ian Sane, Flickr.

of sugar. History's first recorded successes in germinating grains and using malted grain to brew beer can be traced as far back as 1800 BC in the "Hymn to Ninkasi," whose description of malting and brewing accurately portrays how the process is performed today. However, archaeological discoveries—including buildings constructed for the specific purpose of malting—dated to the very beginnings of grain agriculture more than 12,000 years ago give us tantalizing evidence for grain malting thousands of years before researchers' first estimates.[1] To understand the significance of this recent research, it helps to understand how malting works in modern times.

The Malting Process

How exactly is whole grain turned into a sweet liquid that can then be fermented into beer? To obtain the sugars from grain needed for brewing beer, you must first malt it. The process is generally the same whether it's performed on a home scale or an industrial scale.

First, the grains—barley, wheat, or otherwise—need to be sprouted. Sprouting is encouraged by moistening with warm water (about 65°F/18°C) over a couple of days and in two or three successions, with a desired goal of about 45 percent moisture. Once the grains begin to swell due to the growth of an embryo in each kernel, it's time to drain the water and dry the grain with heated air (usually a blower is used)—maintained at a consistent temperature of 55–60°F (13–16°C). During the drying process, the grain must be turned every few hours to prevent molding. On a small scale, you can accomplish this by simply drying the grain on low heat in an oven and turning it by hand. On an artisan scale, maltsters turn the grain every couple of hours, either by shovel in cases where the grain is laid flat on a concrete floor to a depth of about 6 inches (15 cm), or turned in the tank in which it was malted. Industrial systems use automated stirrers. Care must be taken to break up any clumps of rootlets (referred to as bricks) to keep the grain from molding. During this stage, which lasts about five days, the seeds begin to sprout and enzymes begin breaking apart the starch and protein molecules in each kernel.

The sprouting process will continue during brewing when it is restarted through the introduction of hot water to continue breaking the starch down into sugar (subsequently, the yeast will work together with the enzymes in the sugars extracted from the grains to turn it into alcohol), but for now the process needs to be halted. When little shoots begin to sprout from the grain kernels—the same as when you moisten a seed for gardening and it begins to sprout—the grains are dehydrated in a kiln at temperatures ranging from 115°F (46°C) to as high as 210°F (99°C). This brings the moisture level down to about 3 percent, halting the embryos' growth, but also imparting stability and varying degrees of flavor and coloring.[2] The kilning stage—in both style and temperatures used—is tweaked by each malt house to develop unique, often proprietary characteristics. Munich and Vienna malts, for instance, may come from the same grain source—barley—but the process by which they're malted is what provides for the unique flavorings they impart in beer.

After kilning, further character can be introduced by roasting, smoking, and other techniques. The primary sugar providers are known as *base malts*, and are set aside while the rest of the grain is developed into specialty malts. These are used chiefly for flavoring, and provide each malt house with its own claim to fame. The number of specialty malts available when I started homebrewing was somewhat limited, but now

A malt floor at Laphroaig Distillery in Scotland. Courtesy of Stephan Ridgway, Flickr.

Malt Your Own Grain at Home

It's quite simple to malt your own grain. All you need are whole, unhulled grains, water, and a bit of patience. Barley works best due to its high potential for enzyme conversion, but other grains such as sorghum or field corn (dried, not sweet and right off the cob) will work as well. I recommend starting with enough for a 1-gallon (4 L) batch of all-grain beer, as it will help you to understand the process before you try malting larger amounts. Once the grains are malted, you can follow my technique for 1-gallon all-grain brewing in chapter 8, and you'll have the pleasure of being able to say that you made a batch of beer entirely from scratch! You can easily scale up from there. The whole process should take two to three days.

INGREDIENTS AND EQUIPMENT

2 pounds (1 kg) unhulled barley or other whole grain
Around ½ gallon (2 L) warm springwater or dechlorinated tap water (enough to cover the grains)
Widemouthed 1-gallon (4 L) or larger glass jar
Cheesecloth or dish towel with a rubber band, or sprouting lid (basically a lid with a fine-mesh screen)

PROCESS

1. Fill the jar with grains up to about 2 inches (5 cm) below the opening, to allow room for them to swell. Cover the grains with the water and secure a sprouting lid, or use a rubber band to secure a cloth, over the jar's opening.

2. Let the grains soak in a warm area (60–70°F/15–21°C or higher) for 12 to 24 hours.

3. Sometime between the 12- and 24-hour mark (wait longer in cooler temperatures), drain all water off, or the grains will ferment and eventually rot. To do this, let the jar sit upside down in a bowl or draining rack, making sure it is not resting in the drained water. The grains will only germinate if they're moist but not covered by water, as they require both water and oxygen to sprout.

4. Place the jar back in its warm area and proceed to rinse the grains two to three times (or more) a day; be sure to drain off all water each time. You want them to stay moist, but keep from molding.

5. Watch for sprouts (*tails*) to start emerging from the seeds. Once the tails are about three-quarters the length of the seed, they are at peak fermentation viability. Use them within a day or store them for a couple of days in a refrigerator, as the enzymes and sugar will diminish quickly.

6. If you plan on saving them for later, dry them in an oven at about 150°F (66°C) or in a dehydrator. Dry them until they are too hard to bite through when put between your teeth.

7. If desired, roast the grains before storing (using the Roasting Your Own Malt guidelines on page 64).

8. Store the grains in an airtight container in a cool place until you're ready to use them.

To malt grain at home, start by soaking grains in water.

Next, drain the water, but keep the grains moist to ensure sprouting.

Once the grains start producing sprouts (tails), dry them with heat and store them, or brew with them right away.

Dry malted grains in an oven at about 150°F (66°C), or in a dehydrator.

with the Internet and the rise of artisanal malt houses, the breadth of available malt varieties harks back to the olden days when every region or farmhouse malted and roasted its own specialty grains and brewed its own unique beer. Admittedly, you would have to travel for days or months to truly experience all that variety, but it would be a fun trip! The range of nuances possible in specialty malts is quite broad. Not all varieties are readily available (see tables 3.1 and 3.2 for some of the more common ones), but many are simple to reproduce at home by roasting your own grains.

Table 3.1. Barley Malts

Malt Type	Description
Munich	Large amounts in a grain bill will give the beer a light orange color and a toasty, nutty flavor. However, Munich has lower enzymatic power than Vienna, so use caution when determining how much to use in a grain bill. If you're not a fan of malty beers, use in small amounts. Its color profile is broad, ranging from a rich orange to a dark reddish hue.
Vienna	Rich, caramel-like, and sweet (but not cloying when mashed efficiently). A more gentle malt aroma than Munich. Light to rich orange in color (depending on the amount used), Vienna imparts a milder toasty and nutty flavor than Munich. Can be used as most or all of a grain bill due to its high enzymatic capability for starch conversion. Popular in Munich-style beers such as Märzen lagers. This malt shows up a lot in beers made for Oktoberfest celebrations, particularly due to its tendency to make a highly drinkable and refreshing beer.
Aromatic Munich	Roasted longer than regular Munich for darker coloring and a fuller, richer flavor and aroma.
Amber/ biscuit	Lightly roasted while dry, ambers and biscuits are toasty and nutty with a subtle aroma. Although very similar, biscuit malts impart a slightly drier flavor profile than ambers. Popular in English ales.
Brown	In olden times brown malt was made by rapidly heating pale ale malt over an oak fire and then cooking until it reached a rich brown color. It was also the dominant malt in porter. Very nutty in flavor, it is ideal for (what else?) brown ales. It is roasted longer than amber for more color, flavor, and aroma.

Chocolate	Not actual chocolate, although it can be used alongside real chocolate in brewing. Its name comes from its chocolate-brown coloring and roasty flavor, akin to dark-roasted coffee. Can be a bit harsh, so use sparingly.
Pale chocolate	Less harsh than regular chocolate malt but still with the nice flavor and aroma of roasted coffee beans.
Black/ black patent	The darkest, bitterest of all malts. These malts are made by roasting— and nearly burning—pale malt at a high temperature until deep black in color. Use sparingly or look for the de-bittered version for a smooth, rich dark ale or stout. Even ¼ pound (113 g) in a 5-gallon (20 L) batch of beer can impart significant degrees of dark coloring and rich flavoring.
Crystal/ caramel	Crystal (or caramel) malts are available in varying degrees of lightness and flavor. Created by soaking the malt prior to roasting, these malts can add some very interesting and unique flavors to beer. Lighter crystal malts can be used in higher percentages and still provide a clean, crisp flavor profile, while the darker malts should be used sparingly as they can become overbearing.
Roasted barley	Barley that is roasted before being malted. Milder than roasted malts, it has a tendency to impart acrid, dry flavors. A key component to dry Irish stouts.
Acidulated	Also known as *sauermalz* or sour malt. This is a malted barley that contains a small proportion (about 1 to 2 percent by weight) of lactic acid. It can be used to lower the pH levels of high-alkaline water, or to intentionally add a sour edge to beer. Very small amounts can impart a barely noticeable sharp, acidic edge, balancing out a beer that might be a bit lackluster otherwise.
Smoked	Just what it sounds like. Various smoked grains are available with flavors ranging from cherry-smoked to peat-smoked. German smoked malts are traditionally smoked over beechwood. If you already have a smoker, you can smoke grains in whatever fashion you desire. Most commercially available smoked malts have little to no "true" smokiness and may have been produced using liquid smoke. For a strong smoky flavor, or to emulate older styles, smoke your own.

Note: This table is based on my personal experience, research, and discussions with brewers. While the core aspects of each malt's description can be considered accurate, the flavor profile imparted in the final product is debatable. For instance, descriptions of Vienna from one brewer can sound exactly like descriptions of Munich (one is super malty and rich, the other less so) and vice versa.

Table 3.2. Non-Barley Malts

Malt Type	Description
Wheat	Brewers can generally only find a few variations on malted wheat (those with milder flavor profiles), but wheat can be roasted by all of the same methods as barley. It doesn't tend to be as popular as barley, though—except when pursuing a specific wheat-style beer such as *Weizen* or Berliner Weisse. In small amounts, wheat can improve head retention due to its high protein content. However, this quality, along with its lack of a husk, also causes it to gum up a mash tun, making for less efficient lautering process (the process whereby clear wort is drawn from the mash); rice hulls can help speed up the process.
Rye	Imparts a spicy, robust flavor to beer. As with wheat, few varieties are generally available to brewers. It also lacks a husk, so use sparingly or add rice hulls to the mash.
Oats	Commonly available unmalted, oats can be used as an adjunct to impart a soft, full mouthfeel. If you can find malted oats, use them to give your beer a granola-like flavor. As with wheat and rye, lacks a husk, so be prepared to curse or stock up on rice hulls.
Sorghum	Malted sorghum is hard to come across in the US, but the kind found in grocery stores (sugary juice that has been pressed from the cane and boiled down) works well as a substitute for the syrupy extract found in beer kits.

Roasting Your Own Malt

Since specialty malts are generally used in small amounts, it's not a daunting task to roast your own if you can't find the variety you're looking for in the homebrew store. Just follow some simple steps and roast at the appropriate length of time and temperature for your desired malt. You can also smoke your own malt in the same manner that you would smoke meat in a smoker.

Different complex chemical processes lead to different flavors through the various stages and temperatures of roasting. However, you need only be concerned with some basic parameters. One is that the high temperatures of roasting can kill the enzymes present in malt, which won't be a problem if you're simply roasting for flavoring and coloring qualities. If you choose to roast a base (fermentable) malt, consider adding some adjunct sugars or prepare to spend twice as much time to reach complete starch conversion during brewing.

To roast malt, all you need is a cookie sheet and oven (or an open wood fire if you wish to impart smokiness as well). Use unground pale or lager malt, spread the grains evenly at about 1-inch (2.5 cm) depth, set the oven's temperature and a timer as appropriate for your intended outcome, and place the cookie sheet in the oven. Stir occasionally for an even roast. To increase aroma, mist the malt every few minutes with water, as roasting moist malt can result in a richer, more intense scent.

Crystal malt requires pre-soaking; misting won't be enough. Soak crystal malt in dechlorinated water or springwater for 24 hours and then roast while moist in a deep pan such as a bread pan. Start at a low temperature (around 150°F/66°C) for an hour or more, raise to 170°F (77°C) for about another half hour, and then raise to 350°F (180°C) for at least another hour until your desired color is reached.

Always give any roasted grain a rest period of a week or two before using for brewing or you could impart some unpleasant flavors in your beer. The plethora of flavor variations possible by simply manipulating factors such as time, temperature, and moisture is astounding. Combining various grain types and then adding in the fermentation process, along with the use of hops, herbs, spices, and other ingredients . . . you can begin to see just why there are so many beer styles.

We can throw those styles out the window, though, and work toward creating our own unique styles. The more artisanal malt houses, farmers, and brewers work together in local communities across the United States (and, hopefully, the world!), the closer we'll get to the days when every farmhouse and region had its own unique style.

Barley

Barley has long been the primary grain used for fermenting beer, although corn and wheat were some of the earliest grains used, going back to Neolithic times. Historians are conflicted as to whether or not barley is the oldest cultivated grain, but most agree that it is. Regardless, it is an ancient grain and has been extensively adapted for a wide range of climates. "Barley can grow inside the Arctic Circle and barley can grow in the tropics. There are varieties suited for Montana and Arizona, New York and Georgia, Tennessee and Minnesota. And all points in between," wrote Gene Logsdon in his book *Small-Scale Grain Raising*.[3] Barley doesn't do quite as well in the American South, as it requires cool weather for ripening and prefers moderate moisture. While it is highly adaptable, it has its limits. In Kentucky, where I live, several local breweries and distilleries work to source all of their ingredients locally, but barley has to travel a bit. The problem with growing malting barley in the temperate climate of the southeast United States is that the high levels of summer heat and humidity can cause the grains to mold once harvested. To ensure that it fully dries before harvest, barley should be left on the plant as long as possible. This can cause problems for farmers who want to plant cover crops in time for winter, and leaves little time for harvesting.

Barley can be grown in two varieties: two-row and six-row. The two-row variety has only two spikelets on each stalk that are fertile and can germinate into seeds, while the other four are infertile. These two spikelets are consistently large and plump, though. Six-row varieties have six fertile grains, but the grains are smaller and less consistent in size, and don't produce as much starch as two-row. Since we need fermentable starches to convert into sugar to make alcohol, it makes sense that two-row is the preferred choice for most brewers. Another advantage of two-row is that it contains less protein (nitrogen and beta-glucan),[4] as too much protein can cause cloudiness in beer, referred to as *haze*. The effect on the flavor is negligible, but who doesn't like a glass of clear, sparkling beer?

The brewing industry and homebrewing community have both long preached that the best beer comes from two-row barley. However, six-row has in recent years been recognized as an acceptable alternative. Research into and experimentation with multiple varieties are key strategies for determining what works for a particular region. Andrea Stanley of Valley Malt in Hadley, Massachusetts, told me in a phone conversation that the difference between six-row versus two-row is not as critical an issue as it's often made out to be. There are too many other factors to take into account in selecting an ideal grain for malting, she explained. "It was a much more important conversation when people were actually growing grains," she told me.

"If they grew a six-row variety that could be both a malting variety and a feed variety, then it made a lot of sense to have this conversation of six-row versus two-row because there was actually a market for feed barley. There's no market for feed barley anymore." She also feels it's an issue of history and ingrained (my pun, fully intended) thought. "It used to mean more when six-row had higher enzymes. . . . All the modern two-rows have similar enzyme packages to six-row." When people ask her about the two varieties, she likes to bring up that two-row is actually much older than six-row, as it's closer to the wild barley that first grew in the Fertile Crescent. Six-row came about through selective breeding; it's not what ancient brewers would have been using.

Adjuncts: Rye, Wheat, and Other Grains

While barley is the workhorse of modern grain-based beers, other grains can be used for added depth and flavor. Malted and unmalted grains of all kinds can be modified through techniques such as roasting, smoking, and souring to make for a more varied grain bill. While these additional grains can provide a degree of starch for conversion into fermentable sugars, they are primarily used for flavoring, coloring, and texture, and are referred to in the brewing world as *adjuncts*.

Barley has become the go-to for most modern brews in part due to its fermentable qualities but also because much of the modern brewing world has been so heavily influenced by Western brewing traditions that other grains have fallen by the wayside. Historically, people brewed with whichever grains were most prevalent in their area of the world, and found ways to convert the starch into sugar. This is why we have millet beers in Africa, rice beers in Asia, and high usage of rye, wheat, and oats (along with some barley) in Northern Europe. Even in the modern United States, major commercial breweries use up to 60 percent unmalted rice or corn as a substitute for barley in their grain bills to produce low-cost lager beers.

Rye and wheat are common adjuncts in homebrewing. Both belong to the same tribe (Triticeae, in the grass subfamily Pooideae)

Table 3.3. Alternative Grains Used in Brewing

Grain	Description
Buckwheat	Related to sorrel and rhubarb, buckwheat is not common in modern brewing, but was historically used by the Dutch for "black beer," and in small quantities for a type of white beer. It is also sometimes used for kvass, a Russian beer (sometimes made as a non-alcoholic soda) fermented from stale bread. It is gluten-free, very aromatic, and doesn't store well due to high fat levels. Use sparingly.
Maize (corn)	First domesticated from wild grass in Central America, in malted form it can be used to make *tesgüino* and in unmalted form to make chicha (the enzymes are provided by human saliva via chewing and spitting the kernels into a vat). Corn can also be used as an adjunct for American-style beers in small quantities. Due to difficulties in obtaining quality barley or wheat malt in colonial America, corn was used often in brewing, along with molasses and sorghum.
Oats	A late cultivar, oats originated as a "weed" in Western Asia like so many other grains, but the oats we use today more likely came from a wild oat domesticated in Russia and Germany. It was grown extensively in Northern Europe during the Middle Ages, and during the early settling of the US (it's become less prevalent as a cash crop since the advent of 20th-century monoculture-intensive agriculture). If you can find it malted, use it for oatmeal stouts or for low-alcohol "small" beers. In unmalted form it imparts a thick, oily texture, and can cause difficulties with sparging. Both forms can be used to aid in head retention. Oat malt still has the husk attached, but unmalted oat may require the use of rice hulls. In unmalted form, use rolled, old-fashioned, or instant, all of which are precooked. Other forms require precooking.

but have significantly different effects on a beer's flavor profile. Rye is a fall-seeded cereal and is closely related to barley and wheat. It's easy to grow, even on poorly nourished soil, and thus is often called "poverty grain." It germinates rapidly, even at low soil temperatures, so it can continue growing into late fall. Early Scandinavians and Russians were fond of it for these reasons; it grew better than most other grains and was a trusted go-to in hard times. Its tendency to produce lots of leafy biomass makes it ideal for use as a cover crop for organic farming.

Quinoa	Not common in North American beers, quinoa is related to spinach and beets, and is highly revered by Andean peoples, who call it the mother grain due to its high nutritive values. It is sometimes used as an adjunct in chicha.
Rice	Long used for rice beer and spirits in Asia, the American variety is primarily grown as an adjunct for the beer industry and has little aroma or flavor. Look around for specialty varieties from Asia. Used sparingly, rice can make for some nice flavor profiles. As mentioned previously, rice hulls can be purchased to aid in filtering thick, gooey mash during the lautering process (the process whereby clear wort is drawn from the mash). Use about 1 pound (0.5 kg) per 5 pounds (2.5 kg) of grains, or more if needed.
Sorghum	Often called the poor man's grain, sorghum has long been recognized as an easily grown crop for use in hard times. Underappreciated during good times, it is a highly versatile grain and has a soft spot in the heart of most Appalachians. In early America (and today in Africa), sorghum beer was a nourishing traditional drink. It can be an acquired taste for modern Western beer drinkers. Use a lot of hops or other flavorings if you need help adapting to the taste.
Spelt	Related to durum wheat, spelt is an ancient grain more akin to rice. High in protein, the kernels are harvested and roasted for *Grunkern*, which is used to make nourishing soups and breads in Europe. Holland, Germany, and Belgium all have traditions of making beer with malted spelt, often along with wheat.

Domesticated rye is younger than its cousin wheat, having been first domesticated (or so historians theorize) in Southern Asia, after showing up as a weed in wheat and barley fields. From there it traveled north to Western Asia and Eastern Europe, where it thrived in cold and wet environments. Historically, rye doesn't appear in writing until around the Bronze Age (1800 to 1500 BC). Rye was referenced by Pliny as being one of the main crops of the barbarian tribes that eventually sacked Rome,[5] along with barley, which the barbarians made into beer

that the Romans referred to high-handedly as "rotted barley water."
An acquired taste (which I have acquired in spades) to some, rye can be
used in beer to impart a spicy, robust flavor. When incorporating it into
a grain bill for all-grain brewing, you will likely not want to use a large
amount of it. This is for both flavoring and practical reasons, as it can
become quite sticky.

Wheat shares rye's affinity for cold, arid climates and therefore is a
staple crop throughout the world. In North America it narrowly trails
rice and corn in terms of volume produced. A highly versatile and nutri-
ent-dense crop, it is used extensively for baking and in not-too-shabby
amounts for brewing. A descendant of wild grasses originally found in
Southwest Asia, wheat has evolved over time through cultivation and
repeated sowing, first by hunter-gatherers and eventually by settled
agricultural societies. This humble grass grew into a powerhouse of
modern settled society through thousands of years of work by farmers,
vigilantly going through the seeds at each harvest and selecting the
largest, plumpest kernels for replanting.

Wheat is almost as viable as barley for use as a primary grain in
brewing, as it contains a high percentage of enzymes once malted.
Unmalted wheat, like unmalted barley, can be used in small amounts
for color, texture, and, to a degree, flavor. It is most commonly used in
witbiers and *lambics*, giving them their characteristic cloudiness and foamy
head. It can also be used in small percentages to improve head retention
in light beers. Malted wheat can be used in large percentages, but, like
rye, can quickly become thick and sticky due to its lack of a husk and
high levels of gluten. Careful filtering of the grain bed can help alleviate
this. Unlike the sweetness that large amounts of barley malt can impart,
a primarily wheat-based beer can be heavy in texture, but light in cloy-
ing sweetness, meaning the use of hops or bittering herbs to counteract
sweetness can be minimized, and flavorings such as coriander, allspice,
star anise, and orange zest (or the zest of other citrus fruits) can be used
to create a light, zesty, and very thirst-quenching beer.

Oats, corn, quinoa, sorghum, spelt . . . the list of grains that have
been domesticated by humans is rather long. Nearly every one of them
can be used for brewing, some as the primary starch source, and others
as adjuncts. For a summary of each and their recommended and traditional uses in brewing, see table 3.3.

Artisanal Malt Houses

Most malthouses in the 19th century began as attachments to breweries and distilleries to ensure their own malt supply. In 1833, there were 13,242 official malting licenses taken out in the UK for this purpose. . . . Since then, worldwide consolidation has occurred in the malting business. . . . Today, the top 20 worldwide malting companies are all sales maltsters, producing an average of five million pounds of malt daily.

—*Dave Thomas,* The Craft Maltsters' Handbook[6]

The industrialization of malting and brewing caused the traditional malt house to go out of style, making the process almost invisible to the public. In the past, small-scale malting was the norm, performed along with other brewing and cooking tasks. An early description of the malting process provides a fair amount of detail as to how it was done. It's interesting to note the steps that had to be taken to ensure a quality malt during the days before industrialization and climate control (although we can see how malting is already being done year-round on a larger scale):

> The best barley . . . is steeped in a cistern, in greater or less quantity, by the space of three days and three nights, until it be thoroughly soaked . . . [then] the water is drained from it by little and little, till it be quite gone. Afterward they take it out, and, laying it upon the clean floor on a round heap, it resteth so until it be ready to shoot at the root end, which maltsters call combing. When it begin-neth therefore to shoot in this manner, they say it is come, and then forthwith they spread it abroad, first thick, and afterwards thinner and thinner upon the said floor (as it combeth), and there it lieth (with turning every day four or five times) by the space of one and twenty days at the least, the workmen not suffering it in any wise to take any heat, whereby the bud end should spire, that bringeth forth the blade, and by which oversight or hurt

of the stuff itself the malt would be spoiled and turn small commodity to the brewer. When it hath gone, or been turned, so long upon the floor, they carry it to a kiln covered with hair cloth, where they give it gentle heats (after they have spread it there very thin abroad) till it be dry, and in the meanwhile they turn it often, that it may be uniformly dried. For the more it be dried (yet must it be done with soft fire) the sweeter and better the malt is, and the longer it will continue.[7]

A simpler way of understanding and remembering the malting process was through rhyme. This 13th-century English poem, "The Treatise of Walter de Biblesworth," sums it up nicely:

> Then steep your barley in a vat,
> Large and broad, take care of that;
> When you shall have steeped your grain,
> And the water let out-drain,
> Take it to an upper floor,
> If you've swept it clean before,
> There couch [shovel into a heap], and let your barley dwell,
> Till it germinates full well.
> Malt now you shall call the grain
> Corn it ne'er shall be again.
> Stir the malt then with your hand,
> In heaps or rows now let it stand;
> On a tray then you shall take it,
> To a kiln to dry and bake it.[8]

Before industrialization and our current understanding of the science behind the process, poor-quality malt was very common, to the point that laws, regulations, and taxes had to be instilled to prevent maltsters from distributing bad product. With all of the moisture inherent in the malting process, mold was very common (the smell of early malt houses was often described as "musty"), and malt could easily be dried out too much during the kilning and roasting processes. But folks had a hankering for beer, and persevered nonetheless. Over time, through much trial and error, the optimal times, temperatures, and techniques were perfected, just in time for brewers to scale up during the industrial era.

By the late 1600s and early 1700s, in-depth manuals were written on brewing (with substantial sections devoted to malting). What made these books stand out from earlier writing was the attention paid to quality control through careful scientific study and minute adjustments to temperature and environment. Not all brewers were so keen on these new approaches, though. Younger, innovative brewers were often chastised by their elders for bringing newfangled inventions such as thermometers and hydrometers into the brewery.[9] This Luddite approach was to be artisanal malting's downfall. Breweries were quicker to adopt new technologies, but maltsters stubbornly stuck to the manual, intuitive approach that worked well enough for them rather than succumb to the slide toward mechanization. As automation, kilning, and environmental-control technologies were developed, more and more agrarian maltsters were left in the wake of commercial brewing. Transportation that allowed for large amounts of malt to travel great distances, along with heavy industry taxation and regulations, was the final death blow. It was no longer viable to malt, brew, and sell beer all within one small region.

The Return of Artisanal Malting

Artisanal malting has experienced a comeback in North America via the craft malt movement. As with the local foods and craft-beer movements, innovators who want to return to the days of localized malting and brewing (along with a focus on well-crafted malt) are taking lessons from the past while not completely leaving behind modern technology and scientific understanding.

Andrea Stanley, along with her husband, Christian, launched Valley Malt in the small agricultural town of Hadley, Massachusetts, in 2010. The first malt house in New England in more than 100 years, Valley Malt has more than quadrupled its production size since opening, and continues to grow due to demand from consumers and breweries thirsty for beer made from all-local ingredients.

In 2009 Andrea, a social worker at the time, and Christian, a mechanical engineer, began to look into starting up a malt house after wondering why, with all of the grain being grown around them, none was being malted for brewing. They quickly discovered that there were simply no facilities nearby to use for malting. While small malting facilities in Europe and the British Isles have continued through the industrial revolution, America's localized malt houses vanished with Prohibition. Until the artisanal malt house movement, the only malt that could be purchased by brewers and distillers on any scale came from massive industrial operations located mostly in the midwestern and western United States and Canada, or shipped from Europe. Andrea and Christian had a monumental task ahead of them.

Andrea began doggedly researching the malting process and pursuing as many leads as she could with local grain farmers, librarians, historians, and college professors—earning the nickname of Stalker Babe. Christian, meanwhile, spent what free time he had researching the technical aspects of building a malting system, ultimately cobbling together a small all-in-one tabletop system that enabled the couple to hone their malting skills and test their malt by brewing beer. After fine-tuning the prototype, Christian designed and built a 1-ton system based on the prototype. He outsourced the steel cutting, rolling, and welding, and built an electronics-control system for monitoring temperature and moisture levels. The system worked well but they needed a larger version to meet their growing needs, so they elected to retire the all-in-one system and switched to a three-part vat-malting system: one for steeping, one for germinating, and one for kilning. Everything in the new system runs on pneumatics (which uses forced air to germinate the malt), allowing them to focus more of their time on running the business.

Obtaining enough grain to provide all-local malt was the next hurdle. What had once been a commonplace practice—growing, malting, and brewing grains all in the same general vicinity—was practically nonexistent due to the globalization and industrialization of agriculture. But before they knew it, Andrea and Christian were growing grains on a small scale, and experimenting to determine the ideal varieties for malting. Finding farmers willing to produce and store the grains they needed in the fashion required for creating quality malt was tough. Most were tied up in production for bakeries and cattle feed. Local farmers wanted to help, but growing grains for malt just wasn't a viable prospect

continued on page 78

Peterson Quality Malt

Andrew Peterson's farm and malt house are nestled in the countryside of the Champlain Valley, at the foot of the Green Mountains, just south of Hinesburg, an idyllic Vermont town with signs offering fresh eggs, cheese, and maple syrup.

Locating Peterson Quality Malt here was intentional. Andrew wanted to avoid what many breweries and some malt houses have done, setting up shop in a warehouse in an industrial area. "I felt that if I was going to do this, I wanted to walk outside and see farmland, not a bunch of buildings and traffic," he told me. Pulling into his driveway, I felt immediately at ease. I grew up on a farm (and spent some periods of my life working warehouse temp jobs), so commercial and industrial areas don't gel with me. I felt an immediate affinity with Andrew as well. Laid-back, with shaggy reddish hair and a beard, he could be my twin.

Andrew Peterson stands in front of his grain silos and grain smoker.

At the time I visited, Andrew malted only barley, wheat, and rye, but was looking into malting some adjuncts; he just needed to convince some farmers to grow these for him. After quickly attending to various electronic beeps that he says pull him in every direction throughout the

Andrew Peterson demonstrates some malted grain.

day, he took me into his environmentally controlled germination room, which has two large, rectangular, stainless-steel, false-bottomed vats. Resting in one was barley that was currently in the germination stage. It was slightly moist; you could see the telltale "beards" that keep barley's hull intact. The room was cool, and a fan occasionally kicked in. Andrew explained that the temperature and the fan (which pulls out built-up CO_2) help keep the barley from fermenting. As the malt germinates, Andrew and his assistants occasionally sift it to keep it from bricking up.

Peterson Quality Malt is a somewhat more mechanized operation than some of its peers. "Every micro malt house operates a bit differently," Andrew told me. Since each started with few to no modern-day precursors to draw from for information and equipment, they all pieced together their operation in whichever way they saw fit. Some malt houses, like Asheville, North Carolina's Riverbend Malt House, practice floor malting, where the malt is laid out on a concrete floor and raked with a large wooden rake. Peterson practices vat malting.

When we stepped back outside, Andrew showed me where they collect the excess water from moisturizing the malt, which is sent off to farms for increasing the nutrient content of manure. They also bag the culms from the culming machine and set it out for local farmers—who race to be the first to nab it for animal feed. Andrew then posed for a photo next to his smoker, which he uses for smoking meat and specialty malt.

Artisan malt houses enable homebrewers and craft brewers to brew more sustainably and locally, adding to the terroir (French for "earth" or "soil") of beer. In the wine industry *terroir* is used to denote the effect of a region's climate, soil, and other localized factors on the flavor of wine. With this new ability to source malted grains locally, the craft-beer industry can now proudly adopt this term. Not only do artisan maltsters like Andrew provide quality local grains, but they enable a more localized infrastructure, thus minimizing the use of fossil fuels. Craft malt houses also build relationships with local farmers and regional brewers, enabling progress toward a closed-loop production system. It's a win-win-win for all.

at the time. They began to get creative, and looked for what was already available from local farmers. Since not many locals were growing barley (until they convinced some farmers to grow it for them), they went with the ample wheat supply and began malting wheat. This allowed for a localized character in beers brewed from the grains they malted. In turn, consumers were willing to pay a bit extra to drink something truly local.

Andrea and Christian are now able to generally acquire the types of grains they—and their brewing customers—want, in part by sharing the risk with some farmers by purchasing the seeds for the grains they want to grow. They also started a brewer-supported agriculture (BSA) program, based on the community-supported agriculture (CSA) concept. For BSAs, brewers help fund the production and malting of the grains they in turn make into beer.[10]

In 2013 Andrea helped found the Craft Maltsters Guild (CMG), after finding other people across the country interested in starting malt houses but lacking the resources to do so on an artisanal scale. The guild provides a centralized set of resources and networking opportunities for artisanal maltsters, and in five years has grown to include malt houses (including breweries and distilleries with their own malting operations) across the United States and Canada, with over 30 active members, including Blacklands Malt in Leander, Texas; Eckert Malting & Brewing Co. in Chico, California; Riverbend Malt House in Asheville, North Carolina; Haus Malts in Cleveland, Ohio; Horton Ridge Malt in Hortonville, Nova Scotia; and Peterson Malt in Monkton, Vermont.

CHAPTER FOUR

WATER

Water next to Malt is what by course comes here under Consideration as a Matter of great Importance in Brewing of wholsome fine Malt-liquors, and is of such Consequence that it concerns every one to know the nature of the water he Brews with, because it is the Vehicle by which the nutritious and pleasant Particles of the Malt and Hop are conveyed into our Bodies, and there becomes a diluter of our Food.[1]

—William Ellis, The London and Country Brewer, 1736

Who wants to read an entire chapter about water? That was my thought when I first convinced myself to sit down and research water and its use in brewing. It may at first seem the least interesting ingredient in beer, but it is a large component of the final product and, if not approached with the proper respect and knowledge, can have a very real effect on the outcome of that (hopefully) tasty beverage in your pint glass. A cursory understanding of where water comes from and what it's made of is important for the brewers who not only want to understand the role of water in their brewing endeavors, but also hope to brew sustainably and efficiently while minimizing waste.

All alcohols are related to water in their chemical makeup. The difference is simply that one or both of their hydrogen atoms have been replaced by carbon. When scientists first began classifying organic compounds in the 1800s, alcohol, along with ether, was classified as belonging to the "water type." Before this classification, the word *alcohol* was used to reference a single substance, ethyl alcohol (C_2H_5OH), rather than an entire class of organic compounds.[2] Over time scientists began to realize that alcohol and water were closely related. After all, alcohols all start as water. The water is simply "enhanced" through fermentation, although technically it becomes a different chemical substance.

There's a reason water was one of the core components of the Reinheitsgebot—you can't make beer without it! Yet this strict law had an unintended effect when it was first instituted—it prohibited the addition of *anything* extra, even very minor components that were intended to improve quality, including the brewing salts most brewers added to their water, which improved the final product and helped with brewing efficiency by balancing pH levels. No matter; the ingenious Germans learned to acidify their malt through the addition of sauermalz (sour malt—see the previous chapter), and alternatively to employ a long acid

Tonelagee, the third highest of Ireland's Wicklow Mountains, whose springs source the water used to make Guinness. Courtesy of Joe King, Wikimedia Commons.

rest to promote lactobacillus growth.[3] Fortunately, if you're reading this book, you're (hopefully) not bound by the Big Bad Law. We'll discuss pH balancing further on; first, let's delve into a bit of the history and science behind water.

A Brief History of "Demon Water"

Historically, water (or *liquor* as brewing water is properly called) was prepared for use in brewing in various manners—namely boiling and the addition of brewing salts. As a matter of fact, brewing itself was seen as a way to make water potable. Because of this, beer and other fermented beverages were looked at as safe and healthy and water was eyed with suspicion; even clean springwater was considered unhealthy when compared with wholesome beer. In Anglo-Saxon times, when populations were just beginning to concentrate in cities, water was certainly drunk, and much work was done to gather, store, and transport it, but it was still looked at by many as a less-than-desirable substance. It was generally drunk for penitence or as a punishment for offenses such as speaking in church, with offenders being obliged to spend anywhere from a day to a week imbibing nothing but bread and water. In *Regimen Sanitatis Salernitanum*, a poem on healthful living written in the 12th or 13th century, readers are advised to drink diluted wine with meals, rather than water, as water was thought to chill the stomach, making food indigestible. Historical records show that water was used primarily as a base for fermented drinks, soup stocks, gruels, teas, and other liquids—even before it came to be associated with sickness.[4]

Upon arriving on American shores, the Pilgrims were very concerned about their shortage of beer, even after discovering springs and pristine streams full of fresh, potable water. Their fear of water was deeply ingrained due to centuries of pollution in European cities. They knew that boiled and fermented water kept them alive and healthy, while straight water had a habit of sickening or killing people. Nearly every new colony commissioned a brew house as one of its first structures. In sea voyages to and from the New World, it was considered disastrous to stock a ship with only water to drink. The idea that boiled and cooled water could be drinkable without being fermented into beer was close to nonexistent. By 1638 the notion that every sailor must be

On Boiling of Water for Historical Beers

Nearly every contemporary book, article, or blog on historical beer brewing refers to water being boiled to make it safe for drinking and brewing. Yet recently researchers have started to question whether this was always the standard. For one thing, boiling water for safety really only became prevalent as people started settling in cities and polluting their water sources. Most early cities—and temporary settlements for nomadic peoples—were situated near springs and other sources of clean water. In addition, humans figured out how to purify water by methods other than boiling. Through ancient Sanskrit, Greek, and Egyptian writings, we know that early peoples boiled water, but they also purified it by filtering it through gravel and sand; with precious metals, by dropping hot rocks or dipping hot iron into it; or by using additives such as alum or the seed of the clearing-nut tree (*Strychnos potatorum*, a bushy tree native to India, the seed of which purifies water instantly).[5]

While early written and anecdotal evidence exists that demonstrates humankind's dislike of water, let's be honest, water is pretty boring on its own. When we drink water, we drink enough to satisfy our thirst and then our bodies are done until they need more. When we drink a well-crafted fermented beverage, tea, lemonade, soda, or the like, we continue to drink because our bodies crave good flavors and the nutritive (or non-nutritive) substances in these "enhanced" waters. It may not have always been the case that beer was thought of as necessarily safer than water, but it was certainly considered to be more enjoyable and healthful to drink. Lengthy boils are a fairly modern innovation and are only really necessary to draw out the properties of hops. Boiling is also very resource-intensive. Even with modern range tops and propane burners, it can take some time—and a fair amount of fuel and energy—to bring a large kettle of water or wort to a boil. Think of how much precious fuel it would have taken without these modern innovations.

One of the reasons for soaking grains in hot water is to draw out the enzymes that will convert starches to sugars. However, we know that chicha, the beer made by indigenous South Americans, is made by chewing corn kernels, which not only exposes the germ for fermentation but also provides necessary enzymes that occur naturally in human saliva. Granted, beers made this way are lower in alcohol and tend to be cloudy, as boiling also concentrates the wort and kills any remaining enzymes, allowing for a clearer beverage with higher alcohol content due to more concentrated sugars. It is highly unlikely, though, that Neolithic beers were boiled for any amount of time.

Dr. Martin Zarnkow, a brewing historian in the Center of Life and Food Sciences at the Munich Technical University, notes that beer is still brewed at ambient temperatures in Africa today, but it is drunk young while still foaming, as it is the yeasty "head" that keeps spoiling microorganisms out.[6] Most other ancient cultures would have drunk their beer this way as well, and few, if any, would have boiled their wort. *Sahti*, a traditional Finnish beer, was customarily made without boiling the wort, and is still made this way in some parts of Finland today. Billy Quinn and Declan Moore of Moore Environmental and Archaeological Consultants in Galway re-created a prehistoric beer for which they heated the wort by dropping hot stones in it (more on this in chapter 8). It would have been far too labor-intensive to bring the wort to a boil using this method. They found that the act of fermentation and the fact

that they used a clean water source kept the beer from spoiling.[7] Many of the recipes in this book call for a one-hour boil, primarily because this is the standard for most brewing recipes today, particularly those that use hops. For those that don't require any boil or don't need a 60-minute boil, I'll make a note. It doesn't hurt to understand that boiling wort isn't needed to initiate fermentation, but that there are often good reasons for doing so.

Illustration of *Strychnos potatorum* by William Roxburgh, 1795. Public domain.

provided with beer was set into law, with an agreement being set forth between shipowners and crews that every sailor aboard New England sailing ships receive a quart of beer per day. Hence, a large portion of each ship's store was devoted to beer.[8]

It wasn't until the early 19th century that water began to have its day as a healthful substance. Piped water began to make its way into cities, starting with Philadelphia in 1799, and technology for the safe storage of potable water was developed. The old fears still ran deep, though. A French visitor to Philadelphia noted that handbills were passed around to visitors, warning them "either to drink grog or add a little wine or some other spirituous liquor to their water. Sometimes notices are placed on the pumps with the words: 'Death to him who drinks quickly.'"[9] Strangely, river water was considered by some to be drinkable. Travelers of means whiling away the hours on riverboat rides spent their time in the lavish saloons drinking cocktails and wine and gambling, while the less fortunate stayed on the main deck along with their livestock and luggage, where the only drinks available were whiskey and river water. Drinking it sediment and all, one traveler preferred it "fresh out of the river, with the true Mississippi relish."[10]

By 1867, spurred by the recent discovery by Louis Pasteur that bacteria can be killed in liquids via what came to be known as pasteurization (heating it to between 147° and 212°F / 64° and 100°C for 32 minutes), Paris underwent an ambitious remodel, building broad new streets with water lines beneath that pumped fresh water via aqueducts to residences and other buildings, paving the way for modern cities and water-treatment facilities.[11]

The Water Cycle and the Chemical Makeup of Water

There's no way around it, brewers use a *lot* of water: Water not only goes into the beer itself, but is also used for brewing the wort, cooling the hot wort, cleaning, rinsing . . . and more cleaning . . . and more rinsing. And let's not forget the water that is lost, whether it's trapped in spent grains, evaporated during the boil, or left behind in the equipment. Most brewers estimate that cleaning constitutes anywhere from 75 to

90 percent of brewing. So when we consider the water cycle, we need to include both the natural water cycle and the cycle once people take over. Water begins its cycle in the skies above us, when pure H_2O in the form of vapor in the clouds condenses to form water droplets, and falls from the sky as rain or snow. As it falls, it gathers various substances from the atmosphere before landing on the earth, where it either evaporates or soaks into the ground, watering plants and becoming groundwater. In the ground, water picks up more substances, from organic matter and various minerals to herbicides and pesticides. Most organic materials and contaminants are filtered out as the water soaks deeper into the earth, while minerals continue to accumulate over time. Groundwater then resides in aquifers for hundreds, even thousands, of years. If not brought to the surface manually by people, it eventually seeps up through wells, springs, rivers, and streams, becoming surface water. At any point this water can evaporate into the atmosphere and start the cycle anew.

So what does this mean for the brewer (or brewster)? Each phase of the water cycle changes water's levels of pH, sediment, dissolved minerals, and so forth. Environmental conditions and human activity also have varying degrees of impact on water quality. Water for brewing and drinking has traditionally come from surface and groundwater sources. In the past boiling was the primary method to ensure water was as clean as possible (it was subsequently, but not always, brewed it into beer). Today municipalities in the United States and other countries are required to treat water for contaminants before distributing it. This doesn't necessarily mean it's ready for drinking right out of the tap; often it's not appropriate for brewing or other types of fermentation without additional treatments. This is why it is important to obtain a water report from your municipality and learn how to read it. Although water treatment processes vary somewhat by municipality, there are certain steps required by law. Generally it works as follows (with the order varying depending on the municipality and the types of contaminants identified):

1. Water is filtered through screens to remove debris.
2. Activated carbon is used to remove organic taste and odor compounds.
3. The water is aerated/ozonated to oxidize soluble forms of iron or manganese into their insoluble forms so they can be filtered out.
4. Overly hard water is softened with lime.

5. Fine particulates are coagulated with alum (aluminum sulfate), ferric chloride, or polymer additions.
6. The water is then filtered through fine sand or media filters to remove micro-particles and microbes.
7. The water's pH is adjusted through lime, caustic, or acid (this is primarily to prevent scaling or corrosion of pipelines and plumbing).
8. As a final check against bacterial growth, a disinfectant (usually chlorine, but sometimes chloramine, aka monochloramine) is run through the utility's pipelines.

The last step is something conscientious brewers should take note of upon first drawing water from the tap. By nature, chlorine and chloramine are both fermentation inhibitors. Generally, chlorine isn't a concern for brewing beer since it evaporates during boiling (or even if left for a few hours in an open container), but chloramine (chlorine bound with ammonia) is a more complex chemical that doesn't dissipate with ease. Municipalities in warmer regions may be more likely to use it, as summer heat can cause chlorine to dissipate quickly. And because chloramines are less effective at removing bacteria, they are used in larger amounts than chlorine.[12] The EPA regularly conducts studies on the safety and effectiveness of using monochloramines in drinking water and is open to questions from the public.

The safety of drinking unfiltered tap water with high levels of chlorine or chloramine in it—and the government's role in regulating dosages—is up for debate (just pay a visit to your nearest conspiracy-theory chatroom), but when it comes to brewing, you should filter your tap water to some degree. One safety concern, which has been addressed by environmental regulations such as the US Clean Water Act, is that hypochlorite (free chlorine) can form potentially carcinogenic compounds known as disinfection by-products (DBP) when reacting with organic compounds in surface water such as lakes and streams. Since chloramine is less likely to break down when interacting with organic compounds, municipalities with large amounts of organic matter in their water supplies are more likely to use it (along with additional measures such as ultraviolet light and ozonation).[13]

There are various methods for removing disinfectant chemicals in preparation for brewing. One is to use sodium metabisulfite or potassium metabisulfite (aka Campden tablets); used by many wine- and mead makers to remove wild yeast from *must* (unfermented wine or mead), it also serves as an antioxidant in beer wort and is useful in breaking down chlorine and chloramine in water. Another technique that works to remove chlorine, chloramine, and other contaminants is activated carbon. Most breweries pump their tap water through granular activated carbon (GAC) filters. The carbon in raw organic materials such as wood, nut shells, or coal is increased or "activated" through heat. The heated surface, minus the presence of oxygen, serves to adsorb (trap) chemicals as water passes through the filters. Since the process essentially creates charcoal, these filters are also known as "charcoal" filters.[14] There are two primary ways homebrewers can employ GACs in their home. One is a whole-house system, which is installed at the water supply point of entry, serving to filter all water in the house (usually with the exception of outside faucets). Another is a point of use (POU) filter, such as an under-sink unit or GAC pitcher filter. The latter is tedious for filling a large brew kettle, and is much less effective at removing all contaminants. When I first started brewing with extract, I simply brought tap water to a boil and proceeded. The beers I produced were quite tasty, but lately I've been using a faucet filter to ensure that as many contaminants as possible are removed before I heat the water. For one, boiling doesn't necessarily remove everything, but if I'm intending to mash any grains, I'd rather just heat the water to the proper mash temperature rather than boil it and wait for it to cool. Personally, I haven't felt the need to make pH-balancing additions, but many brewers swear that mashes tend to be more efficient with fewer off flavors in the final product if a few minor pH adjustments are made.

Dude, That's Some Pretty Kickass Metal

Metal is not a bad thing. Metal is actually pretty awesome if you can learn to appreciate it. Or at least that's what I keep trying to tell my wife. Whoops, I think I may be talking about the wrong kind of metal. . . .

With the exception of distilled water, in which pretty much everything is stripped out (one reason why it's not ideal for brewing), nearly all water contains some degree of minerals and metals. Depending on what you're brewing, and what type of metal we're talking about and what your personal preferences are, this can be a good thing or a bad thing. Trace amounts of metals such as copper and zinc can serve as yeast nutrients, making for a more vigorous and complete fermentation, while too much can cause flavoring and fermentation problems. Iron can often be found in well water, and should be removed before using it for brewing. Manganese is also unwelcome, as it can cause cloudiness and off flavors and doesn't get along well with yeast (this is usually removed from municipal sources through oxidation or greensand treatment). Aluminum has been unfairly maligned due to its supposed link to Alzheimer's disease, but isn't harmful in brewing (or drinking) in trace amounts. While many brewers prefer stainless-steel brew kettles to aluminum pots, aluminum is actually a very strong metal and very little if any of it leaches into beer wort due to the near-impenetrable layer of nonreactive aluminum oxide that surrounds it. Tin also is not dangerous, but can cause haziness in beer.[15] Heavier metals (my favorite kind . . . assuming we're not talking about minerals) such as lead, calcium, and mercury won't necessarily cause problems with brewing, and are okay in trace amounts in water, but should be avoided at high levels. Get an analysis of your water and invest in a higher-grade filter (charcoal alone won't do it) if you need to remove any of these, or remove them through lime softening or reverse osmosis.

Adjusting Mash pH

The meeting of hot water and grains is when pH really starts to matter, so from here on out when I mention pH I am referring to mash pH. Extract brewers need not be concerned about mash pH, as the work has already been done for you. Even if you're adding small amounts of adjuncts, you shouldn't be concerned. Just be sure you're using quality water.

For all-grain brewing you probably don't need to adjust your mash's pH unless you have a particularly high level of alkalinity in your tap water or are using a mineral-heavy water such as well water or water from a mineral-intensive spring. Godfather of modern homebrewing Charlie Papazian writes, "Most beer yeasts enjoy an environment that is acidic at a pH of 5.0–5.5. This environment will occur naturally in all beer worts. The homebrewer need not make adjustments,"[16] while *Radical Brewing* author Randy Mosher says, "Fortunately [pH] doesn't require a lot of managing. Use proper techniques in other respects, and pH will usually take care of itself." He goes on to say that pH "can have a modest effect."[17] Some, though, feel that brewing a truly great beer is all about paying attention to the "modest effects," which include:

- Enhanced enzyme activity, which leads to higher conversion of starches to sugars.
- Improved yeast health and reduced potential for bacteria growth during fermentation.
- Better hop extraction rates in the boil.
- Improved clarity, stability, and flavor during aging of bottled beer.

In *Designing Great Beers*, Ray Daniels writes that for a mash containing only a primary malt such as pale malt, pH adjustments will always need to be made, and provides mathematical equations for calculating the proper adjustments. He goes on to add, though, that "Even in fairly modest amounts, specialty malts . . . can drop the pH up to 0.5. . . . Many recipes have enough specialty malt that I don't need to worry about further reductions of the mash pH."[18]

So let's say you feel you have a reason for adjusting your pH, or you're just the kind of geek who enjoys doing that sort of thing. There are only three compounds you really need to worry about when adjusting your mash pH. Once you have learned them, you can promptly forget them, as all you really need to do is analyze your mash's overall pH, make the necessary adjustments, and move on (use a pH meter; pH strips aren't accurate and will waste your time). The first compound is bicarbonate (HCO_3-), referred to as alkalinity. The others are calcium ($Ca++$) and magnesium ($Mg++$). Simply put, if you know you have hard water or a test shows high levels of alkalinity (high carbonate), be sure to boil your water first to remove the carbonate and then add brewing salts (usually gypsum, or calcium sulfate, but other salts such as sodium chloride or calcium carbonate will work) to the water. If you really want to go hardcore, pick up a book on brewing chemistry for equations and formulas to help determine the exact amount needed. Most brewers get by just fine with adding about ½ teaspoon of brewing salts to the mash, mixing well, testing, and adding more until the proper level is reached. Don't overthink this. Just get as close as you can and never add more than 2 teaspoons.

Brewing salts can also be added if you want to emulate a style from a specific region, as many traditional European and British beer styles achieve their unique flavor due to the local water they use. Research this if you're looking to brew "to style." The focus in this book, though, is more on traditional brewing techniques, which eschewed "style" in favor of creating a brew unique to a particular brewer (or brewster) and region. Create your own style!

The Terroir of Water

Where water is sourced can have a surprising impact on a beer's flavor. Several European beer styles and brands are still recognized today in large part for the water that goes into their beer. London, Munich, and Dublin, for example, are all known for beers made with darker malts. This is because their water is high in carbonates (high pH) and has what is known as "temporary hardness." This hardness can be adjusted to make a lighter beer with the addition of brewing salts. If the carbonates are left as is, however, they can draw out harsh, astringent qualities in hops. Dark, roasted malts have enough acidity to balance the mash; hence the tendency for these cities to produce dark, smooth, malty beers.

On the other end of the spectrum are beers made with water with "permanent hardness" caused by sulfate. Burton-on-Trent (also Burton upon Trent, or just Burton) in England is famous not only for its beer but for its water as well. An entire style has developed around the type of beer produced there: bitter pale ale, or simply *Bitter*. While the style's parameters have branched out beyond Burton-on-Trent now that brewers know more about water chemistry, this is still the best place to obtain a true English Bitter. At some point after the introduction of hops as a standard ingredient, London brewers discovered that hopped beer made with their water had a bitterness that was far too astringent and harsh. However, in the village of Burton, the hopped beers had a pleasant, aromatic bitterness. Further, the sulfates in Burton's water helped to clarify the beer, resulting in a clear, refreshingly bitter beer. Although many breweries produced a fine Bitter, industrialization and the resultant consolidation of breweries caused most of them to fold or be folded into the premier British pale ale brand of today, Bass, whose signature red triangle was the very first trademark to be registered under the U.K.'s Trade Mark Registration Act of 1875. Bass had a reputation in the 1800s for producing strong, clear beers that held up well to the rigors of travel. They produced some of the first and most popular India Pale Ales (IPAs), pale ales that had twice the amount of hops of a standard pale, as they were made to withstand lengthy ship travels, particularly to the British colonies in India. In addition to doubling the amount of hops, brewers also produced lower-gravity beers, meaning more sugars were fermented out, resulting in a drier, lighter-bodied beer with less likelihood of spoilage by sugar-eating organisms. Anyone wishing to brew a good, strong, and clear pale ale, or IPA, today would be remiss not to add some brewing salts (usually gypsum or Burton water salts), and to first remove any bicarbonates for a true Burton-style pale.

Salt is a little-discussed mineral when it comes to beer, but does play a part in certain styles. In very small amounts it elicits a barely detectable impact on body. In styles such as gose, a white ale from East Germany, enough is added for a detectable level of saltiness. This style may have originated due to the use of salt, along with flour, to clean casks, or because the water had a naturally high salt content.[19]

Sustainability and Wastewater Management in Brewing

Whether you minimize and responsibly dispose of wastewater for environmental reasons (as you should) or to cut down water costs, you should go into each brewing session knowing approximately how much water you'll need (and preparing a couple of gallons more than your estimate), and with a plan for disposing of any wastewater. This should start at the cleaning stage. If you heavily sanitize your equipment with chemicals (I don't—see chapter 5 for my thoughts on this), you'll need to take extra care with cleaning wastewater to ensure you're disposing of the chemical-saturated water responsibly. Try not to use overly hard water for cleaning. The terms *soft* and *hard* when referring to water actually came about as people realized that less mineral-heavy (soft) water tended to better break down soap and create more suds. Hard water was literally harder to clean with. You'll get more efficient cleaning and rinsing with soft water, and won't leave behind carbonates in your equipment. Even

Cooling water from a wort chiller can be used to fill a kiddie pool. Fun for the whole family!

with my regimen of soap and hot water, I go through a lot of water when I wash and rinse my equipment. Some of it inevitably goes down the drain or on the lawn, but I take care to minimize the amount I use when cleaning. Further down the line, I may go through additional water while doing things like cooling down my wort. In this case, I try to use water that is still pretty much the same as how it came from the faucet to fill containers for watering my garden or animals, or I might fill the kiddie pool and let my kids join in the fun. Sometimes I'm just too busy attending to things and it soaks into the lawn. Regardless, I recommend always going into brewing with the mind-set of responsible water management.

Calculating Water Amounts When Brewing

I discussed the basic concepts of all-grain brewing in the last chapter, but here's a quick primer on calculating water amounts while we're on the subject. In the recipes and techniques chapters, I'll address specific amounts of water for the recipe/technique in question. Calculating amounts of water is much more important in all-grain brewing than simpler types of brewing for which the only thing you'll want to be concerned about is the amount you brew with. When you're all-grain brewing, you'll be making all kinds of adjustments to varying amounts of water throughout the process, mostly regarding temperature.

Whatever amount of beer you plan on making, whether it's 1 gallon (4 L) or 5 gallons (20 L), you may as well resign yourself to the fact that the amount you bottle will almost always be smaller, unless you dilute with additional water or another liquid. A savvy, mathematical brewer could probably calculate how much water to start brewing with to come closer to the actual amount of the vessel, but in general you will lose various amounts of water, wort, and beer throughout the brewing and fermentation processes (think of it as the angel's share, which is what whiskey or Scotch lost due to evaporation and soaking into barrels while aging is called by distillers). So let's start with the brewing process. You will experience water loss through:

- Water being soaked up by grain.
- Water/wort being left behind in equipment.
- Water/wort evaporating in the boil.
- Water/wort decreasing in volume as it cools.

After brewing, you'll be transferring the wort (and eventually beer) into various containers. Very small amounts will be lost in hoses, funnels, and the original vessel, but you will also lose minuscule amounts that are soaked up by any plant matter or adjuncts. Once fermentation has commenced, a portion of the fermentation vessel's volume will be taken up by trub (sediment) at the bottom. When racking, you'll want to leave this behind in addition to a bit of the actual beer to ensure clarity. And let's face it, if you want to emulate the ancient practice of drinking beer while it's still fermenting, you'll likely be sampling some of the beer before you bottle it. So with that in mind, whenever I refer to, say, a 1-gallon (4 L) or 5-gallon (20 L) batch of beer, what I really mean is the size of the vessel you're brewing in. You will prepare this amount initially, but the overall volume will change slightly throughout. Does this need to concern you? Not really. In many cases I won't add the full amount of water for the vessel until active fermentation has died down, as some brews will produce a lot of krausen (fermentation foam) and I want to save some extra space to avoid overflow. In other cases I don't mind a slight dilution in alcohol content and flavor intensity if adding a bit of water will result in a bit more beer in the end. These things will be up to you. There are steps you can take to calculate the proper amount of water to start with for each recipe, though. My simple solution is to boil about a gallon (4 L) more water than the amount of beer I want to end up with (with the understanding I will still lose some in the fermentation process). If I end up with a bit less than my intended 5 gallons (20 L), I can simply add a bit to the fermenter. I don't get any more technical than this, but if you do enjoy crunching numbers, there are plenty of calculators and spreadsheets on the Internet for determining amounts of water and grain for a batch of beer. There are also brewing manuals much more technical than this one. I recommend Ray Daniels's *Designing Great Beers*, as he has some very thorough tables and formulas that even number dumbos like me can find useful.

So that's it. One more element of the Reinheitsgebot down, and an ingredient you'll need regardless of whether you follow antiquated, finicky German brewing laws or not. That wasn't so bad, was it?

CHAPTER FIVE

YEAST

east. On one hand it's the simplest and easiest-to-work-with ingredient in beer. Simply add it in powdered or liquid form, or initiate a wild fermentation using airborne yeasts and yeasts that exist naturally on botanical ingredients (provided they haven't been sprayed or sterilized) and let nature do its work. On the other hand it is an incredibly complex microorganism with a rich history of coexistence (even symbiosis) with humankind that we are only just beginning to understand. Beer would not be beer without it. Humans could very well not exist without it. Yeast are living creatures. They run wild in herds (or more accurately, hitch rides on fruit skins and dust motes). They rest in petri dishes and packets of powdered and liquid yeast on the shelves of homebrew stores and in breweries, waiting to be woken and fed. The types of yeast we use, how we feed them and keep them at the appropriate temperature, and how they interact with other microorganisms all can have very real effects on the flavor, drinkability, mouthfeel, and alcohol level of the final product.

In my first book, *Make Mead Like a Viking*, I explored how ancient societies captured, saved, and passed down yeast cultures through generations, emphasizing how simple it is for us to do the same even in our highly sterilized, highly commercialized modern culture. I still hold to my mantra that simplicity is the key when it comes to brewing, even if you want to delve more in-depth into different styles and techniques. Although in researching this chapter I have opened my eyes to the myriad possibilities presented by experimenting with different yeast strains—whether wild or domesticated—and how fickle a creature yeast really can be, it's still simple enough to make a quaffable batch of beer using wild yeast or a domesticated single strain with basic skills and rudimentary equipment. In the end I still hold to a straightforward approach to how I use yeast in my brewing, approaching it more as art— even magic—than a regimented technical process. Learning what these tiny creatures are all about and how they have been manipulated (and how they have manipulated us) through time is a fascinating subject. I think you will agree.

Yeast and the Origins of Life

Picture if you will, deep in the vastness of space, a massive cloud. Not some ordinary earth cloud made up of water vapor, but a booze cloud. Sagittarius B2N lies about 120 parsecs (390 light-years) from the center of the Milky Way and some 26,000 light-years (150 quadrillion miles) from the earth. This is one of many "space clouds," or gas clouds, and consists almost entirely of alcohol, primarily methanol, ethanol, and vinyl alcohols (only one of these, ethanol, can be imbibed safely by humans). Vinyl alcohol in particular is of great interest to scientists, as it is a complex organic molecule and thus a precursor to life. Scientists theorize that vinyl alcohol molecules have the ability to attach themselves to interstellar dust particles, which in turn are picked up by passing comets. To the best of our knowledge it's not yeast that creates this alcohol. The prevailing theory is that when new stars form, these boozy gas clouds are the by-product. Space booze could very well have played a role in the creation of life on earth. Scientists have witnessed comets spewing trails of the stuff. They theorize that these complex molecules could have entered earth's atmosphere via a closely passing (or crashed) comet, creating an organic soup that led to more complex life-forms.[1] While space booze is fascinating to theorize about, what does it have to do with yeast and the production of alcohol that humans can imbibe? Well, for now we have to assume there are two different ways of producing alcohol: harnessing the powers of microscopic herds of wild yeast or growing a new star. Personally, I'm going to stick to yeast herding.

Pillars of Creation, a photograph taken by the Hubble Space Telescope in 1995 (and enhanced in 2014), depicts "pillars" of interstellar gas and dust in the Eagle Nebula, debris from the creation of new stars. Courtesy of Jeff Jackowski, Flickr.

Yeast has played a critical role in the formation (and flourishing) of our species, regardless of whether it came from a passing space cloud. In order for yeast to produce alcohol, it needs sugar to feed on. It gets that sugar from plants—and by-products of plants such as honey, malted grains, sorghum, and cane sugar. Plants are only able to produce sugar through the process of photosynthesis, which requires light, water, and air. Simply put, plants draw what they need from their environment, turn it into the air that we breathe—and into stores of sugar to survive on. We then extract their sugar, and employ yeast (or the yeast goes about it all on its own) to eat it up and produce ethanol and carbon dioxide (that is, booze!).

Since yeast can survive without oxygen, it was most certainly around before people. The breakdown of glucose by enzymes (in other words, the fermentation of sugar), or glycolysis, is theorized to be the earliest form of energy production on earth; primitive single-celled organisms munched on simple sugars floating around in primordial soup and excreted ethanol and carbon dioxide until there was enough oxygen in the atmosphere for more effective methods of energy extraction.[2] As more complex organisms developed, these new life-forms recognized the powers of this primordial booze and began to actively pursue it.

Although humans eventually found ways to control and fine-tune the process of turning simple sugars into booze, they, along with many animals, enjoyed naturally produced ferments when they came across them. Humans may have discovered the power of fermentation by gathering honey, perhaps in a gourd that had other yeast-carrying and sugar-intensive substances such as fruit in it, forgetting about it for a few days, and then taking a drink and noticing a marked difference in flavor and substance. Over time they learned to gather and ferment sugar from other sources, and to let it age long enough for the drink to produce a magical buzz—transporting their minds to other places. Animals of all kinds are known to gather around fruit trees—not just for the freshly ripened fruit, but for the fruit that has fallen and begun to ferment—and then devour as much as they can in a drunken feeding frenzy. Monkeys, our closest relatives, greatly enjoy the boozy by-product of yeast. Charles Darwin noted in *The Descent of Man, and Selection in Relation to Sex* that "the natives of north-eastern Africa catch the wild baboons by exposing vessels with strong beer, by which they are made drunk."[3] In his book *The Drunken Monkey: Why We Drink and Abuse Alcohol*, Robert Dudley hypothesizes that primates are hardwired to pursue fermented beverages because of our ancestors' desire to pursue—and binge on—high-sugar, lightly fermented fruits when they were in season. Through his extensive field studies, Dudley found that howler monkeys would follow the heady, boozy scent of over-ripened fruit for miles, indulge excessively, and show clear signs of drunkenness. Not only did the high-sugar fruit provide them with vital nutrients, but it also served as a social lubricant, causing them to become more social and work as a team. Based on his research, Dudley theorized that over time, as alcohol became more readily available at higher levels, humans continued to pursue the instinct to indulge to excess. Once a nutritional necessity, alcohol is now always "in season" for humans, so when our neural pathways tell us to continue indulging, we're not always able to stop when we should.[4]

Let's Take a Ride in the Wayback Machine

Highly adaptable single-celled organisms that can reproduce at astounding rates, yeast share similar cellular traits with both plants and animals. In the right environment they can ravage through sugar at astounding rates. Researchers are now discovering that there are more species of yeast than we could possibly imagine, but it's only been a couple of hundred years since we figured out how to look at yeast under a microscope and to isolate different strains. It's a popular myth that we had no idea that yeast was its own substance before Louis Pasteur; people were playing around with saving yeast strains and doing their best to keep the ones going that seemed to work best long before. Pasteur's novel discovery was in isolating yeast and other microbes under a microscope and finding that some of them caused what he called "beer disease" (which was part of his overall work on the germ theory of disease). This was a godsend to the rising brewing industry, as the ability to isolate yeast strains and the understanding that heating (pasteurizing) water and wort before pitching yeast would greatly minimize the chance of spoilage.

Before Pasteur, we had a very different relationship with yeast. We knew that certain ingredients and certain conditions would lead to

Saccharomyces cerevisiae as photographed under a scanning electron microscope (SEM). Courtesy of Materialscientist, Wikimedia Commons.

vigorous foaming of a sugary liquid, and that if we cared for this liquid properly, it would change in character over time to become a flavorful, nourishing, and mind-altering beverage. We didn't have a clue as to what caused this to happen but we sure as hell liked it. From ancient brewing rituals to medieval associations of fermentation as a sign of God's approval (the act of alcohol fermentation was referred to as "goddes good," or "God's good," in medieval times), it is clear that yeast was viewed in mystical terms by early peoples. This doesn't mean that we didn't know that yeast was a physical substance, though. The word *yeast* stems from words such as Old English *gist* (froth), Middle High German *gest* or German *gischt* (foam, froth), and related words such as Old Norse *jastr* or Swedish *jäst*. It makes sense that a word describing the physical appearance of an active ferment eventually came to reference the substance that causes fermentation.

Everyone who brews is familiar with the residue that gathers on the bottom of a fermenter, or on the surface of the ferment. Gather a bit of this and save it, or just use a pint or so of the active ferment and add it to your next batch and you'll have active fermentation in no time. Many older beer, mead, and wine recipes reference adding "barm" to start fermentation. The word *barm* originates from the Old English *beorma* ("yeast, leaven," or "head of a beer"), which stems from the proto-Germanic *bhermen*. A related word, *barmy*, meaning "excited," "flighty," or "bubbling with excitement," clearly stems from the foamy excitement of a newly initiated brew.[5]

Historically, barm wasn't only added to the next active ferment; sometimes it was kept alive much longer. If fed regularly with any sugar source (ideally, honey, or beer wort), an active starter can be kept alive indefinitely. To do this in modern times without creating vinegar, you're best served keeping a liquid barm alive in an airlocked container, or in a refrigerator. Or you can do it the way many ancient cultures did, by allowing the liquid to dry out on a stirring stick or in a fermentation vessel. This won't need to be fed the way a liquid culture does. Simply reuse the same stir-stick or vessel, being sure to never subject them to sanitizing chemicals or very hot water (different yeast strains have different heat tolerances, but most don't like temperatures of above 110°F/43°C).

Another ancient technique was to create a yeast log (*Kveikstokker* in Scandinavia), whereby a log, usually birch or juniper, was left to dry out and form cracks and then was set at the bottom of a fermentation vessel. The ferment would be started initially through spontaneous/wild fermentation, but once yeast was acquired, it would gather on the log and in its bark crevices. Each subsequent use would result in a quicker fermentation. Over time people began to realize that if they drilled multiple holes in the log, it would enable the gathering of larger amounts of yeast. The log was then dropped in a brewing vessel with an active ferment to gather yeast, rolled in flour, dried, and dipped again. After repeating this a few times, brewers hung up the log to dry. They could then either drop the log into a new brew or scrape off a bit of dried yeast to use for brewing or baking.[6] Unbeknownst to brewers, over time dominant yeast strains would thrive, and weaker ones would die off. Hence, each stick, vessel, or log carried a strain with unique flavoring and fermentation characteristics that grew more powerful with each use. In some cultures the stir-stick was referred to as a magic stick or totem stick.

Magic stirring sticks are one of the many subjects oft-repeated as fact in writings on brewing history whose sources have uncertain origins. However, as enough evidence exists to show that similar techniques were used to initiate fermentation in ancient societies and still

A *kveikering* from 1877 or earlier in the Nordic Museum, Stockholm, Sweden.
Courtesy of Ambrosiani, Wikimedia Commons.

Susan Verberg

Susan, a self-described independent researcher and historical reenactor, has been of immense service to me in helping to authenticate the historical portions of this book and debunk myths by sharing her knowledge of brewing history and sources I may have not come across otherwise. She and her husband, Rolf, currently homestead in the Finger Lakes region of upstate New York, where they raise their own meat, grow their own greens and fruit, and work hard to live sustainably by reusing and freecycling. They grow and wild-harvest fermentables, and produce raw goat's milk for their family and goat's-milk soap business. They also harvest wool from their Icelandic sheep to turn into fiber that Rolf weaves with on a hand-built warp-weighted loom.

Susan Verberg brewing in her reenactment garb. Courtesy of Susan Verberg.

Interest in sustainable and self-sufficient living led their family to be active in the international medieval-reenactment group Society for Creative Anachronism (SCA). "My interest in wild fermentation and traditional ingredients led me down the medieval brewing rabbit hole," Susan told me, "and I have happily spent countless hours, days, weeks, behind my keyboard and at the Cornell University Library to track down just this specific manuscript or that recipe." Her interest in brewing came about initially from figuring out what to do with a surplus harvest. She first started making meads and fruit wines based on historical recipes. Due to a lack of modern reference material on historical mead making, she wrote and self-published a guide called *Of Hony*. She also enjoys brewing historical beers and is passionate about the history of gruit, particularly in differentiating it from herbal ales, though she enjoys brewing those, too. "I personally do not like hoppy beers," she told me, "which works well for the time period I am interested in [pre-1500s] as European beer was mostly herbed or low-hopped back then."

When brewing historical recipes, Verberg emulates the specific technique and recipe as closely as possible, using traditional equipment to the best of her ability, and only uses modern equipment such as hydrometers for monitoring to ensure the brew is progressing as predicted, "though of course in history that would have been the fresh egg, not a weighted piece of glass!" she said. When it comes to natural ingredients such as honey or fruit, she takes copious notes, including time of harvest and whether it was a dry or wet year. She also primarily uses soap, water, and heat to clean her equipment, avoiding chemical sanitizers except when fermenting in plastic, as she has had acetobacter contamination a couple of times from her plastic containers. All in all, she stresses simplicity. She teaches mead-making classes regularly and always emphasizes that brewing only needs to be as elaborate as you make it. "Brewing alcohol was not discovered by man; nature figured it out all on its own, without pH sensors and hydrometers. With basic kitchen equipment and some key ingredients (quality sugars, whether fruit-, honey-, or grain-based, water, and yeast) you're off to a good start, and when patient you will be happily rewarded!"

are in indigenous societies today, it's sensible enough to be likely. Beer archaeologist Merryn Dineley and her brewer husband, Graham, note that "In the Western Isles of Scotland, a hazel 'wand' was traditionally used to stir brews during fermentation. When a fresh wort is stirred, the yeast dried on the 'wand' would start it fermenting."[7] In her blog Dineley references wooden yeast rings, or kveikering, an ancient technique for inoculating wort that is still practiced in parts of Northern Europe. "Some sources say that the tradition of the kveikering dates back to the 18th century," she says, "although I wonder whether the concept might date even further back. It's difficult to be sure because, of course, a wooden object used to gather yeast and start a fermentation would not survive in the archaeological record. In the Viking era, apparently, a stick was used to stir the fermenting wort. This would put yeast onto the stick. Then, if it was kept dry, it could be used to start the next fermentation by stirring a fresh wort. . . . We did some experiments using a wooden spoon and found that this technique works perfectly."[8]

That's Wild, Man

Over the past 25 years or so, the intentional use of wild yeast in beer has experienced a comeback, although many people still hold to the mantra that all wild yeast and bacteria should be slaughtered mercilessly before adding a commercial yeast strain. As one person put it online after reading one of my articles on making mead with wild yeast, brewing with wild yeast concerned him so much that he thought of it as a "dark art." This was several years ago, so I'm hoping that by now he has changed his mind. Bacteria—and by extension, wild yeast—need not be completely eradicated from our brews so that only commercialized, homogenized strains can thrive. Rather, we must learn to harness them properly, and to work with nature rather than against it.

People have a tendency to want to corral nature into lots and categorize everything into nice, convenient classifications, but we shouldn't confuse categorization with control. Understand what you're working with and follow a procedure, but leave some room for nature to play its course. Just as with botany, isolating strains of yeast and microbes that consistently behave a certain way helps us to create more consistency and reliability, but when we go too far and begin eradicating the strains we don't like, nature loses its rich variety, sickness abounds, disease prevails, and we weaken what was once a powerful work of nature so that it can't thrive without our constant input.

For years I brewed using the strictly regimented techniques espoused by homebrew manuals and homebrew-supply-kit instructions: that is, using specific ingredients, exacting techniques, heavy chemical sanitization, and single-strain packaged yeasts. I'm not saying I didn't make excellent beer this way, or that I don't have great respect for the manuals' authors, but over time I began to lose my passion for brewing because of all the stuff I kept reading (and doing my best to follow) about the things that *have* to be done if you don't want to end up with a "spoiled" beer that needs to be tossed or a beer that isn't "to style."

Along with my newfound understanding that wild yeast is my friend (and can be yours, too!), I have over time renounced the following homebrewing dogma:

- We must sanitize *all* post-boil equipment obsessively, thoroughly, and with chemicals our ancestors most certainly would not have had.
- Beer wort always has to be boiled.
- We should expose fermenting beer to open air as little as possible.
- And, of course, hops are a necessity for beer.

To be fair, not every modern brewing manual goes to these extremes, but many homebrewers spout these "truths" religiously. Exceptions are made for beers such as lambic, which were traditionally brewed in open containers using captured wild yeast, but even in these cases, home-brewers often use packaged and sold "wild" yeast strains from Belgian breweries, and continue to follow the other regimented practices as well.

Lambic is the result of generations-old practices of Belgian brewers who brewed—more by necessity than intention, at least initially—using wild yeast that gathered in the rafters of the brew house from previous brews, floated in from nearby orchards, and was present on the fresh yeast-laden fruit they used in their brews. They also aged their beer in wood casks that were naturally coated in lactobacillus (a bacterium that eats up sugar and spits out lactic acid, giving beer a sour edge), and sometimes blended it with various amounts of sweet and sour fruit to attain a perfect balance (lambic brewed without fruit is known as *gueuze*). Who's to say we can't emulate these practices at home, using our own yeast, water, and fruit, to create beer with our own terroir? Sure, it may not be a legitimate Belgian ale, but I daresay it will taste about the same if done right.

Any kind of alcoholic ferment can be started with newly gathered wild yeast, a barm created from wild yeast, or wild yeast that has been dried on a stir-stick or other brewing implement. I first began exploring fermenting with wild yeast by making wild-fermented mead and wine. The process for wild-fermenting mead and wine is surprisingly simple, and can be adapted for beer easily—but with some caveats. In essence, cultivating a wild fermentation requires employing a natural yeast source, which can't be heated above the point of sterilization. Most modern beer brewing requires sterilizing and boiling the wort, which means killing off any yeast in the ingredients that may help initiate a wild ferment. Even if you're brewing by this method, you can simply follow my wild yeast wrangling technique to create a starter (barm), which you can then add to beer wort once it has cooled to the proper temperature. You may also want to play around with saving yeast on a stir-stick or yeast log, or in a container in your freezer or refrigerator. Once you've broken free from the fetters of regimented brewing technique, the avenues that open up to you are nearly unlimited. But first, let's debunk some persistent myths about wild yeast.

Myth 1: Wild yeast is unpredictable and can result in wildly varying alcohol levels. While I have read the scientific and brewing literature on this, I prefer personal experimentation. I don't exclusively use wild yeast, but I make a lot of wild-fermented mead. In every one I make, I simply add the amount of honey or sugar I understand will reach a certain ABV range along with ingredients containing wild yeast, proceed with wild fermentation, age and bottle (or drink it young), and enjoy. I sometimes test with a hydrometer (a homebrewing instrument for testing potential and final alcohol levels) but pretty much always hit my intended alcohol levels. When I don't test scientifically, the perceived alcohol level is still there.

Myth 2: Brewing with wild yeast that hasn't been examined in a laboratory is a crapshoot, since you never know if it's a viable strain or some low-to-no-alcohol "bad" yeast that will ruin your brew or even make you sick. From time to time

I come across online forums in which comments like "bad idea," "dangerous," or "poison" appear regarding wild yeast. People also approach me at workshops or online worried about the potential dangers of using wild yeast, to which I respond that people have been making alcoholic and non-alcoholic ferments from wild yeast since the beginning of time. Every commercial yeast strain started out as a captured wild yeast, and was eventually tamed and isolated into a single strain in the laboratory. The simple answer is that wild yeast is safe, and it works, but as with any other aspect of brewing, things can go wrong or not quite as expected. Commercial breweries and distilleries examine captured wild yeast in laboratories to ensure it is a viable strain because it can be financially unviable to brew large amounts of product with untested yeast, but you don't need to do that at home . . . unless you really want to.

Myth 3: You must sanitize all equipment and heat all wort (for beer) or must (for wine or mead) to at least pasteurization level to kill off any potential spoilage bacteria and wild yeast to ensure your commercial yeast strain does its job. Do sanitizing, sterilizing, and pasteurizing increase the chances of a problem-free fermentation? To a degree, yes, but this doesn't mean we need to follow these practices religiously. I always encourage people who are new to the idea of avoiding chemical sanitizers to approach the concept from a different viewpoint. The "sanitize, sanitize, sanitize" mantra was adopted early on by homebrewers for a good reason. The pioneers of modern homebrewing noticed that they were less likely to have spoilage or a "bad" batch if they sanitized everything (it's worth noting they were likely often working with plastic, which picks up contaminants more easily). They also believed that the effects of commercial yeast strains were hindered by wild yeast. A commercial yeast strain, though, is by nature a very strong strain. Wild yeast will do the job just as well as, or along with, commercial yeast.

Working with wild yeast is like performing alchemy or witchcraft (in its original sense of working with nature). It's best not to approach wild-fermented brews with a specific flavor in mind. Sometimes the taste may be a bit challenging, but most often it will turn out to your liking (or perhaps to the liking of someone else). That being said, take extra care of any plastic equipment. Clean it well, but not with anything harsh that will scratch the surface and give bacteria a place to harbor. I know wild fermenters who sanitize their plastic buckets because they have occasionally picked up lactobacillus contamination, though I have a plastic bucket I use quite often for all manner of brews and none have become contaminated that I can tell.

The best way to introduce wild yeast to a beer without worrying about over-souring the grains is to create a wild yeast starter. The following section describes how to create one using honey since honey (provided it is raw) is the most natural and traditionally accurate sugar source to use short of acquiring grain from malted and mashed grains. If you go on to add the starter to more honey and water, you've made a mead. Otherwise, you can use this as a barm for other types of alcoholic ferments. I recommend setting aside some equipment, preferably glass, ceramic, or even wood, to use specifically for wild fermentation. For brews you want to intentionally sour, this is partially to avoid "contaminating" your brewing equipment (I've never had this happen but I've heard others have), but also because you'll want to form a relationship with your wild-fermentation equipment, and potentially to save yeast strains you like for future brews.

Creating, Saving, and Reusing a Yeast Starter

Most brewing manuals contain detailed instructions on how to create yeast starters from beer wort or save yeast from a previous batch of beer to pass along to future batches. Excessive sanitation and the use of laboratory equipment (albeit fairly simple and affordable equipment readily available in homebrew stores) are always emphasized. Those methods may work well, but I recommend simply creating a wild yeast starter for your beers, meads, and other ferments. If you want to carefully save a specific type of yeast without any "contamination," you'll want to refer to other sources.

To create your starter, you need a sugar source. I usually use raw honey—natural, unpasteurized honey, full of wild yeast and microbes—but cane sugar or fresh beer wort will work in place of, or alongside, honey. Take a quart (liter) jar and fill it to the one-quarter mark with your sugar source, then fill it to the three-quarters mark with springwater. You may need to warm the water a bit, but I've found that putting

A honey-based yeast starter.

a lid on the jar and shaking it until the sugars are fully dissolved does the job. You can also stir it with a small stick (a twig or a chopstick usually works for me), which you'll need for the rest of the process anyway. While this is technically all you will need to create the starter, adding some other botanicals is always a good idea due to the native wild yeast and yeast-feeding nutrients they provide. Sometimes I'll drop in a small handful of organic raisins or dried berries, but most times I'll also go outside and pick things from my yarden (what I like to call my yard, since many of the edibles growing there occur naturally) or go for a walk in the woods. I pull off a leaf here, a flower there, drop in some berries or other fruit, and enjoy communing with nature while preparing my starter. Just be sure you know *exactly* what it is you're adding. If you haven't wild-harvested before, learn about wild-harvesting ethics and be sure to not pick from areas that may have been sprayed, such as roadsides or public lands. As long as you're adding small amounts (a fingerful or so), they shouldn't have a noticeable effect on the flavor of the final brew. Most fruits are good wild yeast sources, as are edible flowers, tree bark, and pinecones.

For the next few days, use your stir-stick and stir vigorously for a couple of minutes three to four times a day. This provides the aeration necessary for fermentation by invigorating any wild yeast that may float to the bottom or hang out on the surface, in addition to preventing molds from growing on the surface. To keep flies, ants, and bugs out, cover the jar with cheesecloth or other porous cloth when not stirring—this provides additional oxygenation and allows floating wild yeast (technically they don't float but ride on microscopic dust particles and other things floating through the air) to populate the must. Keep the vessel in a warm (60–80°F/15–27°C) area away from direct sunlight, as sunlight can have a negative effect on flavor over time, though I will sometimes place my starter jar in sunlight for a couple of hours early on in the process to draw in warmth. In three to five days (usually sooner in summer and sometimes longer in winter), the mixture should be fizzy and a bit foamy. You officially have an active yeast starter! It's hard not to look on this in wonder, as ancient cultures would have. Seemingly on its own, this liquid went from being inert to being active and alive. Even today, this is often referred to as spontaneous fermentation, although that's technically a misnomer. Still, I like to think of the process as a sort of magic and always get a tingle of excitement when it happens. If you place a lid with an airlock on the jar, you can keep it alive indefinitely without it turning to vinegar. Just be sure to feed it a tablespoon or two of honey every couple of weeks to keep the fermentation going. Any time a recipe calls for yeast or barm, add some of your starter. Usually a tablespoon or two will work for a small (1–2 gallon/4–8 L) batch. Use about a cup for a 5-gallon (20 L) batch and more if you're making a particularly large batch (10 gallons/40 L or more).

I usually let my starter go for a day or two longer to ensure a strong ferment. Although the foam that forms on the top (krausen) is a protective layer that keeps out acetobacter while the fermentation is at its most active stage, I still stir or swirl the jar a couple of times a day. Sometimes you may see a bit of mold or a thin white film form on the surface. The mold is not dangerous and can be skimmed off or just stirred back in. The white film is actually a type of yeast, or *pellicle*, an oxidative yeast barrier that prevents acetobacter from turning your mead into vinegar. In beer brewing this is known as *Brettanomyces*, referred to by beer brewers as "the Brett" and by vintners as "Flor" (flower). It should be left intact until ready to rack or bottle so that it may achieve its purpose of keeping out souring organisms.

Don't Mess with the Brett

While a little bit of Brett forming on the surface of barm or fermenting beer won't cause the entire beer to go funky (I often find it forming on the surface of my non-sour beers), it can be intentionally nurtured and harnessed to achieve its full potential, resulting in all manner of funky and sour beers. This funkiness comes from Brett's tendency to acidify beer. Acidification can be used to build body in a beer with no noticeable sour effect, to achieve a subtle level of sourness or tartness, or to go full-on sour.

There are four prevailing classes of microorganisms that can ferment and acidify "wild" beers, of which *Brettanomyces* is one. The others are *Lactobacillus*, *Pediococcus*, and *Saccharomyces*. *Brettanomyces* and *Saccharomyces* are both strains of yeast, and contribute to fermentation when used in combination with *Lactobacillus* and *Pediococcus*, which are bacteria. *Saccharomyces* is a predictable, easy-to-manage, fast-acting category of yeast that most beers made with a "clean" flavor employ for fermentation, while *Brettanomyces* ferments slowly; it takes time for Brett's full character to come out, often not until well after the beer is bottled. *Lactobacillus* and *Pediococcus* are the motley fools of brewing, imparting all manner of unpredictable funk to beers brewed with them when used in combination with fermenting yeasts.

There are many, many more key players of yeast and bacteria in the wild-brewing symphony. When you're wild-brewing at home, your best bet is to follow traditional procedures and initiate your own experiments. While some brewers prefer to be specific and scientific about which strains they seek out for dominance, I prefer to work with nature rather than try to control it. Scientists continue to identify more strains of yeast and bacteria in traditional Belgian lambics, while Belgian brewers themselves simply continue brewing as they always have, letting the native yeasts and bacteria that have gathered in the nooks and crannies of their breweries over hundreds of years of brewing do most of the work.

Depending on what type of beer they're after, brewers have differing relationships with Brett. Most avoid it like the plague and sanitize religiously to kill it off. Others purposely seek it out in order to achieve a desired "wild" effect in their beers. I'm ambivalent; I don't mind if it gets in my beer, as I know I can control its presence with the proper technique, and that I can allow it to flourish if I so desire. When the Carlsberg brewery's laboratory director Niels Hjelte Claussen first isolated the Brett microorganism in a slow-fermenting British beer in 1903, he gave it the name we know today, which translates to "British

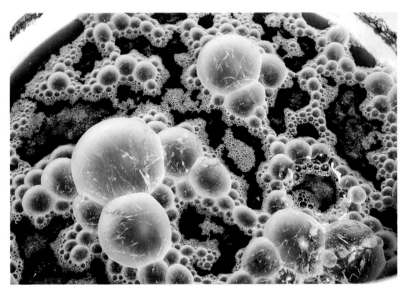

Some brews, particularly those brewed with wild yeast strains such as *Brettanomyces*, will often grow a "pellicle," which is, in microbiology terms, a biofilm (a community of interconnected microorganisms).

brewing industry fungus."⁹ It was henceforth known and vilified by brewers as a beer-spoiling organism. As Belgian brewing began to reenter the consciousness of the general public in the late 20th century due in large part to the pioneering beer writer Michael Jackson ("the one without the glove" as he liked to refer to himself), Brett was finally given its due once again as an important element of brewing. While you can go out of your way to obtain a specific Brett strain, it occurs naturally in the environment around us pretty much everywhere.

Since Brett relies on oxygen to thrive, it will cease its work if placed in an airlocked, anaerobic (without air) environment. If you want it to grow and continue to consume sugars, it needs to do its work in an aerobic (with air) environment, such as a widemouthed open container (or, as in the case of Belgian breweries, a large, shallow copper vat called a coolship). Like any alcoholic ferment, though, if it's left to ferment in an open container longer than three to four weeks, an acetobacter will take over and either turn it fully to vinegar or impart a sharp, vinegary taste that not even all sour-beer lovers enjoy. Brett also prefers a low-pH environment (after primary fermentation); anything below a post-mash pH of 3.4 and it will stop reproducing.¹⁰ My low-tech recommendation is to take small taste samples while it is in open fermentation and move it to an airlocked environment when you're ready. A safer way to ensure you don't over-sour a large batch of beer is to set aside a portion of the main batch in a separate vessel, allow to sour, and then mix to taste.

Brett also often resides on the skins of fruit, along with various other strains of wild yeast. This is likely one reason fruits such as cherries are used by Belgian brewers to achieve a desired level of sourness. Many Brussels breweries initially situated themselves near cherry orchards for this very reason—the theory is that the yeast "floats" through the air on dust particles or possibly on the feet of fruit flies, eventually settling on the floors, equipment, walls, and rafters of breweries.¹¹ Many of these orchards have since disappeared, but the breweries see no reason to relocate. When fermentation revivalist Sandor Katz asked the master brewer and owner of Brewery Cantillon, Jean Van Roy, about whether or not he had considered moving closer to a cherry orchard, his response was an ardent no, as he felt the yeast he needed were firmly entrenched in the building.¹²

Commercial Yeast

Though I'm an advocate of wild fermentation, I can't deny that I use a lot of commercial, single-strain *Saccharomyces* yeasts in my brews as well. They're tame, they're predictable, and they don't tend to just go off and do their own thing like Brett and other wild yeasts do.

There are a multitude of *Saccharomyces* yeast strains available to the modern brewer, though I don't go out of my way to hunt down a specific strain when I'm planning a batch of brew. I simply purchase a variety when I go to the homebrew store—a packet or two of wheat yeast, some British ale yeast, some Belgium yeast, et cetera—and use what's available (even if it doesn't match the style I'm brewing) when I brew a batch. If it's viable, it will initiate fermentation and that's all I'm really after. To be clear, however, different yeasts result in differently flavored beers, so go with the recommended yeast strain for the beer you are brewing *if you're shooting for a specific style.* Remember, though, isolated yeast strains are still a fairly modern concept. There's a reason that older recipes never (that I have seen) mention specific yeast strains except when differentiating between ale and lager yeast. All earlier brewers knew is that if they pitched yeast (that is, added barm) and followed the proper procedures, the brew would ferment.

I've outlined some categories of yeast strains in the following section so that you can understand what strains to use when seeking out a certain style of beer. Short of buying a packet of yeast for every single new batch of beer, however, there is no definitive way to know that a given strain of yeast will result in a certain flavor profile, as even highly technical, detail-focused brewers admit. Yeast is a living substance that changes over generations (in yeast years, not people or dog years). Breweries with on-site laboratories (or that contract out to off-site laboratories) are able to keep strains consistent through careful monitoring, but homebrewers, unless they are very technical- and scientific-minded, have much less of a chance of keeping alive a yeast strain that will continue to have the same results over several batches. As Ray Daniels notes in *Designing Great Beers*: "If you reuse the same yeast over a long period, its very character may change. This is because the conditions of fermentation, harvest, and storage exert selection pressures on the yeast. The specific members of the strain that like the conditions they are subjected to will thrive while others die out."[13]

Common Yeast Strains and Their Suggested Uses

The selection in a homebrew store yeast case or on a homebrewing website can be bewildering. This section breaks down the basic categories of yeast generally available to the homebrewer, but keep in mind that when you go to buy yeast, each manufacturer has its own description. A strain for a wheat yeast from one manufacturer, for example, will have a different flavor profile than one from another manufacturer. This is why my personal belief is that homebrewing is more about experimentation and going with the flow than about chasing elusive flavor profiles with a hyper-specific goal in mind. That being said, the descriptions I provide should at least give you an idea as to the general flavor parameters each style of yeast will impart in a brew.

Yeast are extremely robust creatures; they need very little help to do their job. Just stick within some fairly broad parameters and they'll do what you need them to do. Yeast will certainly behave differently across different temperature ranges, and may need to stay within certain parameters if you're pursuing a specific style. In general, though, pretty much all yeast will ferment well in warm temperatures and slow down (or completely stop) in colder temperatures. Some types of yeast have higher *attenuation* (the percentage of sugars they can consume); some have better *flocculation* rates (the efficiency and rate at which they drop to the bottom of the fermenter upon completing fermentation); and some aren't strong enough to fully ferment large amounts of sugar without additional nutrient input. There are many, many discussions in brewing magazines and on the Internet about this, and there are books that cover it in detail. As with all other aspects of brewing, I prefer to keep things simple. If you're interested in getting more technical, there are plenty of resources out there.

ALE YEASTS

The recipes in this book by their nature pretty much all call for ale yeasts, which are the oldest style of cultivated yeast. They ferment at warmer temperatures than lager yeasts and are known as top-fermenting yeasts due to their tendency to hang out at the top of the fermenter as opposed to lager yeasts, which are bottom-fermenting. Note: You will notice several references to *attenuation* and *flocculation* in the following. For details on these terms, please see the glossary at the end of this book.

American. A good all-purpose yeast for making American-style pale ales, IPAs, ambers, browns, and other ales requiring a clean, crisp, neutral character to allow malt and hop flavors to dominate. Some describe this as having low fruitiness and minimal ester contributions. It has low to medium flocculation and medium attenuation. While the recommended temperature range for these yeasts is 60–72°F (15–22°C), it can handle temperatures as low as 53–55°F (12–13°C).

Belgian. Substantial levels of fruity, estery, clove, and phenolic notes. They have high alcohol tolerance along with medium to high flocculation and attenuation levels. Sometimes sold as Abbey or Trappist.

British. Likely due to Britain's significant history with its ale, there are a number of British yeasts available, all with their own unique characteristics. Often they're sold as "British ale yeast," but you can sometimes find them in the following subcategories (many more than these are available): *Whitbread* (crisp, clean, tart, fast-fermenting; medium attenuation and flocculation), *London* (crisp, tart, woody, fruity; medium attenuation and flocculation), and *London ESB* (malty, fruity; high flocculation and medium to high attenuation).

Canadian. Clean, crisp, somewhat fruity. High in attenuation and flocculation. Best for light ales, including cream ales, bitters, and pales.

German. German yeasts are generally available as dry and sweet strains. Dry strains are crisp and dry, with a complex but mild flavor. They ferment at temperatures as low as 55°F (12–13°C). They are high in flocculation and medium to high in attenuation. The sweet strain creates full-bodied, complex ales with a spicy sweetness. It is high in flocculation and low to medium in attenuation.

Irish. Somewhat woody with slight diacetyl notes; usually imparts a degree of dryness preferred in stouts; also imparts subtle fruitiness at lower temperatures and high levels of fruitiness at higher temperatures. Some have high levels of attenuation but others are much lower. Most have medium to high flocculation levels. These are ideal for darker ales, particularly porters and stouts.

Scottish. Very malty with low attenuation, medium-high flocculation, and the ability to ferment at lower temperatures, similar to American yeasts. Creates strong, complex flavors and can handle high alcohol levels. Some have woody, oak esters reminiscent of malt whiskey.

LAGER YEASTS

Scientists classify all ale-brewing yeasts as *Saccharomyces cerevisiae*. Lager yeast (or *S. pastorianus*) is closely related, but can handle a much colder environment (39–54°F/4–12°C) than ale yeast (59–68°F/15–20°C), although it will still ferment at warmer temperatures. The temperature preferences of each require that we distinguish between the two when it comes to brewing, as the flavor and character of beer produced by each differ significantly. In order to be comprehensive, I will outline some lager yeasts here, even though I don't include any beers in this book that require lagering. It's good to know about them if you decide you want to make lagers, or if you want to use lager yeast for a warmer ferment (as do some traditional German beers).

American. Clean and crisp with slight fruitiness. Tends toward high attenuation and medium flocculation levels.

Bavarian. Strong malty character with rich, full-bodied flavor. Medium flocculation and attenuation.

Bohemian. Produces a smooth, clean, full-bodied beer with strong malt flavors. Low attenuation and medium flocculation. Some suppliers also provide a Pilsen strain that has a drier, crisper flavor.

California. Ferments warmer than most lager yeasts (up to 66°F/19°C). Primarily used to create California Common, a style of lager brewed at warmer temperatures still being made by the Anchor Brewing Company in San Francisco today. Has a malty profile with a bit of fruitiness.

Munich. Provides a very smooth, soft character with some body, but not a lot. It's one of the reasons true German lagers are so drinkable. Nothing overly stands out, but you can't help but down another right away. Medium attenuation and flocculation.

Working with Yeast

The following are some of the core principles you'll need to understand when working with yeast.

Temperature. In general, the ideal temperature for fermentation is 60–80°F (15–27°C). Some yeast strains prefer the lower end of the spectrum while others like things a bit warmer. This doesn't mean they won't do their job at the wrong temperature. They may ferment slower if it's too cold or they may produce a different flavor if not at their optimal temperature range. For instance, many yeasts will impart a fruity or clove-like flavor if fermented above their preferred temperature range due to the production of ester (ethyl acetate). This is sought after in many Belgian brews and in *Hefeweizen*, but not everyone likes it. My homebrewing setup has remained fairly rudimentary throughout my brewing life and I doubt it will change much. Many people purchase special equipment to maintain strict temperature parameters but I prefer farmhouse and caveman brewing so I'll stick with my fluctuating temperatures, thank you very much.

Pitching. This is simply the act of adding yeast to the wort. There are various ways of doing this, and various forms that yeast can come in. This is another thing that can quickly become complicated if you read too much into it. Every time I read up on pitching, I come across something different regarding best practices. Some say dry yeast is best; others, liquid yeast. Some say to start your yeast in a small amount of wort or water warmed on the stove first; others advise pitching it directly into the wort. I've tried them all and can't say any had a noticeably different effect on yeast activity or the final flavor of the beer. Most times I just sprinkle dry yeast on the wort after aerating it, put the lid and airlock on my brewing bucket, and leave it be. Creating a liquid starter from scratch (described earlier in this chapter) or starting dry yeast in a small amount of liquid is a surefire way to ensure a strong ferment, as it helps to significantly increase the cell count of your yeast. If I'm using liquid yeast or a starter, I simply pour it in, cover, and wait. There are also different opinions about pitching rates, meaning the amount of yeast to add.

More is always better in my opinion, but you don't need a lot except for very high-gravity beers, meads, or wines. The standard beer-yeast packet contains 11 grams of yeast, although some contain as few as 5. If you're brewing something with an intended ABV of less than 10 percent, 11 grams (per 5-gallon/20 L batch) usually does the trick. Anything higher and you should double the amount. For liquid starters, use a cup (250 mL) for lower-gravity beers and 2 cups (500 mL) or a bit more for higher-gravity beers (such as bragots).

Aeration. Yeast need oxygen to thrive, but they need it at the proper rates. Too much and they may sour the beer; too little and they may give up early or produce high levels of ester. It's important to aerate your wort before pitching, which can be accomplished simply by pouring the wort from the brewpot into your fermenter, or giving it a good stir before adding the yeast. Generally, you won't need to worry about anything beyond this. If a yeast is slow to ferment, aeration is one of the first things you should try when troubleshooting, either by stirring it, or by pouring it into another container and then back in the fermenter. Most homebrewers do just fine without worrying about it.

Feeding. This is rarely of concern when brewing beer, but often discussed by wine- and mead makers. Essentially, yeast—like any living creature—require nutritious food to stay healthy. If they just indulge in empty calories, their health will be in jeopardy. Fortunately for them, beer wort is full of nutrients such as amino acids, lipids, vitamins, and minerals. Just be sure to use the proper amount of yeast for a high-gravity beer such as a bragot, and remember that dropping in some nutrients in the form of a cup or so of dried fruit never hurts.

For all aspects of brewing, but yeast treatment and fermentation in particular, something that may be important for large- or even midscale commercial brewing is often negligible for homebrewing. When you're dealing with larger volumes, you have the potential for larger issues. And then of course there's the cost factor. Commercial breweries, even small craft breweries, require consistency, with the exception of special limited releases. If their customers can't come to expect a certain flavor from their favorite beer, or if a large volume of beer comes out tasting less than desirable, it can be disastrous to their bottom line. Often I come across debates in online forums that are eventually resolved when people realize they're trying to replicate what is being done at large breweries, and even after a lot of time and expense their efforts make little—if any—difference. My mantra is to brew how you want to brew, and simple is best. If you want to scale up your brewing, definitely do some research and take extra precautions. If you're brewing on a small scale for the fun of it, follow the wise words of homebrewing guru Charlie Papazian in the introduction to the second edition of *The New Complete Joy of Homebrewing*: "I encourage all of you to never forget that homebrewing is fun and rewarding and that worrying can spoil your beer more than anything else. Relax. Don't worry. Have a homebrew."[14]

CHAPTER SIX

HOPS

Hops are what makes beer *beer*, right? By now you should know that this isn't entirely true, but many who haven't studied beer history or brewing are surprised to learn that beer and ale don't necessarily need to contain hops. Those who suggest that perhaps an overabundance of hops in beer isn't always a good thing—particularly

Hops growing at a hop farm in Oregon. Note how they grow straight up.
Courtesy of Visitor7, Wikimedia Commons.

when talking to aficionados of American craft beer—are often met with confusion or even vociferous disagreement. When my IPA-loving friends learn of my desire to make beer with little to no hops, they tend to hold tightly to their IPAs and look at me with great concern. However, I've found that there are plenty of people out there who are not hop lovers—or who are more interested in the idea of historical beer made with herbs and other traditional bittering and flavoring agents. I enjoy the flavor of hops in beer, and appreciate the bittering they provide to counteract the sweetness of malt. However, I'm also a fan of the underdog—all those other herbs that haven't been given their due—and of re-creating history in a bottle. The intent of this book is not to be "anti-hops" but rather to step back and learn to use hops for balance and nuance—or primarily for their antibacterial properties—rather than focusing on "hop-forward" beers. And of course, you can forgo hops altogether and use other ingredients for their bittering, flavoring, and preservative properties.

A Brief History of the Hop Plant

According to archaeological evidence, *Humulus lupulus*, better known as hops, has been harvested wild since Neolithic times. However, there is scant evidence that they were used in brewing beer, and the time period during which they were first used for brewing is difficult to peg down. The first written reference to the hop plant appeared in AD 77–79 in Pliny the Elder's 37-volume encyclopedia *Naturalis Historia*, in which he explores all manner of subject matter pertaining to the natural world. Pliny also references a liquid that Western Europeans use to intoxicate themselves, which he says is made from "grain and water" but makes no reference to hops.[1] Instead, Pliny refers to hops as *Lupus salactarius*, or "wolf of the willows," due to the hop plant's tendency to climb and overtake any plant or tree it encounters.[2] *Humulus lupulus* is a bining plant that grows horizontally along the ground via a combined root-and-rhizome system until it encounters an object it can wrap itself around via shoots that sprout from the rhizome, grow into leaves, and climb, climb, climb. A hop bine will climb as high as its support allows, growing as much as a foot a day in late spring and early summer and reaching heights of 40 feet (12 m) or more. The root and rhizome system, meanwhile, penetrates deep underground for nutrients and water, as much as 15 feet (4.5 m).

Since hops grew wild and plentiful in the thick woods of early Europe, there is no doubt early Europeans explored methods for using them in food and drink. Before their preservative qualities were known, people used hops to treat a variety of ailments. Although the cone of the female hop plant contains the oils that are used in brewing and other applications, other parts of the plant have their uses as well. The bright green leaves of the female plant, for instance, can be used to help fermenting pickles stay crisp due to their high levels of tannin. The antibacterial properties (from the compound *humulone*, found in hop resin) of hop cones make them effective as poultices for treating wounds. The hop cone is also a soporific, emitting an aroma that can cause drowsiness and help with insomnia. Hop tea, hop tincture (hops soaked in distilled alcohol), and pillowcases stuffed with dried hop cones have all been used to help people with sleeping problems. Picking hops can also cause drowsiness, however, as workers in hop fields can attest.

Another interesting characteristic of hops is that they contain phytoestrogen, a botanical version of estrogen. Historically, they were used to treat menopause and other "female problems," and the leaves were fed to dairy cows to help with milk production. Even today, some doctors (the pediatrician for my first two children with my wife, Jenna, for example) recommend drinking a stout a day while nursing, as the combination of grains and hops helps stimulate milk production. Modern research has also shown that the flavonoids in hops have high levels of antioxidants. One flavonoid found only in hops, xanthohumol, has a protective coating that can survive longer in the body than other flavonoids, making it an excellent cancer-fighter.[3] It's no wonder people have been cultivating and harvesting hops since practically the beginning of humankind.

Initially, the hop plant was more likely to be harvested wild, as it grew so abundantly there was little need to cultivate it (some monastery tenants were expected to "gather hops in the wood"), but written evidence does exist of hops grown in gardens in monasteries around the eighth century, and even of hops being used for barter.[4] No one knows for sure when people realized hops' preservative and antibacterial properties, which enable beer to keep longer and allow brewers to produce lower-gravity, lower-alcohol beers. We do know that hops were used in beer to some degree in fermented grain beverages as early as the eighth century, and were harvested and traded for what may have been other purposes much earlier. In writings from Viking-era Denmark (AD 800–1066) and Anglo-Saxon-era England (AD 410–1066), there are references to what may have been hops, although evidence that they were used in brewing is weak. The hop plant, like its cousin hemp, has many non-intoxicating uses that have fallen by the wayside that were once critical to daily life—and thus important in trade. In addition to the aforementioned medicinal and edible uses, the fibrous stems were used for rope making and clothing. In 1970 the Graveney Boat, dating back to around AD 900, was excavated by archeologists in the Kent village of Graveney. Analysis showed evidence of a significant amount of hops onboard during an era in which there is no evidence that hops were used in brewing. Given the many other uses of hops, there is really no way of knowing for sure what the intended use of the hops onboard the ship was. The hop plants, argued one researcher in a 1975 article for *The New Philologist*, may very well have been used for temporary binding of the brushwood platform of the Graveney Boat or to make repairs, although hemp or leather would more likely have been used. Hops could also have been used for bedding, insulation, or packing purposes, as there is evidence that early hop growers sometimes placed spent hop bines under straw for cattle.[5]

Whether they were used primarily for brewing before or after the 10th century, hops slowly became an accepted ingredient in beer and ale; after experimenting with hops in fermented beverages over the centuries, things began to click. As early as the 12th century, Saint Hildegard, the abbess of the Benedictine convent of Rupertsberg—a brewster and student of science and medicine—advised the use of hops as a preservative for beer and other beverages. In her extensive study on the science of her time (much of which is still considered accurate today), *Physica*, she said that hops' "bitterness keeps some putrefactions from drinks so that they may last much longer." However, she cautions that its overuse "makes melancholy grow easily in man and makes the soul of man sad, and weighs down his inner organs."[6]

Commercial hop gardens, according to the best understanding of historians, were prevalent in Germany between the 12th and 15th centuries, but didn't become common in England until the 15th and 16th centuries. In Holland hop plants were grown specifically for use in beer by the 1300s. Hops were becoming serious business, to the point that manuals were being written on proper cultivation. The first book in English written specifically on hop growing, *A Perfite Platform of a Hoppe Garden*, was published in 1574 by Reynolde (Reginald) Scot, and covered practically every aspect of hop cultivation.[7] The use of hops in beer, at least to the degree that it had a noticeable effect on flavor, and the plant's subsequent ascendency to near-universal recognition as *the* plant to use in flavoring and preserving beer, took several hundred years to become accepted in Europe and held out longer in England.

John Wesley, the 18th-century Anglican evangelist and founder of the Wesleyan tradition, was a strong believer in the healthful qualities of beer and wine and vehemently protested the use of hops in beer. In letters to the *Bristol Gazette*, he railed at great length not only to defend hop-less ale as an intoxicating beverage, but to convey his concern for the health of a nation, as the Temperance movement hadn't yet reached full swing and ale was still considered more a healthful meal than an intoxicating beverage:

> Forty years ago, I well remember, all the ale I tasted [in Yorkshire and Lincolnshire] had a soft, sweetish taste, such as the decoction of barley will always have if not adulterated by bitter herbs . . . whereas all the ale in Yorkshire as well as in other counties is now quite harsh and bitter. . . . No bitter is necessary to preserve ale, any more than to preserve cider or wine. I look upon the matter of hops to be a mere humbug upon the good people of England.[8]

Despite the protests of Wesley and others, opposition to the idea of hops in beer eventually vanished except in small corners of England devoted to keeping "true English ale" alive. By the 17th century—after taking note of volunteer hops that occasionally popped up due to cross-pollination—hop growers began to breed distinct varieties to provide brewers with different flavor profiles. When Europeans began migrating to North America, they discovered entirely new flavor profiles in that continent's wild hops and eventually in the new varieties they produced by cross-pollinating American and European varieties. Commercial beer production, and thus commercial hop cultivation, was

Hop Holiday

There was a period when a visit to the hop yard was both a popular family outing and a way to make a bit of extra cash. In his 1889 book *The Curiosities of Ale & Beer*, my good-but-long-dead friend John Bickerdyke describes the practice of entire families escaping the foul living conditions of industrial London by taking "workcations" to the countryside of Kent, Surrey, and Sussex to work in the hop yards. Traveling in droves by train, these happy throngs would spend the day picking hops while breathing in the fresh air of the country . . . and the lush fragrance of fresh hops. It was such a popular pastime that people would sign up months in advance and hop growers would pick names from a basket to determine the lucky winners. While picking, they sang and took care to work in such a manner that they would be invited back. One hop-picking song goes thus:

> And far and near
> With accent clear
> The hop-picker's song salutes the glad ear:
> The old and the young
> Unite in the throng,
> And echo re-echoes their jocund song,
> The hop-picking time is a time of glee,
> So merrily, merrily now sing we:
> For the bloom of the hop is the secret spell
> Of the bright pale ale that we love so well;
> So gather it quickly with tender care,
> And off to the wagons the treasure bear.[9]

The short "holiday" in the country worked wonders for the soul. Laughing and dancing gaily upon their return to the train station, "Young men and girls, invigorated by their sojourn in the bracing country air, alike garland themselves with hops, and decorate themselves with gay ribbons. Laughing, dancing, and singing, they hurry to the station, or along the road to London."[10] Today there are still hop festivals in England, Germany, and other parts of Europe to celebrate both the growing and the harvesting seasons. The Faversham Hop Festival in Kent celebrates the nostalgia of Victorian-era hop-picking excursions but also acknowledges some of the hardships hop pickers experienced, including the sparse pay and the tendency of hop farmers to press down the highly compressible hops in the picking baskets so they could pay the pickers less.

Yet despite the difficulties and the long days, there was a certain mystique to a hop-picking excursion. The aroma of the hop oils drifted through the fields while pickers filled their baskets with the soft, pillowy cones, singing songs and losing themselves in the soporific aura of the hop haze. At the end of the day, they would head to their campsites, makeshift huts, or haylofts and stay up late around groups of campfires singing, drinking, and eating. Then it would be up before dawn to start anew. An influx of June babies became a trend among hop pickers, with that same month also seeing a sharp uptick in the number of babies abandoned at hospitals and orphanages.

A group of hop pickers near Independence, Oregon. Date unknown. Courtesy of OSU Special Collections and Archives, Flickr.

in full swing by the 18th century. Increased industrial and transportation capabilities allowed for the global transport of hops. New York's Otsego County became a focal point for American trade in hops, producing close to 4.5 million pounds (2 million kg) of hops in 1880. James Fenimore Cooper, author of *The Leatherstocking Tales* (which included *The Last of the Mohicans*), called Otsego County home, as did his grandson (also James Fenimore Cooper), who wrote as part of a series of newspaper articles, "Those were the days when the 'hop was king' and the whole countryside was one great big hop yard and beautiful."[11]

European hop growers settled in the Northeast and hoped to stay, but the inevitable problems of growing a monoculture crop in a temperate, humid climate caught up with them. To escape growing disease and pest problems, New York hop growers pulled up some rhizomes and headed to the Northwest, settling in Washington State's Yakima Valley.[12] The dry, arid climate and Cascade Mountain snowmelt of the Yakima River were perfect for hop production. The deserts of Washington, Oregon, and California—which weathered Prohibition better than New York—became the new epicenter for hops. Only now in the early 21st century are hop growers beginning to experiment with growing hops in the Northeast and Southeast (albeit on a much smaller scale than Pacific Northwest growers), thanks to the locavore and local brewing movements. Laura Ten Eyck and Dietrich Gehring, co-owners of Helderberg Hop Farm and Indian Ladder Farmstead Brewery near Albany, New York (and co-authors of *The Hop Grower's Handbook*), have been cultivating hops commercially since 2012, and for the 20 years prior on a small scale. They supply local breweries with standard varieties such as Brewers Gold, Centennial, and Cascade—and their own heirloom Helderberg variety. University agricultural extensions, such as Cornell University's, are also conducting research on the viability of growing hops beyond the Pacific Northwest and providing support to hop growers. Additionally, Cornell, along with the University of Vermont Crops and Soils Team, serves as adviser to the Northeast Hop Alliance (NeHA). In the South, the North Carolina Hops Project was launched in 2010 through the establishment of an experimental hop yard at NC State University's Lake Wheeler Road Field Laboratory in Raleigh. The hop yard consists of 200 hop plants comprising 10 US varieties on ¼ acre (0.1 ha). The parameters of site selection were to determine varieties

A Hallertau hop near Hallertau, Germany, the largest continuous hop-planting area in the world. Courtesy of LuckyStarr, Wikimedia Commons.

best suited for North Carolina's unique growing conditions and with the greatest potential for commercial production, as well as featuring a range of alpha acid content, yield potential, disease and pest resistance, total US production, and demand by local craft breweries.[13]

Variety Is the Spice of Beer

There are more than 200 hop varieties—both wild and domestic—with more being developed and tested in beer all the time.[14] Of these, around 30 to 40 have become brewing standards and thus are readily accessible to commercial and homebrewers, while others have lost their popularity and been cast aside. Beer flavors are dizzyingly diverse due not only to the nuances of each variety, but also variations in timing when they're added to the wort during the brewing and fermentation processes.

Although hop cones contain many compounds, the ones that are of primary interest to the brewer are the alpha acids in the soft-resin portion of the hop. These acids, humulone, cohumulone, and adhumulone, are primarily responsible for providing bittering in beers, but only after they've been boiled. Boiling hops causes them to undergo *isomerization* (the process whereby one molecule is transformed into another molecule that has exactly the same atoms, but in a different arrangement), which brings out bittering compounds called iso-humulone, iso-cohumulone, and iso-adhumulone. Hop cones also contain beta acids that undergo isomerization during boiling, but these are less soluble in wort and contribute little to bittering. Hence, when you're buying hops, your primary concern should be the level of alpha acids; this will determine how much of a bittering effect the hops will have. Some hops are subtle and mid- to low alpha, some are high alpha and bitter, some are citrusy and aromatic and ride high on the "nose" when you sip, some are well balanced and "noble" (*noble* is a classification of traditional European hops known for their low alpha acids, soft well-rounded flavor, and subtle aromatic qualities), and some just march to the beat of their own drummer. Although many herbal additions and adjuncts such as honey provide their own antibacterial properties, hops can also be used in small amounts to ensure that a beer such as a long-aged Belgian will keep over time (though, again, there are many factors and ingredients other than hops that will ensure a "clean" aging). One technique Belgian and other European brewers have taken to is using stale hops early in the boil. This imparts little to no bittering or aroma, but still has the antibacterial properties necessary for long-term aging.

In modern brewing, particularly modern American craft beer, hop varieties play a huge role in the overall character of the beer. In traditional European brewing, hops tend to be more of a supporting player and—as we've seen—didn't necessarily play a role at all historically. The recipes in this book, based primarily on early European and colonial American brewing, consider the characters of malt, adjuncts, and herbs and spices in determining the flavor of a beer rather than those of hops.

For most beers, I recommend low-alpha varieties unless you want a high level of bitterness. I will also look for low-alpha-range varieties (Germany's Spalter and Tettnanger are good ones) if I want to use hops primarily for their preservative effect. Hops aren't actually bitter until they've been boiled, so if you do like a bit of a hoppy aroma, you can always adjust any of these recipes by adding ½ ounce (15 g) of low-to-mid-alpha hops during the last two minutes of the boil, or after cutting off heat. If I'm looking for hops that provide just a hint of bitterness and aroma, I look for mid-alpha-range varieties (British varieties such as Kent Golding and Fuggle are some of my favorites).

When purchasing hops, your basic choice is between hops in their original leaf form and hops in pellet form. Which of these is better is a matter of some debate among homebrewers and even professional brewers. When hops are pelletized, the leaves are run through a machine that crushes and compresses them into a small pellet. In the process they are subjected to heat and oxidation. This helps concentrate the oils and preserves their flavor longer than if left in leaf form. Some feel the mechanization involved in pelletizing hops brutalizes them and either removes or harshens some of the delicate flavors from the resin, while others feel it draws out and concentrates all of the flavor by opening up every lupulin gland and releasing their oils, enabling a more powerful, consistent product. For some it's more a matter of less messiness in the brew kettle. Pellets tend to drop to the bottom as part of the trub while leaves float around and need to be filtered out (this can be avoided with the use of a mesh bag). For me it's one of those "to each their own" things.

There are a number of different qualities hops can impart depending on when they're added. Notwithstanding the additional effects different varieties and alpha levels can have, the overall effect of any hop addition can be summarized as follows:

- When added pre-boil (*first-wort hopping*) hops impart a well-rounded balance of aroma and bitterness.
- When added at the start of the boil, the primary effect will be bitterness.
- When added at mid-boil, hops impart a fairly equal degree of both bitterness and aroma.
- When added during the last five minutes of the boil or just after cutting off heat, hops provide primarily aroma.
- When added to the secondary fermenter (*dry-hopping*), hops provide a high level of fresh, crisp aroma (be sure to add after active fermentation has commenced, or most of the oils responsible for aroma will exit along with the CO_2).

So what does this all mean for the brewer who just isn't all that interested in hops or, like me, is more interested in experimenting with other flavoring and preservative ingredients and doesn't feel the need to get all geeky-techie? First off, if you want to experiment with brewing without

International Bittering Units (IBUs)

In modern brewing, the international standard for describing the level of bitterness in a beer is the International Bittering Unit (IBU). When referring to IBUs, only bitterness from hops is considered, as it is a measurement of the concentration of iso-alpha acids in a finished volume of beer. Commercial breweries measure IBUs for their recipes using expensive, complicated laboratory tools. For homebrewers, it is pretty much impossible to measure IBUs to any degree of certainty. We can come pretty close to a planned bitterness profile if we select hops that are known to have a certain degree of bitterness, but it's futile to sweat it this much. Even the most sensitive palates have difficulty detecting subtle shifts in bitterness, and, like any other aspect of taste, bitterness can be highly subjective. In addition, IBU tests can only determine the amount of bittering qualities that exist in a beer; they

hops, but don't want to give up on them altogether, it is of paramount importance to know what effect *any* addition of hops will have on the final product. Second, although we're talking primarily about the effect of adding hops to the boil, there are some similarities in the timing of additions of herbs, spices, and other ingredients. Botanical ingredients with any degree of bittering impart a much greater degree of bitterness if added early in the boil. On the flip side, whether an ingredient has a noticeable bittering effect or not, its flavor and aroma will usually be lost or barely noticeable if added anytime before the last 5 to 10 minutes of the boil. Preservative/antibacterial effects will be present no matter when you add them. The bulk of modern research on this subject has been done on hops, although we know a fair degree about the effects of other ingredients. With the vast array of potential ingredients you can add to a brew, it would be a daunting task to outline all of their effects to the degree that has been done with hops. However, many have similar qualities that help us estimate the effect each will have. For more on these, see chapter 7.

don't take into account other ingredients that can balance bitterness. For instance, a high-malt beer can handle a larger amount of hops without becoming excessively bitter than can a lighter beer. Other factors that can balance bitterness include water chemistry, residual sugars, and bottle aging. In our current IPA-crazed times, many breweries have responded to consumer demand by listing the IBUs of each of their beers right on the can or bottle. This helps drinkers determine (to a degree) what is about to hit their taste buds, but it can also be used as a gimmick that gets in the way of simply enjoying beer. The best bet for determining the proper amount of bittering and other flavoring elements in creating a homebrew is experimentation, careful recipe formulation, and—in the end—appreciating a beer for what it is. The rest is just marketing.

To Hop or Not to Hop?

I'll admit, I still find it difficult to completely forgo hopping my homebrews. Maybe it's that hops were a big part of the magic when I made my first brew many years ago. Adding hops has its own *schedule*, its own set of specific instructions and warnings that if not done just right . . . well, the beer might taste a bit different than it was supposed to. Though over the years, I've come to find that there are many other ingredients that can lend their own mystique to a brew, sometimes I want a hint of hoppiness to balance out another flavor, such as when I make a spruce beer, as spruce and hops complement each other well. Other times I may want to use hops strictly for their strong antiseptic properties. To put it simply, if I want to use hops, ain't nobody stopping me, but if I'd rather not, well, ain't nobody stopping me from that, either. Mostly, though, I hope more people come to understand that hops are by no means required for beer and, even when they are used, can be considered for balance and nuance rather than the dominant flavor.

As with grain, it's hard to find hops that have been grown locally and sustainably, and when you do find them, they can be expensive. Seek out local hop growers, grow your own, or simply substitute other ingredients. When you're brewing with hops, perhaps minimize the focus on specific varieties called for in recipes and instead seek out lesser-known varieties that have similar characteristics. Embrace the fact that even established varieties of hops undergo subtle shifts in flavoring as their genetics change over time, and short-term factors, including soil health, weather, decrease of oils due to drying, and supply and demand, can also lead to inconsistency. The good news for US hop lovers interested in brewing with local ingredients is that—thanks to the locavore and sustainability movements—local hops at an affordable price are becoming more prevalent. In addition to the small-scale hop farms popping up throughout the United States that supply directly to brewers, some homebrew suppliers are beginning to offer their own locally grown hops. For those of us not on the West Coast, there is still a lot of work that needs to be done, but if consumers keep making their voices heard, prospective hop growers will be encouraged. In the meantime, I suggest pursuing beer as it was brewed before hops took over the beer world.

CHAPTER SEVEN

FLAVORING INGREDIENTS AND ADJUNCTS

The richer sort generally brew their small beer with malt, which they have from England, though barley grows there very well; but for the want of convenience of malt-houses, the inhabitants take no care to sow it. The poorer sort brew their beer with molasses and bran; with Indian corn malted with drying in a stove; with persimmons dried in a cake and baked; with potatoes with the green stalks of Indian corn cut small and bruised, with pompions [pumpkins], with the Jerusalem artichoke which some people plant purposely for that use, but this is the least esteemed.

— Governor Sir William Berkeley, on the brewing habits
of Virginians in the 1600s[1]

Even if you're planning on making beer from "standard" ingredients (what most modern peoples assume beer to be), there is a plethora of ingredients you can add that affect flavor, body, and mouthfeel. Many of these ingredients will have a fairly minimal impact on the flavor of the final product if not overused, some are not entirely predictable due to seasonal changes in flavor (such as spruce and pine needles), and others I'll simply say require an adventurous spirit and forgiving taste buds.

Some of the ingredients in this chapter are considered *flavoring ingredients* while others can be referred to as *adjuncts*, according to technical brewing terminology. While brewers tend to have differing ideas as to what exactly an adjunct is, the general definition is an ingredient that is fermentable to some degree but has not been malted (however, malted "alternative" grains such as wheat and rye sometimes fall into this category, as do other specialty grains). Adjuncts can be either *kettle adjuncts* (simple sugar sources such as honey or molasses that can be added directly to the kettle or fermenter) or *mash adjuncts* (adjuncts such as corn or oats that contain starches that need to be broken down into sugars during the mashing process). Flavoring ingredients impart few to no fermentables, but subtle to big flavors.

Herbs, Spices, and Wild-Foraged Edibles

> *When Hops have been dear, many have used the Seeds of Wormwood, that they buy in the London Seed Shops, instead of them: Others Daucus or wild Carrot Seed, that grows in our common Fields, which many of the poor People in this Country gather and dry in their Houses, against their wanting of them: Others that wholsome Herb Horehound, which indeed is a fine Bitter and grows on several of our Commons.*
>
> —William Ellis, The London and Country Brewer,
> The Seventh Edition, 1759[2]

Just as our ancestors did, you can use pretty much any edible botanical to flavor a brew. If you are a forager or herbalist, you likely already know a number of botanicals that are ideal for cooking, medicine, or tea. Nearly all of these can be used in brewing as well. Regardless of your level of knowledge, however, take care to fully understand the effects of these botanicals, and any potentially dangerous interactions with other herbs or pharmaceuticals (contraindications), as well as their recommended safe dose. Be sure you've identified any plant you're considering using for brewing with 100 percent certainty, never harvest and ingest a plant that may have been sprayed with pesticides, and avoid harvesting from roadsides that see a lot of traffic. Even once you have correctly identified a plant, sample a little bit of it before eating or brewing with large amounts, as even plants that are safe to eat can cause allergic reactions in rare cases. If you are pregnant or may be pregnant, research a plant to see if it has qualities that may cause a problem with your pregnancy or create a hormonal imbalance. Many plants were used traditionally for abortive purposes, so we have a pretty comprehensive understanding of which ones to avoid.

Learn and practice foraging ethics and sustainability when harvesting wild plants. There are many online foraging guides. The respectable ones state their stance on foraging ethics up front. Be sure to double-check sources, particularly as each should have photos of wild edibles you can use to compare. There are also several books on foraging, one of the most respected and comprehensive being *The Forager's Harvest* by Sam Thayer. I also recommend *The New Wildcrafted Cuisine* and *The Wildcrafting Brewer* by Pascal Baudar as comprehensive guides on how to use wild edibles for both food and beverages. One of Baudar's mantras is to "taste the forest," using not just fruits but bark, grass, leaves, twigs, tree sap, and stones (for heating and grinding ingredients). However, you'll need to pursue advanced foraging on your own. An expert understanding of the environment of the forest, and how materials interact with one another (as well as which are deadly if used in more than very small amounts), is essential if you want to pursue forest brewing. As with any subject, start with the basics and build from there.

Although what follows is by no means a comprehensive list of herbs and spices that can be used for brewing, I've outlined the core ingredients that have been used traditionally, as well as my experience with them where applicable. If you have an interest in herbs for cooking or medicinal purposes, that interest can easily cross over into brewing. Experiment with single herbs and then with combinations in small batches to discover flavors you like, or create brews with intentional medicinal benefits. Keep in mind that when you're brewing with herbs or spices of any kind, a little goes a long way. For most, just a teaspoon or two per gallon will do, particularly when added to the end of a boil or during secondary fermentation. A good way to test the potency of an herb or spice's flavor is to make a small batch of tea first, measuring both the water and ingredients carefully, and then scale up for a full batch of brew when you've found the right balance.

Alehoof (*Glechoma hederacea*) can be found in many yards and wildlands throughout North America and Europe.

Alehoof (*Glechoma hederacea*)

As do many plants with a long-running history of use in brewing and medicine, alehoof goes by many names, including tunhoof, creeping Charlie, and ground ivy. Commonly found in most wildlands and in many yards in North America and Europe, it is considered by many to be a weed. A member of the mint family, it can be identified by its delicate light purple flower and square stem. Traditionally, alehoof was used for both its bittering and its preservative effects, and it works well as a substitute for hops. Its bittering effect is mild, though, as is its flavor. It can hence be used in minimal amounts without concern that it will overpower other flavors. Don't just throw in handfuls, however.

Allspice (*Pimenta dioica*)

Heady and flavorful, allspice complements similar spices such as cloves and cinnamon. Along with cardamom, nutmeg, and star anise, allspice can be used to really give a brew an exotic kick. However, these are all flavorings that should be employed such that their presence is barely noticed (even a bit extra of any of them can be overpowering).

Bayberry (*Myrica cerifera*)

Related to the traditional brewing stalwart *Myrica gale*, bayberry is an astringent and is anti-inflammatory. Like alehoof, it can be used in brewing as a substitute for hops, but it has more of an astringent than bitter effect, so take care not to overdo it.

Bog Myrtle (*Myrica gale*)

Often referenced in brewing literature as sweet gale, bog myrtle was one of the herbs purported to have been a standard in gruit recipes. It has similar properties as bayberry. Both the leaves and flowers of the plant can be used for brewing, with the flowers having a bit more of a sweet flavor, and the leaves having more of a grassy/herbal flavor.

Broom (*Cytisus scoparius*)

Broom is a small woody brush that gets its name from its traditional use in making brooms (and baskets). The tips of its young branches were historically used as a bittering agent. If you're harvesting, take care not to mistake it for its cousin Spanish broom (*Spartium junceum*), which is mildly poisonous and can cause vomiting.

Caraway (*Carum carvi*)

One of the known historic gruit components, caraway can be used effectively in brewing, particularly alongside rye. Like dill, fennel, cumin, and anise, it has carminative properties, meaning that it helps with indigestion and is . . . ahem . . . a fart-stopper.

Cardamom (*Elettaria cardamomum*)

Also known as green cardamom, cardamom is a relative of ginger with an aromatic, pungent, citrusy flavor. If you like Indian food, you're probably already familiar with its flavor, as it is native to India and Sri Lanka and a standard component in Indian cooking.

Chamomile (*Chamaemelum nobile*)

Fragrant and sweet, chamomile can add a certain fruitiness to beer, but can also be overdone and make your brew taste more like a very herby tea.

Cinnamon (*Cinnamomum zeylanicum*) / Cassia (*C. cassia*)

Both cinnamon and cassia are the powdered bark of their respective trees. The former is true cinnamon, while cassia passes for cinnamon, and is marketed and sold as such in most American grocery stores.

While not as strong as the other exotic spices, it provides a nice festive flavor and can make for a warming holiday-themed ale.

Cloves (*Syzygium aromaticum*)

Cloves provide a deep, rich, aromatic flavor to beer. A couple of the tiny pods go a long way. It can be used in combination with other exotics to provide a festive flavor to holiday ales. While they can be used to provide a subtle effect to lighter beers, they shine best paired with dark malts.

Coffee (*Coffea arabica*)

The fermented, roasted beans of a modest shrub from Ethiopia, coffee is the elixir of life and keeps many a writer from falling asleep on the job (or just staring blearily at the strange glowing object in front of him/her). Also, it's good in beer. Although best for adding depth to brews made with darker malts, it can be used to impart subtle effects to lighter beers. In my personal experience, it's better added to the wort boil, although some brewers think this imparts too much bitterness and prefer cold extract added to the secondary. Personally, I have found this results in a stale coffee flavor. The type of coffee used, how much to use, and when to add it are all factors that you can vary greatly; no choice is better than any other. Personally, I like adding coarsely ground espresso beans during the last 10 to 15 minutes of the boil, preferably for stouts. However, brewers have tried all manner of variations. Experiment away! Highly roasted malts such as chocolate and black patent will both impart a coffee flavor without the use of coffee as they have been processed in a similar manner to roasted coffee beans.

Coriander (*Coriandrum sativum*)

The seed of cilantro, coriander is traditionally used in Belgian witbiers and complements any wheat beer nicely, particularly when used with additional ingredients such as orange peel.

Ginger (*Zingiber officinale*)

The part of the ginger plant used for brewing and cooking is the rhizome. While a very popular flavor in traditional beer brewing, it should be used sparingly unless you want ginger to be the dominant flavor, as with ginger beer. In small amounts, it works well in various styles, particularly wheats, along with flavorings such as coriander, orange peel, grains of paradise, and licorice.

Grains of Paradise (*Aframomum melegueta*)

A relative of ginger, it has a similar potent flavor but is a bit more subtle and therefore more forgiving. Its flavor and bite are really more akin to black pepper, for which it can be used as a substitute in both cooking and brewing. It's very common in British beer recipes, and I have added it to many of my brews since discovering it.

Licorice/Liquorice (*Glycyrrhiza glabra*)

Taken from the root of a herbaceous perennial legume native to Southern Europe and Asia, it shows up in a number of traditional beer recipes. It has a unique sweet flavor that can easily overpower a recipe. Use sparingly.

Meadowsweet (*Filipendula ulmaria*)

A much-heralded precursor to hops as one of the core components in beer as both a preservative and flavoring, meadowsweet shows up in many early brewing recipes, and is often found in the analysis of brewing-vessel shards in archaeological digs. Very aromatic, it is often a component of Scottish heather ales.

From bottom left corner clockwise: cloves, cardamom, allspice, cinnamon, grains of paradise, fenugreek, and star anise (center).

Mugwort (*Artemisia vulgaris*)

Related to wormwood (and sometimes called common wormwood), mugwort shares wormwood's bittering powers, but is tamer in flavor. As with wormwood—and any other bittering herb for that matter—I've found that my herbalist and brewing friends have differing opinions as to just how bitter mugwort is. It's one of my favorite substitutes for hops, for its bitter and preservative effect more than its flavor. It is generally best to balance it with a more aromatic herb such as meadowsweet.

Nutmeg (*Myristica fragrans*)

The seed of an evergreen indigenous to Indonesia, nutmeg is very strong and aromatic and should be used sparingly, or along with spices such as allspice, cinnamon, and cloves to brew holiday ales.

Rosemary (*Rosmarinus officinalis*)

Both the stem and needles of this small evergreen shrub—a woody perennial herb—can be used to flavor beer. The flavor is potent and aromatic either fresh or dried. A little bit goes a long way! Not to be confused with the mildly toxic wild rosemary.

Sage (*Salvia officinalis*)

Most often associated with cooking today, sage was very commonly used to brew with in ancient times. While *Salvia officinalis* is the type of sage most Westerners are familiar with, there are many other plants that take the name sage. Not all of them are related, or even have the same medicinal properties. Take care when selecting a sage plant for brewing that you understand its true properties. Spanish sage (*S. lavandulifolia*) is the common culinary variety, and is the only variety that doesn't contain thujone, which is toxic in excess amounts and can cause breast milk reduction. Thujone, however, is strongly antiseptic and stimulates digestion, and can therefore be used for medicinal purposes in smaller amounts.

Saint-John's-Wort (*Hypericum perforatum*)

We know Saint-John's-wort has a rich tradition in brewing, since it lent its name to unfermented beer: *wort*. It was a traditional component in Scandinavian beers such as sahti, and likely showed up in gruit recipes. Traditionally, and even in modern medical usage, it has been used as an antidepressant, so why not put it in your beer? It's important to note that, according to the NCCIH (National Center for Complementary and Integrative Health), Saint-John's-wort can interact negatively with a number of pharmaceuticals.[3]

Sassafras (*Sassafras albidum*)

Both the roots and inner bark of this shrub found in the eastern US have traditionally been used to make medicinal teas and can be used in brewing beer, including root beer. The FDA doesn't permit its sale, as studies on rats have shown that it is carcinogenic in very large amounts, and thus it was banned in 1960.[4] Considering the much larger amounts of carcinogens that surround us on a daily basis—and that we're not rats being forced to ingest massive doses of it—a little bit of sassafras shouldn't be much of a concern. If you compare drinking modern root beer to a sassafras tea or beer, you may notice that they did a surprisingly good job of imitating the flavor of real sassafras. One way I've heard the flavor described is as tasting like soft licorice or aniseed (which licorice candy is flavored with), but to me it has its own unique flavor.

Vanilla (*Vanilla planifolia*)

The pods of a species of orchid native to Mexico and Central America, vanilla can be used in whole form or as an extract in brewing. Although its flavor is soft and mild, it can easily overpower other flavors (which makes it useful for covering up off flavors before bottling).

Wild Rosemary (*Ledum palustre*)

Another reputed gruit ingredient, and a common ingredient in many other traditional herbal ales, it is toxic if consumed in large quantities. Although it probably won't kill you, drinking too much beer with wild rosemary is alleged to cause dizziness and headaches. One of those traditions it's probably best not to emulate. A related plant is Labrador tea (*L. groenlandicum*), a member of the heath family.

Woodruff (*Galium odoratum*)

Often referred to as sweet woodruff, it is best known for its use in May wine. Known in Germany as *Waldmeister*, it was traditionally used to flavor Berliner Weisse beer.

Wormwood (*Artemisia absinthium*)

Legendary as a component in absinthe and other herbed beverages, wormwood was also traditionally used as a bittering component in beer. Its reputation as being dangerous due to having some degree of toxicity and supposed mind-altering abilities is overstated. Due to its high level of bitterness, it should be used sparingly in beer. One thing I have discovered in my personal experience is that wormwood I purchased from a home-brew-supply store produced an almost undrinkable beer due to excessive bitterness. When I ordered some from a reputable herb supplier, I made some beer with a small amount and the bitterness was barely discernible. I decided to sample a pinch of each to see if there was a difference. The stuff from the homebrew-supply store tasted awful; the other just had an herbal (and not overly bitter) flavor. Maybe I got a bad batch. Still, in general I recommend ordering dried herbs from a reputable supplier, and sampling a bit before using—if a bit on the tip of your tongue tastes awful, chances are you're not going to like it in your brew.

Yarrow (*Achillea millefolium*)

Another classic gruit herb, it has a mild bittering effect and is a good candidate to counteract the sweetness of malt and other ingredients in place of hops.

Forest Brewing: Tree Leaves, Bark, Needles, and More

Many old brewing recipes call for the addition of items such as bark, leaves, and pine needles, so brewing with forest materials is a well-established tradition. Even today brewers, vintners, mead makers, and distillers use oak and other wood to impart flavoring through the use of barrels and wood chips. The only difference is that these woods are a bit more processed than what you can find in the forest. Many of the other ingredients you can brew with are very common and can be grown yourself or purchased from an herb supplier. Learn to identify them in the wild and you'll never need to buy or grow them, provided you only pick small amounts to allow them to continue to propagate. Although you can use the roots of some plants for brewing, such as dandelion, it's generally best to avoid uprooting any wild plants. While I use most of these ingredients in smaller batches of simple wild brews (or primitive wild beers, as Pascal Baudar likes to call them), ones that I have experimented with and ascertained acceptable ratios for brewing with often end up in my larger grain-based brewing batches.

Tree Bark

The bark of most deciduous trees (trees that shed their leaves every fall), and of most conifers (trees with needles that stay on the tree year-round), is edible and good for brewing. Oak, walnut, willow, alder, sycamore, and birch are among the various tree barks that were used in traditional brews. Cambium, the inner, living bark, is edible and nutritious and can be eaten as an emergency food source (in small amounts) or brewed with. The rougher outer bark can be used, but contains a higher level of tannins, which means more bitterness; it also provides less flavor than the inner bark, as it is essentially the dead "skin" of the tree.

Try to avoid taking bark from live trees. As long as it is fairly freshly fallen, a dead tree will serve you just as well. If you do elect to take a small amount from a live tree, try to go with some bark from a branch, or scrape a bit from the trunk. If you were to take bark from the entire circumference of the tree (which you shouldn't), you would be cutting off its food source and will likely kill the tree. As with any

The inner layer, or cambium, of tree bark can be procured by carefully scraping off the outer bark with a knife, and then shaving strips of cambium.

wild harvesting, borrow what you need and let nature keep the rest. Just remember that bark will be crawling with all kinds of bacteria that you don't necessarily want. While you *can* sterilize the bark by boiling it in the wort, this will also release tannins that can lead to excessive bittering. I've made flavorful enough (and not overly bitter) beers this way, but you'll get a more balanced flavor if you heat the bark in an oven at 250°F (120°C) for 20 to 30 minutes and add it as a flavoring component after the wort has cooled. You can experiment with various quantities to use for brewing. It's tough to give specifics on how much to use—as tree type and age, time of year, and other environmental factors can affect the flavor—but I generally go with a small handful (about 0.5 ounce/14 grams) per 1-gallon (4 L) batch.

Tree Leaves

Many older brewing recipes call for floating an oak, walnut, or maple leaf on top of a new mead or wine for tannin. Along with tannin, leaves provide additional nutrients and flavoring qualities. Beers don't generally need tannin, although non-grain-based beers (such as simple ales) can benefit from some, or can be flavored with only tree leaves. I like to work with leaves that have already fallen, although green leaves will work as well. When they've fallen and have begun to decompose, they start producing a musky, earthen flavor. Walk through a forest in the autumn and take a deep whiff. That's the flavor you're looking for.

Coniferous Needles

The needles of conifers (spruce, pine, and cedar trees) have long been used for brewing, and to make teas. Spruce beer recipes abound in historical brewing literature, and spruce was often used instead of or alongside hops, for both its preservative and its flavoring qualities. Spruce was commonly used to prevent scurvy on long sea voyages due to its high vitamin C content. While nearly all conifers have edible needles, I usually use the word *spruce* in regard to brewing for simplicity's sake and because nearly all recipes—new and old—use that word primarily.

Please check a reputable source to identify a tree before brewing with its needles. The toxicity of some types of conifers, such as the western ponderosa pine and the southeastern loblolly pine, is a matter of debate (you would have to ingest a *lot* of "toxic" needles, which you should

Spruce and pine needles come in a large variety of shapes and sizes. All of them can be used in brewing, with the possible exception of the western ponderosa pine and the southeastern loblolly pine.

never do anyway). The yew tree, easily identifiable by its red berry with a single seed, is a well-known toxic conifer with a rich history in folklore. Ingestion of the needles of any conifer on an extended, regular basis can potentially be toxic, and conifer needles of any kind should be avoided by pregnant women. Just as with any other edible plant, though, you should be fine unless you're consuming very large amounts on a daily basis (with the exception of yew). Also, as with any other plant, research contraindications before consuming. If you're unsure or don't live in an area with easy access to conifer needles, visit Spruce on Tap (spruceontap.com). They provide sustainably harvested spruce tips from Colorado, as well as a number of other wild-harvested ingredients such as juniper berries and yarrow (along with recipes for brewing with spruce).

As with bark, the recommended amount of needles to use for brewing is hard to peg down. If it smells strong, it will likely have a strong flavor. The most flavorful needles for brewing are those harvested in the spring (although they can be harvested and used in brewing year-round). Gather several of the tips (the new-growth ends of a branch, which will be tender and bright green in the spring) and toss as many into a brew as you dare. Flavors imparted by needles range from citrusy, to floral, to resinous and piney. If you don't want your beer to taste like Lysol, be sure to not use too much if the needles have a strong flavor, and avoid adding them to the full boil (adding them at the end as the brew begins to cool, and leaving them for 30 to 45 minutes is best). The most consistent way to get the exact flavor you want is to make a spruce tea or purchase some spruce essence from a homebrewing store. Add very small amounts at bottling and taste until you're satisfied. Spruce essence is a concentrate, so start with *very* small amounts (around ¼ teaspoon). For spruce tea you can be a little more liberal. To make a spruce tea, simply take several spruce tips, boil them in about a gallon (4 L) of water until the bark peels off easily, strain, cool, and keep refrigerated until you're ready to bottle.

EASTERN RED CEDAR (*JUNIPERUS VIRGINIANA*)

Not a true cedar, but a member of the juniper family. European settlers mistook it for a cedar and the name stuck. Like European junipers, the eastern red cedar can be identified by the berrylike cones on the tips of the shoots of female trees. True to its name, it is most common in eastern North America, with the Rocky Mountain juniper (*J. scopulorum*) more common in western North America. Traditional Scandinavian recipes often call for juniper branches and berries. In North America cedar branches can be used as a substitute for juniper, but take care with how much you use. In my own brews I've found that it can add a very strong woody, piney, almost dirtlike flavor if not used sparingly. In checking with Finnish sahti brewer, blogger, and author Mika Laitinen (brewingnordic.com), I discovered that other North American brewers have reported similar flavor profiles.[5] Although it is not as authentic, I prefer the flavor spruce imparts in my Scandinavian-style brews, unless I'm able to procure true Scandinavian juniper. If you use eastern red cedar or Rocky Mountain juniper, I suggest just using the branches as a filter and only adding a small amount to the wort to avoid a brew you may want to toss down the drain.

Fruits and Vegetables

Most technical brewing books I've read say there is little historic precedent for brewing with fruit or vegetables, probably because they tend

Mushrooms

Capturing the rich diversity of mushrooms is far beyond the scope of this book. There are many excellent books and several reputable websites on the subject. I grow my own mushrooms and forage for them from time to time, but I'm much more a hobbyist than an expert. As with other wild edibles, I work with what I know and slowly build my repertoire. My favorites to brew with (mostly because they're the ones I'm most familiar with) are shiitake, oyster, wine cap stropharia, and turkey tail. Some species add a heady dose of earthiness, some impart a nutty flavor, some are more delicate, and most impart some degree of bitterness. Try out different varieties to determine the flavors that work for you. It doesn't hurt to chew on a mushroom and slowly savor its juices to ascertain the flavoring qualities and degree of bitterness it is likely to give a brew.

Mushrooms can be used fresh or dried (whole or powdered) with about the same effect but, as with herbs, dried mushrooms have more concentrated flavors, so you should use about half the amount. They can (and should, if raw) be heated in the full boil, as this will draw out their medicinal and flavoring qualities, and kill off any live bacteria that may or may not lend positive qualities to the final product. If you decide to add mushrooms to the secondary fermenter, first be sure to cook them in the oven, dehydrate them, or cook them in water to make a mushroom tea. Most mushrooms are indigestible raw, and even edible ones can be mildly toxic if not heated first.

to focus on specific styles and beers that were produced commercially (exceptions are given for Belgian beers, which often contain fruit such as raspberries and cherries). I have found quite the opposite to be true in my research, but perhaps that's because—like most early brewers—I don't have a regimented concept of what I consider to be a beer. Most people today consider any alcohol brewed with fruit and (nonmalt) sugar to be wine—or mead if made with fruit and honey (which technically makes for a type of mead called a melomel). While I agree with these designations, when we brew, we can work with whatever combinations of sugars and ingredients we desire. If we're brewing for ourselves and our friends and family, it doesn't matter so much what we call it (although, like myself, you likely have friends and family members who are stuck on the aforementioned designations). The point here is that fruit and vegetables have been used extensively in brewing throughout history. We know that as far back as Neolithic times fruits were used not only for flavoring and an additional sugar source, but also to initiate fermentation due to the wild yeasts that like to colonize their skins. Residue from pottery shards found in early Bronze Age Northern Europe, for example, reveals a prevalence of beerlike beverages (grogs) that contained fruits such as apples, cherries, cowberries, cranberries, and lingonberries. These grogs also contained grains, along with herbs such as meadowsweet and bog myrtle, as well as honey.[6] Given that grains were often included in these brews, I would say that there was a very early precedent for fruit beer. Another ancient brew, discovered from analysis of pottery jars found in the Neolithic village of Jiahu in northern China, was an early rice beer, but also had elements of wine and mead, as it contained honey, grapes, and hawthorn berries.[7]

For small craft breweries, the cost of procuring enough fruit or vegetables for a beer—along with the cost of lost profits due to potentially unpopular beer—can be high. Many fruits, for example, grow mostly in the wild, grow only in certain regions, or aren't generally grown on a commercial scale. The good news is that you've got a leg up on commercial breweries. For you, if it's edible and you can forage or grow it, you can brew beer with it. You don't even have to gather enough for a 5-gallon batch. For my fruit beers, I often just gather what I need and throw it into a 1-gallon batch. Quick, easy, and dirt-cheap. But while brewing with fruits and vegetables is a simple prospect, there are some things you'll want to take into consideration when formulating a recipe.

Let's start with fruit, since fruits are a bit different than most vegetables in how they affect a brew. First, do you want the particular fruit you're using to be the highlight of the drink, do you want it to be more of a subtle afterthought, or are you more interested in its fermentation-enhancing and flavor-balancing properties? Depending on the beer you have in mind, you'll need to decide not only how much to use but also the point of the brewing process to add it. As with wine and mead, most of the flavor will be lost if the fruit is added at the beginning of the fermentation process, but you can add fruit, or fruit juice, all the way up to bottling. The further along you add it, the more it will contribute to the flavor. There are brewers who steep fruit during the last 15 minutes or so of the boil, although others argue that this brings out high levels of pectin, which can contribute to haze. The general consensus seems to be that adding to the secondary is a perfectly valid—and likely the best—option. Juniper berries are cooked in Scandinavian beer worts, but remember that these are actually a type of pinecone, not a true berry.

Try to procure quality fruit at peak ripeness and either add immediately to the fermenter or freeze until you're ready to use. Not only does this give you time to gather enough for the brew but freezing also breaks down fruit's cell walls, allowing more of its essence into the brew. Be sure to allow the fruit to fully thaw before using it, however, as you may shock the yeast if you drop it in cold. Concentrated juice or fruit extract will also work, as will regular old fruit juice (with no preservatives). If you're using concentrated, check the container for the equivalent amount of fruit.

I prefer to avoid extract, as I feel it imparts a syrupy, soda-like flavor to my beers, but it's good to use at bottling if you have a specific amount of fruit flavoring you're after. Since extract has no fermentable sugars, it won't restart fermentation. Just add a bit at a time, stir, and taste until you're satisfied (or take a sample of the beer, measure how much you add, and when you like it, scale up for the rest).

The amount of fruit you use can vary depending on the fruit and your preferred flavor profile. Start by following someone else's recipe (there are lots of fruit-beer recipes in online brewing forums), or experiment. A good place to start is 1 to 2 pounds (0.5–1 kg) per gallon (4 L). The worst that can usually happen is that you make a beer that is too fruity, that comes out bland, or has too much tartness or sourness. There are various ways to balance these undesirable flavors when it comes to bottling time so that you're not left with a bunch of *blah* beers. Wine- and mead makers create balance by adding acids and tannins. Most beer won't need tannin because grains usually provide enough, and any herbs or hops have a similar effect. However, citric and malic acid additions can make just the difference you need. Fruits such as lemons, limes, oranges, and grapefruit provide citric acid, while malic acid comes

Brewing with Oranges

Oranges are a very popular fruit to add to farmhouse ales and any light, refreshing summer ale. When brewing with oranges, or any other citrus for that matter, most brewers use only the zest, or colored outer rind. The inner white rind, or pith, should be avoided or used carefully in very small amounts, as it can add a bitterness you probably don't want. Scrape the outer rind off with a zester, or buy the zest of exotic oranges such as Curaçao at an herb or homebrew-supply store. You can also use orange juice for additional orange flavor, but this can be easy to overdo. I recommend waiting until fermentation has died down and adding it to taste.

I've heard of some people brewing with whole oranges but I've had whole-orange brews that have come out far too pithy, so I can't provide any personal advice on how to do that. I have made small meads, though, to which I add several orange wedges at the beginning of the fermentation process. These are quite enjoyable drunk young as intended, but can start to turn pithy with aging.

from apples. Malic provides more of a soft flavoring effect if you just want to round the flavor out a bit. If the brew seems bland at bottling, any citrus fruit will do, although lemon is the most common. Adding a high-acid fruit such as raspberries (a very popular fruit for beer on its own) during fermentation can be a good way to avoid needing to make adjustments at bottling. Use juice when adjusting at bottling, not whole fruit. Start with a teaspoon per gallon, stir, taste, and adjust until satisfied. Or adjust a small sample and scale up.

The next question is: What type of malt should you pair with fruit? In general, lighter barley and wheat malts meld better with most fruits, but more robust fruit flavors can handle darker malts. For instance, cherries work remarkably well with dark beers. One of my favorite stouts to brew is a cherry-espresso stout. I was living in Washington State the first time I made it, and I brewed it with large, plump, sweet bing cherries that my wife and I had picked and canned in syrup. Tart cherries will also work well with dark grains, but they may require a bit more of a balancing act. When brewing with fruit, I recommend doing some 1-gallon (4 L) test batches with dry malt extract (DME) until you reach the ratio of fruit to malt that you like, then scaling up to 5-gallon (20 L) extract or all-grain batches if you have enough fruit. Generally, dark grains should be avoided when you're brewing with lighter-flavored fruits, even as adjuncts, as they can conflict with the fruit flavor. Careful, small additions don't hurt to experiment with, though. Wheat and pilsner malts are some of my favorites for fruit brews, particularly since their flavors hark back to traditional Belgian and French farmhouse brews.

Most of the so-called vegetables that are most often used in brewing are actually fruit. Pumpkins are fruit. So are other squash such as zucchini. Peppers are fruit. Tomatoes are fruit. Fruits contain seeds, as opposed to vegetables, which are parts of the plant such as roots, stems, leaves, tubers, and flowers. The reason people think of certain fruits as being vegetables is because these types of fruits tend to be less sweet, so they usually suit different culinary purposes. Oh well. Call them what you will; they're still fair game for brewing. I can't say I've brewed with a lot of vegetables (or fruits that are actually vegetables), but I do play around with them some. For instance, rhubarb ferments into a nice tart, slightly sour flavor reminiscent of a good Belgian ale (see the Rhubarb Ginger/Simple Ale recipe in chapter 9). Many brewers brew with peppers, but they definitely require careful balancing; I like to smoke various types of chili peppers and use one to two per gallon. The pepper flavor should complement the rest of the brew, not overwhelm it.

Come fall, the craft-beer market is inundated with pumpkin ales. While pumpkins have been used for brewing in the US since the colonial era, I don't think their brewing potential has been fully realized. I find most commercial pumpkin beers a bit bland, although I have tasted exceptions. The trick is to use pumpkin as a base for other flavors, as it doesn't have much of its own. Just as with pumpkin pie, if you add the right amounts of spices such as allspice, cinnamon, nutmeg, and coriander (usually around ¼ to ½ ounce/7–14 g in a 5-gallon/20 L batch), you can give a pumpkin brew a nice well-rounded flavor. Pumpkins, and other squash, should be cooked before being used in brewing to break their flesh down and to caramelize them. Split them in half, scoop out the seeds, and lay them flat on a cookie sheet lined with foil. It's best to not grease the pan, as that may impart flavors you don't want in the brew. Bake them pulp-side down for an hour or two in an oven at 300°F (150°C) until the pulp is soft and mushy. Let it cool, scoop it out, and add it to the mash (or wort if you're brewing with extract).

Adjunct Grains and Sugars

As we've learned, the process of breaking grain starches down into fermentable sugars takes a bit of work, especially when you're brewing with highly starchy grains such as corn, rice, unmalted wheat, or oats. For the most part, these grains won't do you much good in extract brewing, and they may very well cause some problems. While oats can be used in small amounts to build up body in a beer such as a stout, most of these starch grains will contribute little more than haziness and instability. Unlike barley, which stores its starch in granules, these adjuncts keep their starch in a well-organized, tightly bound structure. When creating a mash in all-grain brewing, we are introducing grain-derived enzymes (alpha and beta amylase) that degrade starch into simple sugars. The best way to make starchy unmalted grains accessible to these enzymes is to precook them in water before adding them to the mash. Soaking starchy foods allows the starch to absorb water, while the granules remain intact. The starch's structure then begins to break down and the water molecules begin to disperse. Since starch-degrading amylase enzymes are water-soluble, they are now able to get to the starch and begin degrading it.

Corn

Corn gets a bad rap today, with good reason. It has become a monocrop in the United States, taking up vast fields to supply manufacturers of high-fructose corn syrup, as well as a multitude of additional additives and sweeteners. Not to mention that mega-breweries use large amounts of corn (and some, rice) as filler for fermentable sugars in their beers to keep costs down and production up. When the first American craft breweries began introducing their all-malt beers, the flavor was a shock to the drinking public. Some embraced it while most stuck to their adjunct-heavy lagers. Time turned the tide, though, and now big breweries have been forced to play catch-up. For a long time, craft-beer geeks turned their noses up at the use of corn or rice in beer, and no craft brewery dared use any. However, as craft breweries (and homebrewers) become more innovative and interested in the use of traditional ingredients, corn is becoming accepted again, provided it is in small amounts or is used to re-create a traditional recipe and not simply as filler.

There are many examples of corn-based beers in colonial-era United States, including recipes from George Washington, Thomas Jefferson, and Ben Franklin. George, Tom, and Ben were all prolific brewers, as were other founding fathers, and passed down their favorites. Credit must be given, however, to Jefferson's daughter Martha, as she was a well-respected brewster well before her father took to brewing. Martha brewed copious amounts of beer while living in Monticello, serving more than 120 gallons (454 L) in her first year there alone.[8] Since barley wasn't readily available, or was prohibited for use as malt due to scarcity, early colonial brewers got creative, thanks in large part to the Native Americans who had helped them through the harsh early years by teaching them how to grow and use crops such as corn. One of the earliest reports of making beer from maize was written by colonist Thomas Hariot around 1588: "Wee made of the same [corn] in the country some mault, whereof was brued as good ale as was to be desired."[9] While

Dried corn ideal for malting from a corn-harvesting party at permaculture guru Susana Lein's Salamander Springs Farm near Berea, Kentucky.

it is possible to make a flavorful all-corn beer such as chicha or other South American brews (which require enzyme conversion through the introduction of saliva via chewing and spitting), corn is generally best used as a minor adjunct in malt-based beers. Colonial American recipes that call for corn generally also list malted barley, although at times early Americans had to use mostly—if not all—corn. Malted corn isn't common today unless you malt it yourself, so contemporary brewers usually use corn grits (coarsely ground dried corn kernels) or fresh sweet kernels (better used for corn wine than beer).

Various forms of corn can be used for brewing, from cracked corn to corn grits, cornmeal to cornstalks. Cornstalks (according to one early recipe, chopped and pounded so that their juice can be extracted by boiling[10]) must be used early in the season, before they've passed all of their sugars along to the kernels. For brewing with kernels—in whatever form—precook them before adding them to the mash as described on page 155 and in the Modernized Chicha recipe in chapter 9. Flaked maize can be added directly to the mash, as it has already been precooked through a steaming process, after which it is pressed between hot rollers to pre-gelatinize the starches, making them ready for conversion to sugar.

Unmalted Oats and Wheat

Contributing no extractable sugars, unmalted oats and wheat are two prime examples of ingredients primarily used to provide body, with limited contributions to flavor. While they can have some noticeable effect when used in an extract beer, they're best included as part of an all-grain recipe. Take care, though; because they don't easily give up their fermentable sugars, they can become rather gooey and gum up the works of your mash tun. A good way to avoid this is to add rice hulls to act as a sparging filter, about 1 pound (0.5 kg) per 5 pounds (2.5 kg) of adjunct. All unmalted grains, including corn, need a bit of precooking to prepare them for the mash. When precooking, take the amount you plan on brewing with, place it in a pot, and add just enough water to turn it into a thick porridge. Bring it slowly to a boil, stirring constantly, and then cut the heat down to an occasional bubble. Leave it like this, continuing to stir regularly, for 15 minutes. At this point, you can add it to your mash, which you should already have heated to about 122°F (50°C). Slowly add the adjunct grains and monitor your temperature until it reaches what your recipe calls for, adding more hot water if needed. Instant, rolled, and old-fashioned oats have all been precooked already and can be added directly to the mash.

Molasses, Brown Sugar, and Cane Sugar

Molasses was one of the main ingredients used for brewing beer in colonial America when malted barley was scarce. Molasses is a syrupy substance derived from sugarcane and a by-product of refined sugar. To produce sugar, juice is extracted from sugarcane or sugar beets, which is then boiled down until the sugars crystallize. The leftover syrup is molasses. The word *molasses* comes from the Portuguese *melaço*, meaning "treacle," and is derived from the Latin *mel*, "honey," likely due to its similar consistency. There are usually three stages of boiling and crystallization during sugarcane production. The excess molasses contains less sugar with each subsequent phase. The further along in the process, the higher the vitamin and mineral content is of the resultant molasses. This is why refined sugar is really a non-food. By the time sugar makes it to crystallized form, particularly table sugar, it is devoid of any nutrients. The forms of molasses are, by order of extraction:

Light molasses: The syrup left over from the first boiling cycle, it is light in color, has a high sugar content, and has the least viscous texture.

Dark molasses: The second by-product, this molasses is darker, more viscous, and contains less sugar than light molasses.

Blackstrap molasses: This variety has the highest mineral content and contains the least sugar. It is very dark in color and highly viscous. It also has the most robust flavor, which can be a turnoff to some.

Sugar production was a major economic powerhouse for the growth of the United States and, along with cotton production, was highly dependent upon slavery. Sugarcane likes warm temperatures, so most sugar was produced in the Caribbean, but it was also grown and processed in the Deep South of the United States. Because of its explosive growth in popularity once colonists realized how easily it could be distilled into rum, it was produced on slave plantations to maximize profit. Initially, molasses was tossed or used as animal fodder until it was determined to be almost as easy to ferment as honey. An early description of the resultant product in a 1651 description of Barbados was none too kind: "The chief fuddling they make in the island is Rumbullion, alias Kill-Devil, and this is made of sugar canes distilled, a hot, hellish, and terrible liquor." As the distilling process became more refined, the tune quickly changed. Rum became extremely popular in England, the American colonies, and even West Africa—where thousands of men, women, and children were sold into slavery in large part to enable its production. By the late 1600s the island of Barbados was transformed from a dense forest into an ocean of sugarcane plantations.[11]

Although many recipes dating back to the 1600s call for the use of molasses—and only molasses—as the sugar source for brewing beer, it can have a strong and off-putting flavor when used in its more concentrated forms. Blackstrap molasses in particular should be used in small amounts in malt beer, or blended with lighter molasses or crystallized sugar in sugar-based ales. This is not only because it has a lower degree of fermentability, but also because the flavor it imparts—sharp, pungent,

Cane sugar, brown sugar, and molasses are all by-products of various stages of the sugarcane-refinement process.

and vitamin-rich—can be difficult to imbibe as the primary flavor in a beer. For malt beers, molasses is best used to add body and flavor to stouts and porters. As it was a common ingredient in spruce beer, I like to add a pound (0.5 kg) of it to my malt-based spruce beers for a degree of authenticity.

Brown sugar can be used in a similar manner as molasses for brewing, as it is simply granulated sugar with some molasses still present. There are two types: *Unrefined* or *partially refined* brown sugar is sugar that hasn't had the molasses fully processed from it, while *refined* brown sugar is refined white sugar to which molasses has been added back. Brown sugar comes with a variety of labels, including *dark, light, natural, turbinado, demerara,* and *muscovado.* The difference in these varieties is negligible when it comes to brewing (with the exception of light brown sugar, which will produce, well . . . lighter-flavored beer than dark brown sugar), so when I reference brown sugar in a recipe, any brown sugar will do. For a simple ale with a lighter, crisper flavor, replace the same amount of brown sugar with raw cane sugar. Feel free to blend various refined sugars and even molasses to come up with your own preferred flavor.

Sorghum

Sometimes sold as "sorghum molasses," sorghum is not actually sugarcane molasses, but is produced by boiling down sweet sorghum, a high-sugar grass similar to sugarcane. As with molasses, beers made with sweet sorghum extract as the sole fermentable can be an acquired taste. The ones I've made have a funky sweet-sour flavor that I can only handle in small doses. It does work well as a low-percentage adjunct to malt-based beers. Sorghum beer is drunk throughout much of Africa, serving as much as food as a beverage due to its high levels of protein, fats, vitamins, and minerals.[12] Sorghum as an agricultural crop has a deep, rich history in sub-Saharan Africa. As Dr. Patrick McGovern notes, "In the eastern Sahel, the semiarid scrub grasslands south of the Sahara Desert, sorghum has been king for thousands of years. It remains the most important crop for all of sub-Saharan Africa, feeding hundreds of millions of people and providing three-quarters of the caloric intake, mostly as beer, in many areas."[13] The sorghum grown in Africa is primarily grain sorghum, which has lower sugar content than sweet sorghum until the grains have been malted. Sweet sorghum is what is primarily grown and sold in the United States, with my home state of Kentucky leading the charge. Although it has been grown in nearly every other state since colonial days, Kentucky is one of eight southeastern and midwestern states that produce nearly 90 percent of the total US output, with Kentucky producing more than $12 million worth of syrup in 2008.[14] Grain sorghum isn't typically produced in the United States, so sorghum beer made from US-produced sweet sorghum will likely differ from that made from African grain sorghum, which is malted rather than cooked down into syrup. If you can obtain some sorghum grains to malt, by all means give it a try. Millet is a more readily available option and would work as an alternative.

Honey

Entire books could be (and have been) written about brewing with honey (shameless self-promotion alert: See my first book *Make Mead Like a Viking*). Although technically a brew made with honey as the sole or majority sugar source would be a mead, it can be used in different amounts to brew beer. There is even a type of mead-beer hybrid called bragot (also braggot, brag, bragio, brakkatt, or bracket) that has large amounts of honey along with large amounts of malt. Reaching alcohol levels of 12 percent or higher, it drinks more like a wine or a mead than a beer. Another brew that was traditionally made with honey is Welsh Ale. As I reference in my discussion on Welsh Ale in chapter 9, it is closely related to bragot and in many senses is one and the same. In my discussions on simple ales in chapter 9, I reference small mead, also known as short mead or session mead. While these aren't technically beer, they have similar alcohol content as a "sessionable" beer and drink very much like a beer. A *sessionable* or *session* beer ranges from 3 to 5 percent ABV; its low alcohol level and refreshing flavor mean several can be drunk in a session without succumbing to overt drunkenness. Call them what you want, but if done right, they're plenty tasty.

I often use honey as an adjunct when I want to increase my wort gravity without overtly affecting the flavor. Usually this means adding no more than 1 to 2 pounds (0.5–1 kg) per 5-gallon (20 L) batch. Depending on the honey and the type of malt, this amount will have little effect on the flavor. In a very malty brew such as a porter or stout or any beer with darker grains, it will add a bit of heft to the alcohol effect and smooth out the rough edges of the grains. In lighter ales and lagers, it will have a more pronounced effect. As with malt, the darker the honey's color, the stronger the flavor. Hence a very dark honey, such as buckwheat, can impart some very strong (and not necessarily pleasing) flavors to a light brew but work well for accentuating a dark brew. A lighter honey works well for both light and dark beers. Most wildflower honeys and honeys derived from tree blossoms (such as orange blossom, sourwood, or tulip poplar) are good honeys to use in lighter beers. When using large amounts, such as for a bragot, take care with honey selection. I find that lighter honeys work well with pale malts to make for a very refreshing bragot that can be enjoyed young or aged to bring out more subtle flavors. I once obtained a large amount of very old, very dark honey in exchange for a presentation on mead making to a group of Ohio beekeepers. The honey had been kept in 55-gallon (208 L) drums in a barn for many years. Since it had grown dark with age (and had caramelized somewhat over years of hot summers), it couldn't be sold as "table honey" but was rather considered less marketable "baker's honey." I've made some meads and bragots from this honey and wasn't initially pleased with the results. It tended to produce a strong flavor reminiscent of cough syrup. I've found, however, that bragots made with this honey aged for six months or more have a mellower flavor. It's still not something I would drink in large amounts, but when sipped like a well-aged wine or mead it can be quite nice.

Honey, particularly lighter honey, can be low in nutrients, so it will need some additional help to ferment properly. Most mead makers purchase nutrients from a homebrew store, which will work just fine. Darker honeys tend to need fewer nutrient supplements, and fermentation of any honey will benefit from the use of raw, unfiltered honey with pollen, propolis, comb, and other bits of the hive still present. Add honey after cutting off the boil or directly to the fermenter to retain its aromatic qualities. When I make mead, I rarely heat it except to dissolve it in the water or if I want to impart a burnt or smoky flavor. Honey has all of the sugars it needs and thus doesn't need to be heated to draw the sugars out as with malt. Excessive heating also detracts from honey's subtle aromatics and kills off the wild yeast that some brewers, like myself, want to aid in a strong fermentation.

While malted grain is the soul of beer, adjuncts and flavoring ingre-dients are the icing on the cake. Beer and ale can be made with just fermentable sugars, water, and yeast—but without anything additional, it will have a tendency to be bland, overly sweet, or sour. The ingredients covered in this chapter, even in very small amounts, will make a beer go from *bleh* to *wow* . . . if used correctly.

PART THREE

TYING IT ALL TOGETHER

CHAPTER EIGHT

BREWING TECHNIQUES

This chapter is all about the nitty-gritty of how to make beer. While some recipes have their own unique techniques that I'll cover when appropriate, here I'll break down clearly the four primary methods for making beer and beerlike beverages using primarily modern equipment and processes. You can then decide for yourself if you want to go fully ancient in your brewing, fully modern, or a combination of the two. This chapter is broken into four sections: Simple Brewing, Extract Brewing, Brew-in-a-Bag (BiaB) Brewing, and All-Grain Brewing, progressing from simple and quick to complex and time consuming. The closer you get to working with all grain,* the more control you'll have over the entire process and the subtle effects of each ingredient. However, you can make excellent beers using all of these techniques.

Simple Brewing

This section covers techniques and equipment for the quickest, simplest no-stress beers you can make. Some will come close to tasting like you'd expect a popular hopped beer to taste, but most won't. While malt is often mentioned in old recipes, many call for brown sugar or molasses

---

* Good news! There are simple methods for working with all grain as well!

as the sugar source, and might be more accurately referred to as *hard sodas* according to modern taste expectations. Some taste more like cider than beer while others, such as those made with molasses, have their own unique flavor. Since all are relatively simple and affordable to make, I prefer to call them *simple ales*. The alcohol content of most of these is fairly low, as they were intended to nourish all members of a family throughout the day—and were purported to have medicinal and healthful qualities.

For simple ale recipes using the following techniques, see chapter 9.

BASIC EQUIPMENT

2–3 gallon (8–12 L) cooking pot (preferably stainless steel or enamel)

3–5 gallon (12–20 L) openmouthed container: glass, ceramic, or food-grade plastic

A lid, towel, or cheesecloth to cover the container

A vessel with a spigot for bottling (you can also bottle from a spigot-less container using vinyl tubing or just by pouring carefully into the bottle through a funnel)

The basic equipment for a 1-gallon (4 L) batch of beer or simple ale.

1-gallon (4 L) glass or plastic jug (optional; can be used along with or
 instead of the openmouthed container)
Bottles (see page 169 for a discussion of bottles)
1 stirring spoon long enough to reach the bottom of your cooking pot
 and brewing vessel

SOME NICE-TO-HAVES

Airlock with rubber stopper, 4–6 feet (1–2 meters) of food-grade
 vinyl tubing with rubber stopper, or a balloon
Bottle capper and new caps
Thermometer
Hydrometer (for measuring alcohol level; see "Determining Alcohol
 Level" sidebar on page 170)
Funnel and sieve

BASIC INGREDIENTS (SEE RECIPES FOR SPECIFICS, OR EXPERIMENT AWAY)

1 gallon (4 L) clean springwater or dechlorinated, filtered tap water
1–2 pounds (0.5–1 kg) liquid or dry malt extract of your choosing, or
 molasses, sorghum, light or dark brown sugar, honey, maple syrup,
 or any combination of these (when starting out, err closer to 1
 pound/0.5 kg for both sugar- and malt-based beers; this will give
 you around 4–5 percent ABV)
1–2 ounces (28–57 g) herbs and spices (use hops instead of or along
 with these if you so desire), taking care to fully understand the
 flavoring and bittering qualities each will add
Fruit (depending on the recipe), of any variety and as much as you dare
Yeast; about ½ teaspoon of brewing yeast, ale yeast, or bread yeast will
 do, or ½ cup (125 mL) barm (wild-fermented starter or from an
 active ferment)
1 teaspoon (per bottle) white, corn, or brown sugar, or honey for
 bottle carbonation

PROCESS

1. Clean all equipment with hot, soapy water and rinse well.
2. Warm the gallon of water, add your sugar source, and bring to a boil.
3. Stir thoroughly to ensure that nothing sticks to the bottom or
 foams over, and reduce to a just barely rollicking boil.

4. Add the herbs, spices, and other ingredients, depending on what type of boozy beverage you're making. (Some of these, particularly hops, will need to be added later in the boil.)
5. Cut off the heat after about half an hour.
6. Cool the wort quickly by placing the hot pot in an ice-water bath in the sink or a larger pot.
7. Monitor the wort with a thermometer until it reaches 60–80°F (15–27°C), or simply wait until it feels warm to the touch.
8. Strain out the whole ingredients you don't want in the primary fermentation by pouring the liquid through a sieve or cheesecloth into your fermentation vessel.
9. If you want to check for potential alcohol level with a hydrometer, go ahead and take the original gravity (OG) reading now (generally you can have a strong indication of the likely alcohol level based on the amount of sugar you add, but you can increase the potential amount of alcohol by monitoring with a hydrometer and adding more sugar).
10. Add powdered yeast by sprinkling it over the surface of the wort, add barm from an actively fermenting batch, or create a wild yeast starter (see chapter 5) if that is your preferred method of obtaining yeast.
11. If you're using a bucket, simply cover it with a cloth or place a lid with an airlock on it; if you'll be fermenting in a 1-gallon (4 L) jug, place an airlock in the opening.
12. Place the container in a warm, dark spot (60–80°F/15–27°C); it should start showing signs of active fermentation within a few hours.
13. In 1 to 2 weeks, it should have begun clarifying; go ahead and transfer it to a secondary fermenter (a clean jug with an airlock) to finish clarifying. Or skip this step if you aren't overconcerned with clarification.
14. Taste and drink as is at any point if you like it and don't want to deal with bottling and carbonating. Otherwise, when there are no signs of active fermentation (CO_2 bubbles rising to the top), prepare to bottle.
15. An hour or two before bottling, warm 2 tablespoons of sugar (white, corn, or brown) or honey in a cup of water and stir it into the beer to prime it for bottle carbonation.

16. Let any remaining yeast residue settle, then bottle straight from the fermentation vessel with a siphoning tube (keep it an inch or two from the bottom to avoid the yeast cake), or transfer it with a siphoning tube to a vessel with a spigot.

17. Bottle, cap, cork, or screw, store in a cool, dark spot, and open in 1 to 2 weeks; open each bottle carefully and have a glass ready, as the amount of carbonation can vary by bottle.

Bottling and Priming for Carbonation

I tend to be a little more lax about bottling my small-batch simple ales than I am with larger grain-based beer batches. The process is the same, but more time, effort, and money go into the larger batches and I want to keep my simple ales true to their name. For some I begin tasting after a week or two of fermentation and continue to pour straight from the container while still fizzy and fermenting if I like the flavor. Often, though, I'll let them fully ferment and dry out, and then restart fermentation with just a bit of sugar or honey so that it will carbonate in the bottle. The amounts can vary depending on how much carbonation you want, the type of sugar used, and other factors that are a little harder to predict (such as the type of sugar you initially fermented with and the ingredients themselves). Really, though, it's mostly a foolproof process. Just don't expect consistency. Rarely do I make the exact same recipe, but even when I do repeat one, the results vary from just a bit of carbonation to a gushing bottle. Thus, it's very important to be safe when carbonating in bottles. Generally I try to carbonate my simple ales in thick-glassed bottles with flip-top lids. They can handle a lot more pressure than regular bottles, and I can pop the opening quickly and reclose it if need be to give it more time to carbonate. When you prime, you are force-carbonating, meaning you are restarting the fermentation in the bottle to produce additional CO_2. You can also practice natural carbonation by waiting to bottle until the brew is mostly finished fermenting (it's fairly clear but you can still see small CO_2 bubbles rising to the top). Take extra care when doing this, as you'll need to develop a feel for when to bottle—and even then the results will be unpredictable. For larger grain-based batches I recommend always waiting for fermentation to end and priming before bottling.

Determining Alcohol Level: The Modern Scientific Method and the Caveman Route

A hydrometer is a cylindrical glass instrument that determines the precise amount of sugar content by measuring the weight or density (gravity) of a liquid destined to become alcohol. Because alcohol is less dense than water, a hydrometer can be used to measure the changes in gravity from when you first prepare a dense, high-sugar wort, and through the various stages of fermentation as sugar is fermented into alcohol. It's also a good method for ensuring fermentation is complete so you can proceed with bottling. Once the hydrometer reading stays stable upon checking over a couple of days, fermentation is complete or very near complete. At this stage you can take a reading and compare it with your original gravity. This is your final gravity.

I used to use a hydrometer religiously in my early brewing practices, mostly because I thought I was supposed to. It's a very convenient instrument, but I find myself relying on it less after realizing I never really needed it to begin with. Brewers accustomed to modern brewing manuals will likely notice the lack of specifics in most of my recipes with regard to *target gravity*, *original gravity*, and *final gravity*. If you're one of those brewers, I hope you're open to the idea of going back to the old ways and brewing without a hyper-specific goal in mind. To put it simply: Certain amounts of sugar fully (or mostly) fermented will result in certain ranges of alcohol. If you've followed all of the steps correctly and see visual signs of a strong fermentation, you will achieve a drinkable, boozy product. That's all our ancestors were after (along with medicinal and sometimes psychotropic effects), and there's no reason we can't be that relaxed about it. Still, if you're seeking a high-alcohol product, striving for a certain alcohol level, or following a modern recipe and want to achieve its intended alcohol level, a hydrometer is a useful tool to have.

Once you've calculated your final gravity, you can then determine final alcohol content. The best way to do this is to subtract the final gravity from the original gravity and multiply the result by 105 (don't ask me where that number came from, but that's what everyone uses). When taking a reading, you can drop the hydrometer directly in the liquid, or take a sample in a cylindrical object (either the container the hydrometer came in or one you purchase that is designed for this). Spin it to make sure any air bubbles are displaced and take note of the number where the liquid crosses a line. If you want to be super-precise, each hydrometer comes with a temperature-adjustment formula, as the reading will change ever so slightly at various temperatures. Hydrometers are calculated to make accurate readings at 60°F (15.56°C), so if you're anywhere near there, don't worry about this. As a point of reference, the scale starts at the gravity of water (1.000), and most ferments end at around 1.008 (this will vary, as some will have higher levels of residual sugar). Most hydrometers measure up to 1.170, or about 20 percent potential alcohol content, although there are special hydrometers for distilling (proofing hydrometers) that go much higher. One trick moonshiners used before hydrometers (BH) was to shake a jar of shine and watch for bubbles. Large bubbles that disappear quickly mean the booze has a high alcohol content; small bubbles that disappear slowly mean low alcohol content. Or there's the old-fashioned method of drinking a certain amount and noting how it makes you feel!

Hydrometers can be used to adjust sugar levels for your preferred final alcohol level.

In his book *The Wildcrafting Brewer*, Pascal Baudar references a similar old-school technique for determining alcohol content. Baudar uses all kinds of ingredients in his brewing, the majority of them harvested from the wild. While he will often use natural sugars such as honey, tree sap (syrup), and even sugar excreted by insects other than bees (*lerp*, or crystallized honey-dew produced by the larvae of psyllid bugs), he also uses processed sugars such as cane sugar, brown sugar, and molasses. He simply determines the ABV range by the amount of sugar he puts in each brew, which he calls the Neanderthal rule. He elected to put his estimations to the test with a hydrometer. Rather than repeating that test myself, I'll just quote him directly, as my experiments have turned out pretty much the same:

- 1 pound (454 g) honey in 1 gallon (3.78 L) of water gives 4.8 percent alcohol by volume (usually abbreviated as ABV).
- 1 pound brown sugar per gallon gives 5.2 percent alcohol.
- 1 pound piloncillo sugar per gallon gives 5.3 percent alcohol.
- 1 pound molasses per gallon gives 5.3 percent alcohol.
- 1 pound white sugar per gallon gives 5.2 percent alcohol.
- 1 pound maple syrup per gallon gives 5 to 5.3 percent alcohol.
- 1 pound dry malt extract per gallon gives 5.2 percent alcohol.[1]

So there you have it—use a hydrometer if you desire, or go primitive!

To prime, add sugar or honey just before bottling. The amount can vary depending on how much carbonation you want. For most brews I want a medium to high level of carbonation. To prime a 5-gallon (20 L) batch, I take 2 cups (500 mL) of warmed water (or take the same amount of beer and warm it) and dissolve ½ cup (125 mL) of honey or ¾ cup (150 g) of sugar in it. I then take this mix and stir it into the beer slowly but thoroughly. For a 1-gallon (4 L) batch, I use around 2 tablespoons of sugar or honey. Proceed with bottling or capping after giving it half an hour or so for any remaining lees to settle to the bottom. You'll need to experiment to find a level of carbonation that works best for you. Try a bit more or a bit less with each subsequent batch and take

Various bottles and types of bottling equipment can be used for bottling beer.

notes. If you're brewing to a specific style, there is usually a carbonation level specific to that style. A good way to determine the appropriate amount of priming sugar is to use an online priming chart or calculator. I prefer the one at Northern Brewer's website (www.northernbrewer. com/priming-sugar-calculator), as it allows for factors such as temperature, your desired level of CO_2 (or you can select a beer style from a drop-down chart), and the volume of beer you're bottling. It then lists several possible sugar sources and the recommended amount for each. Since this book isn't really focused on brewing "to style" and covers types of beer that usually won't show up in priming calculators, you'll have to make your best guess by picking a style that is close to your preferred

Bottling Dangers

Even if you use thick-glassed bottles, please take precautions when storing and opening any homebrewed beverage. Most brews will be fully carbonated within a week, but try to give them at least two weeks. The warmer the area they're stored in is, the quicker they'll carbonate. I usually keep mine at room temperature for a couple of days and then move them to my cellar. When I'm ready to test carbonation, I open them carefully outside or over a sink. If I hear a hissing sound or a pop, I know I have good carbonation. I either recap the bottle and refrigerate it or drink it immediately. Most beers are best at cellar temperature, but my simple ales tend to be better chilled.

You will sometimes open a brew and lose half of it to gushing. Be prepared with a large glass to pour it in immediately and keep a towel wrapped around it should you have an explosion. I've never had a full-on explosion, but some simple ales can build up a lot of pressure and I've heard stories about fermented beverages being bottled too soon, leading to shattered bottles and shards of glass in the wall. This is highly unlikely to happen if you allow your brews to fully ferment and don't use too much sugar when priming, but it's something to keep in mind. The worst I've had happen is a bottle losing its bottom to pressure, likely due to a weak spot in the glass.

carbonation level and enter in the rest of the information appropriate to your brew.

The aforementioned flip-top bottles are ideal, as they don't require special capping equipment or new caps. The rubber gaskets that keep them sealed will sometimes need replacement, but only rarely. They are a little pricey to buy empty, and pricier to buy full (but often well worth it), so you'll likely use other types of bottles if you brew a lot. The standard pop-top (requiring a bottle opener) beer bottle that most craft brews come in is ideal. Save as many as you can and ask friends to save theirs for you. I don't recommend screw-top bottles, as they rarely keep the bottle completely sealed and tend to be made of thinner glass.

Still, they'll work in a pinch if you still have the original lid. You can also use Belgian-style bottles and even champagne bottles with wired-down corks or caps. For caps, purchase standard crown caps from a homebrew store, as pop-top caps aren't reusable. Oxygen-absorbing (also known as oxygen-barrier) caps, for high-alcohol brews you intend on aging for several months or years, are another option. To cap bottles with these, you will need a handheld wing-style capper. There are other types of cappers out there, but many homebrewers use these. They're simple, sturdy, and affordable. If you plan to cork, there are more options available, and some corkers come with capping attachments. When bottling, fill each bottle using your bottling container's spigot or a siphoning tube to about ½ inch (13 mm) below the lid or about 1 inch (2.5 cm) below the cork bottom. Carefully cap or cork it, and move on to the next bottle. Bottling can be tedious, and many brewers transition to mini keg CO_2 systems, but I brew too many small and experimental batches, so I've become accustomed to spending many an evening bottling while watching a movie. I also try to collect bottles larger than the standard 12-ounce beer bottle to lessen the number I use.

Extract Brewing

Extract brewing is a good place for any brewer to begin, and many people prefer to stick with it. Instead of using malted grain, extract brewing involves cans of thick, syrupy (or dry and powdered) malt extract, along with a few other basic ingredients. We'll start with 5-gallon (20 L) batches, as this is what most beer recipes are designed for. With some basic calculations, you can convert 5-gallon recipes into 1-gallon (4 L) recipes if you're looking to try some experimental flavoring or simply want to save some space and money.

EQUIPMENT FOR A 5-GALLON (20 L) BATCH

4–7 gallon (16–28 L) stainless-steel, aluminum, or enamel cooking pot (now officially a *brew kettle*)

5-gallon (20 L) food-grade plastic bucket (from a homebrew store or restaurant that has used it for food or drink storage *only*) with a lid and a spigot

5-gallon (20 L) glass or food-grade plastic carboy (essentially a large jug)

5–6 feet (about 2 meters) of ⅜- to ⅝-inch (9.5–16 mm) ID (inner
diameter) vinyl tubing

Airlock or 4–6 feet (1–2 m) of additional vinyl tubing

Rubber grommet (for buckets only) that your airlock or tubing can fit
snugly into (drill a hole in your bucket lid just large enough to give
the grommet a snug fit; buckets from homebrew kits will generally
already have this)

Drilled rubber stopper (aka *bung*) that fits snugly in the opening of your
carboy, and which in turn holds your airlock or plastic tubing snugly

Funnel

Funnel screen, or a sieve or colander

Long stirring spoon

Hydrometer (optional)

Scent-free dish detergent, hydrogen peroxide, or no-rinse cleaner and
sanitizer (optional)

Fine-mesh nylon straining bag or cheesecloth

High-temp brewing or candy thermometer

60 new or used 12-ounce (350 mL) beer bottles (avoid screw-tops) or
25 cappable champagne bottles

60 unused bottle caps

Bottle capper

BASIC INGREDIENTS FOR A 5-GALLON (20 L) BATCH

5-gallon (20 L) extract, partial mash, or BiaB brewing ingredient kit

Or build your own kit with:

Liquid or dried malt extract of your choosing (the amount will vary
depending on your recipe)

Flavoring / adjunct grains (optional)

Hops, herbs, spices, etc.

Yeast or barm

Corn sugar, plain dried malt extract, or honey for priming when bottling

You will also need:

6 gallons (24 L) springwater or filtered tap water (the extra volume
is to allow for loss of water due to evaporation or being soaked up
by ingredients)

Ice, or 2–3 gallons (8–12 L) very cold water from the initial 6 gallons (24 L)

Equipment for brewing 5-gallon batches of beer.

BREW DAY

Ah, brew day. It sounds so romantic. If you're anything like me, images of clichéd Norman Rockwell farmers quaffing ale while chewing on a piece of straw and attending to bubbling pots of brew float through your head while you prepare for an exciting-yet-relaxing day of brewing. Knock that thinking out of your head. It'll never come close to this. No matter how many times you brew beer, the big day will inevitably feature some kinks, cursing, even shrieking. To make sure you're not caught by surprise, there are a few things you should do before every brew day:

1. Set aside a full day so you have time to take care of any last-minute items; you may not always need a full day, but for your first couple

of tries, don't plan anything else that may be time consuming. Shoot for starting by at least early afternoon, unless you're a night owl.

2. Plan carefully at least a day or two in advance. Look through whatever recipe or process description you're following, and double-check all equipment and ingredients.

3. On the night before brew day, or a few hours before you begin brewing, clean, sterilize with heat (or sanitize with chemicals if you desire), and rinse all equipment that will come in contact with the wort; this is a good opportunity to make sure you're not missing anything vital.

4. Prepare yourself mentally. Your first couple of brew days will likely be chaotic, but they needn't be. Something unexpected will always come up, usually during a time-sensitive part of the process. The trick is to give yourself the time and mental preparation to react without turning your kitchen into something akin to a war zone (which it will likely look like by the time you're done regardless).

5. Come time to start, put on some good music, grab a beer, and get started.

Once you're ready to delve in, set out all equipment that you will need for the wort-boiling process (and have equipment needed for the next steps on hand) and make sure anyone else who may want your attention is aware that you need to spend the next hour or so boiling wort. This is *critical*, as an unattended pot can lead to disaster. Start by bringing 2 to 6 gallons (8–24 L) of water to a near boil in your brew kettle.* If you're brewing on a standard stovetop, start on the lower end (this is called a partial boil). It can be time consuming to bring much more than 2 gallons (8 L) of water to a full boil on anything but an industrial stovetop. If you're brewing outside in a large (7- or 8-gallon/ 28 or 32 L) kettle over a propane burner (a turkey fryer), go ahead and

---

* If you're following a partial mash recipe, you'll first want to "mash" the grains by bringing the temperature to approximately 150°F (66°C) and placing the grains into the wort in a grain bag or cheesecloth for half an hour. Remove the bag carefully with a metal spoon and give the excess wort some time to drain off, gently helping it along with the spoon; don't press the bag to get more wort out, as you may extract some unwanted bittering tannins. From here, proceed to the boil.

boil the full 6 gallons (24 L). While waiting, open your bag(s) or can(s) of extract. It helps to warm liquid extract beforehand by placing the can in a pot of water on medium-high heat for a few minutes so you can get as much out as possible. When the water in your brew kettle begins to show signs of boiling, cut the heat off. Open the extract can (or *fully* cut open a bag of dry malt extract / DME), have a stirring spoon ready in your other hand, and pour with one hand while stirring vigorously with the other, taking care to scrape the bottom of the kettle. This keeps the extract from sticking to the bottom and burning, but also prevents boiling over (you won't likely have a boil-over at this point if you've removed the pot from the heat). Once you have as much of the liquid extract into the kettle as you're able, grab an oven mitt and carefully use hot water from the brewpot to work the rest of the extract from the can (unless you're using dry malt extract / DME). Return the heat to medium-high and start stirring like crazy.

Watch wort closely during the early boil stages to prevent messy overflow.

This is absolutely the part of the process that needs to be attended to the most vigilantly. I'd warrant that nearly every beer brewer has experienced a boil-over at some point. When brewing my first batch of beer, I had a major boil-over, but neglected to attend to a full cleanup until after I was finished brewing. Bad idea. Dried extract will turn into a rock-hard, caked-on mess if left unattended. Even with the help of a chisel and plenty of water I wasn't able to fully clean up the mess the next day. Lesson learned: Get the boil under control and clean up any messes promptly.

Continue stirring until the wort reaches a steady, rolling boil. Once you have a steady boil, you can stop stirring constantly, but continue to attend to it and stir every couple of minutes, particularly if you see foam starting to rise on the surface. Go ahead and set a timer for 60 minutes (or set it for the various increments at which you'll be adding hops and other flavoring and bittering agents). I find that it takes about 20 minutes from reaching the initial boil before I'm comfortable stepping away even for a couple of seconds. Keep the lid off (or only partially on) throughout the process, as fully covering the pot can cause the wort to foam over. Be sure you have your ingredients ready to add when they're called for. Don't fret if you're not right on the dot. Unless you've got superhero taste buds, you're not too likely to notice in the final product if you were a few minutes off here and there.

Most brewing recipes call for a 60-minute boil, but there isn't necessarily a reason for this other than that it's a nice solid number, and provides a convenient schedule for hop additions. Prior to the prevalence of the notion that hops are a near necessity for beer, the boil length, if referenced at all, could vary wildly. Some modern home-brewing recipes call for a 90-minute boil, but the vast majority find 60 to be enough. The schedule for adding hops and other ingredients will be different for a 60-minute boil than a 90-minute. Essentially, you will get a higher rate of hop utilization from a 90-minute boil, as well as more concentrated sugars from the grain extract. The difference may be too subtle to matter for most, but for those with sophisticated palates or who want to experiment with big-hopped beers, 90 minutes is the way to go. Throughout the 60 (or 90) minutes, you can add various ingredients, but if you're using a beer kit or following a recipe, add the hops and other ingredients according to the hop schedule.

Hops added early in the process (at the beginning of or 30 minutes into a 60-minute boil) will contribute largely to bittering, while hops added from 15 minutes to the end of the boil will be more for aroma. The most aroma will come from hops that are added within the last two to five minutes. Ingredients other than hops (such as herbs and spices) added during the last two to five minutes will impart aroma and flavor. Ingredients such as mugwort, yarrow, and dandelion greens are intended primarily for bittering and can be added during the last 15 to 30 minutes.

At this point, it's important to lower the temperature of the wort to 60–80°F (15–27°C) as quickly as possible. If you leave it to cool on its own, you run the risk of beer-spoilage bacteria affecting the final product. It will still be safe to drink, but you may not enjoy it. If you pre-cooled 2 to 3 gallons (8–12 L) of water, you can pour it through a funnel into your carboy and carefully add the hot wort if you have a small brew kettle (*do not* add hot wort directly to a glass carboy—it will crack), or you can add as much of the cold water as will fit to the brew kettle. If you're pouring directly into a brewing bucket, add the hot water first for additional sterilization and follow with the cold water. Whether you're pouring into a carboy or a bucket, be sure to slosh the wort vigorously from time to time to ensure an even mix, and to help oxygenate the wort in preparation for the yeast. Another option is to create an ice bath by putting ice and cold water in a bathtub or large sink and setting your brewpot in it. Be sure to have at least a couple of pounds (1 kg) of ice on hand, as it will melt quickly. You can also purchase or build a copper immersion chiller to accomplish this more quickly.

After you have cooled the wort, it's time to check the original gravity (OG) with your hydrometer, which you will later measure against the final gravity (FG) to determine the approximate alcohol content. Follow the instructions that came with the hydrometer. Next, open your yeast packet and sprinkle it over the surface. Place an airlock in the carboy and set it in a warm, dark corner (60–80°F/15–27°C). You may need to rinse out the airlock while fermentation is active, as the yeast may cause the wort to exude excess krausen (foam). Some brews produce a *lot* of krausen. For these you can either wait to fill the carboy up all the way until fermentation slows down, place a 5-gallon (20 L) batch into a 6- or 7-gallon (24–28 L) fermenter, or remove the airlock and insert some vinyl tubing into the stopper, placing the other end into a small pot with enough water to keep the end covered. From here, proceed to secondary fermentation and bottling.

Brew-in-a-Bag (BiaB) Brewing

When you're ready to take the plunge into all-grain brewing, you may become overwhelmed by long lists of essential equipment, highly detailed procedures, and other technicalities that make the whole process seem expensive and time consuming. But while all-grain brewing can require more specialized equipment than extract brewing, takes more time, and does require more attending to, there are simpler, less technical methods of brewing with all grain. The Brew-in-a-Bag method, which we'll call BiaB from here on out, represents an intermediate step between extract brewing and all-grain brewing.

The BiaB process is nearly identical to extract brewing, except that you create your wort by immersing a bag of crushed, malted grains in water rather than using wort extract. BiaB also requires that you use a large (7- or 8-gallon/28–32 L) kettle, although you can get away with a smaller pot if you don't add the full amount of water at the beginning. You can buy BiaB kits, although not all homebrew stores carry them. You can also modify any all-grain recipe into BiaB, or create your own and buy the ingredients individually. Keep in mind that BiaB is not as efficient as full-on all-grain brewing, so you'll likely need an extra pound or two (0.5–1 kg) of your primary grain and possibly a bit more adjunct grains when converting an all-grain recipe to BiaB. If I'm aiming for a target gravity, I make sure to have an extra sugar source on hand—usually honey—in case the grain sugars don't get me where I want to be. While you should try to get the majority of your sugars from the grain, adding a bit of honey and checking the gravity will ensure your beer reaches your desired alcohol level. BiaB is a great way to make bragots (a beer-mead hybrid), which already require a large amount of honey.

A cursory understanding of the all-grain process helps in BiaB brewing, as they share a lot of steps and terminology. When you're all-grain brewing, your primary goal is to extract as many fermentable sugars from the crushed grain as possible. The first step toward ensuring you do this as efficiently as possible is to get a proper crush. Crushing the grains exposes the endosperm that contains the sugar produced from the malting process, though accessing this sugar still takes some work. The sugar doesn't just sit there waiting for you—it's in the form of a complex starch that will need to be broken down by enzymes into a simple sugar, which you can do by soaking the crushed grain in hot water within a specific temperature range. There is a fairly large amount of room for error, although it's worth noting that if you stray too far on the temperature scale or fudge some other part of the process, you may have different results than what you intend. The equipment you will need for BiaB brewing is essentially the same as with extract brewing, with a few exceptions.

EQUIPMENT FOR A 5-GALLON (20 L) BATCH

7-gallon (28 L) or larger stainless-steel or heavy-aluminum pot

Optional: a false bottom for the large pot (I use the false bottom from my pressure canner); alternatively, just be careful to not let the grain bag touch the bottom

A few additional pots of varying sizes, preferably 15–20 quarts (15–20 L) or larger

Large stirring spoon (long enough to reach the bottom of your brew kettle)

Large ladle

Large (18 × 32-inch/46 × 81 cm) fine-mesh grain bag

Large strainer

Propane burner (an electric or gas stovetop will work, but the pot will get very heavy and water is quicker to heat and easier to maintain at a consistent temperature with propane; brewing outside also works better for cleaning up messes)

High-temp brewing or candy thermometer

Hydrometer (if you're shooting for a specific alcohol strength)

PROCESS

1. Clean and, if you desire, sanitize all equipment early on brew day or the night before.
2. If using an electric or gas stovetop, prepare plenty of space; if using an outdoor propane burner, set it up in a well-ventilated area.
3. Prepare all the ingredients from the recipe, and pour the appropriate amount of water (now *liquor* or *strike water*) into the brew kettle. You

can make calculations for the amount of water required through various online calculators and mathematical formulas; I usually pour in about 4 gallons (16 L) of water and then add more to reach 5½ to 6 gallons (22–24 L) of wort when I'm ready to boil, which I will then boil back down to 5 gallons (20 L). If you want to be more specific than that, go the mathematical route while I have a beer.

4. Place the brew kettle on your heat source if you haven't already done so and set the heat level to medium-high (I usually start at high and then move it down after a bit to speed things up). If you're using propane, turn it up as high as you can and adjust the airflow so that you have more blue flame than yellow (yellow flame can cause a *lot* of soot on your kettle).

5. For most recipes you'll want your strike water to stay at about 155 to 160°F (68–71°C), but as long as you don't let it drop to below 145°F (63°C) you should be fine. I usually bring mine to 180°F (82°C), as the temperature will drop once the grain bag is added.

6. Fill the grain bag with the full amount of crushed grains called for by your recipe, shaking out any excess dust (you can also add the grain directly to the bag in the kettle, but I find filling the bag first is less problematic). Lower the bag slowly into your strike water,

When brewing by the Brew-in-a-Bag (BiaB) method, position the bag over the kettle opening to provide space for stirring, and to keep the bag from touching the bottom.

giving it time for the grains to soak up water, and taking care not to let the bag touch the bottom for too long, as it will burn if you're not using a false bottom. Once the grains are fully soaked, tie the grain bag to your kettle's handles or pull the opening of the bag tightly down the outside edges of the pot to keep it from touching the bottom. Add more hot water if needed to fully immerse the grains. Monitor the temperature and adjust the heat until you've reached a temperature within your strike range. Lift the grain bag up and down a few times and move the grains around gently with a spoon to ensure that they're well distributed; then check the temperature again, make any necessary adjustments, put the lid on, and leave it alone. I usually lower the burner heat enough to keep the water within my strike range, but some brewers elect to remove the kettle from the heat source and cover it with an old blanket or sleeping bag (or a fancy brewing insulator). Let it sit for 45 minutes to an hour and then take some wort out and check your pre-boil gravity with your hydrometer if you desire (be sure to check the temperature first for temperature adjustments to the hydrometer reading).

7. Although you can get away without sparging, it's still a good idea if you want to extract as many sugars from the malt as possible. The bag

When brewing by the Brew-in-a-Bag (BiaB) method, a scrap board is helpful for lifting the heavy bag of soaked grain from the wort. Courtesy of Jenna Zimmerman.

can be pretty heavy at this point, so I've found that the best way to hold the bag over the wort while giving it space for the sparge water to drain is to take a scrap board just a bit longer than the kettle's diameter, set it on the kettle opening, and tie the bag to it. An assistant is very helpful here, but you can pull it off on your own with some elbow grease and perseverance. If you have a space where you can set up a pulley system, even better. Once the bag is secure and hanging a bit over the wort, take a gallon (4 L) of water heated to 180°F (82°C) and pour it slowly across as much of the surface of the bag as possible. Let the bag hang over the wort long enough for as much residual wort as possible to drain off, then place the bag in a smaller pot and proceed to work more wort out—but don't be too forceful or you risk releasing excess tannins. I usually let the bag sit for a bit and add any wort left in the bottom of the extra pot to the boil.

8. Everything from here on out is the same as the process in extract brewing. Have at it!

All-Grain Brewing

Congratulations! You've made it! It's now time to cover everything you need to know and more about all-grain brewing. Don't be intimidated; after all, this is just a fancy version of how our ancestors brewed with grain. You can build or purchase equipment that makes modern brewing easier (or more complex?), but if you're feeling adventurous, you can even use rocks, sticks, wooden troughs and barrels, ceramic crocks, and baskets (see the Ancient All-Grain Brewing section later in this chapter). And don't feel you need to jump right into all-grain brewing 5-gallon (20 L) batches (or that you need to at all); you can always skim through this section and go straight to brewing 1-gallon (4 L) all-grain batches using basic kitchen equipment (proceed to page 202) or the simpler BiaB method.

A Primer on Brewing with Grain

Before we jump into what can seem like a complex, time-consuming process, I want you to understand the *nature* of all-grain brewing. Neolithic brewers didn't use terms like *saccharification*, *protein modification*, or *vorlauf*. They didn't use thermometers and other equipment to get precise temperatures, pH levels, or gravity to determine alcohol by volume (ABV). Even up through the early 20th century, most noncommercial brewers didn't concern themselves with any of this. You can brew great beers with only a rudimentary knowledge of these terms and minimal to no specialized equipment.

GATHERING YOUR GRAIN

The first step in preparing for a grain-only brew is to gather your grain. This can be malted or unmalted, crushed or uncrushed, modified or unmodified, lightly roasted or dark-roasted, smoked, soured, or any combination of the above. You will need malted grain as your base malt, as this is where your fermentable sugar comes from. Or you can use another source of sugar such as honey, with grains added only for flavoring and coloring, but some may not consider this to technically be a beer.

Malted grain kernels have a thick, hard casing that protects the partially germinated sprout inside. For brewing to be effective, the grains must be crushed. Crush them too lightly and you won't get a very efficient starch conversion. Crush them too finely and you'll end up with a powder more suited for making gruel or bread, which may clog your *mash tun* (sometimes *lauter tun*), a system—usually homemade—for mashing grains in water and then separating the resulting liquid, or *wort*, from the grains (overly finely crushed grains can also impart excessive astringency due to excess tannins). On the flip side, the finer your grains are crushed, the more efficient your extract will be (it will take less time and effort to acquire the right amount of fermentable sugars). It's a balancing act in the end, but don't overthink it. Always err on the side of undercrushed malt until you get a system down that works for you (just plan on spending a little extra time during your all-grain brewing day). Always have some honey on hand in case the amount of malted grain you end up with does not release enough fermentable sugar to ferment to the level of alcohol you want for your beer. Other sugars will work, too, but I find honey is the best substitute for malt sugars. Anytime I don't quite get the ABV I'm shooting for, I simply blend in honey until I reach the level I'm after.

You can have grains crushed for you at the homebrew store where you buy them, purchase a mill designed specifically for crushing beer grains (standard mills don't generally have precise enough settings), or crush them manually with a rolling pin or stone. The latter can be time consuming and a powdery mess; I only recommend it for small batches (alternatively, try using a primitive saddle quern to crush your grains, seen on page 208).

I avoided buying a grain mill for a long time because of the prohibitive cost of most mills. However, after some research on homebrewing forums, I found that there are some bare-bones mills that sell for around $100. You may want to splurge a bit for higher-quality components, but a grain mill is a fairly simple mechanism and doesn't need too many bells and whistles. The most important aspect of a brewing grain mill

While not a necessity, a hand drill helps ensure quick, consistent grain grinding.

(as opposed to a grain mill for milling flour) is that it has one static roller and another roller that moves when you turn the handle. This feature, along with screws that allow for precision adjustment of the gap between the rollers, enables you to crush grains at just the right consistency. Flavoring grains can be crushed very coarse or not at all, but base malt grains are a little more finicky. For most grains, I find that adjusting the rollers so that a credit card can just barely be rolled through creates the perfect gap (about 0.28 mm).

While grain mills come with handles, it can be a bit of work to grind 10 or more pounds (4.5 kg) of grain. Not that I mind a little hard work, but grinding at higher speeds can help achieve a finer, more efficient grind. To accomplish this, simply remove the handle from the mill and attach an electric drill. You don't want to drill too fast or too slow, but after a few tries you'll get a feel for the speed that works best (about 300 rpm is ideal). Or you can just go the caveman route and crush the grains with a rock. Take note that grains have a much greater chance of spoiling once they're ground. Most will still be viable for a few months if stored in sealed containers, and some can even last a year or two. You will likely lose aroma and flavor if you wait too long, though. Try to use them within a week or two of grinding, or preferably on the same day you brew.

THE MASH

Once you've got your crushed grain ready, it's time to prepare your *strike water*, which is heated water to which you'll be adding grain for the *mash*. This water is often referred to in beer recipes, old and new, as *liquor*. So if you see a reference to liquor in this book or another beer recipe, don't run out to the liquor store and buy a bunch of vodka . . . unless you already have a need.

These days, most malted grain comes modified. Be sure to check the package to see if it is *undermodified* or *fully modified*. If it is undermodified, you will need to take an extra step during the brewing process to help break down the proteins in the grain. This process was standard in the old days, but most maltsters these days have already done this for you. Essentially, brewers used to start with a protein rest phase, mashing the grains at lower temperatures before increasing the water to the saccharification range (the temperature at which starches break down into sugars: around 148–162°F/64–72°C) to continue the process started during malting. You may wish to use an undermodified malt for various reasons, such as if you want to do a multistep mash. For now, let's focus on what you'll be doing for most brews—a single-infusion mash.

The type of beer you end up with will in part be determined by which end of the saccharification range you stay closest to. Sticking closer to the lower end of the spectrum (140–150°F/60–66°C) will result in a higher-alcohol, drier beer, as you will achieve a high degree of fermentability. When staying at the high end (150–160°F/66–71°C), you will end up with a higher-gravity, more robust and filling (but lower-alcohol) beer. What it comes down to is what style and flavor of beer you're shooting for. For most beers, you'll want your strike water to stay in the intermediate range (within 5°F/3°C or so of 150°F/66°C). Usually you'll let it rest at this range (the *saccharification rest*) for 60 to 90 minutes and then *mash out*. You won't always need to perform the mash-out, but it helps to prepare the grain bed for lautering (see the following section), and is a good idea if you are producing a wort with low fermentability. You do this by raising the temperature of the grain bed to 170°F (77°C) by heating a separate batch of water (about a gallon/4 L) to 180°F (82°C) or higher and rinsing the grains by pouring the hot water slowly over them while stirring constantly. Let the mash rest for about 10 minutes before proceeding with the next step.

LAUTERING

The rinsing process is called sparging, but first you must vorlauf, or "recirculate." The combined process of the mash-out, sparge, and vorlauf is referred to as lautering. The vorlauf is intended to drain out any husks or grain chunks in the grain bed until the wort runs clear. Drain a couple of quarts through your mash tun's spigot into a container that you will then pour back over the grains. Once the wort is clear (with no grain particles), place your brewing kettle under the spigot and sparge, which is the process of rinsing the grain bed with hot (180°F/82°C or higher) water, about ½ gallon (2 L) per pound (0.5 kg) of dry grist, to draw out as much of the converted sugars from the grains as possible.

There are two methods of sparging. Both can be equally effective—mostly it depends on which works best for your particular needs and equipment setup. The first is *continuous sparging* or *fly sparging*, which is partially opening the valve of your mash tun to allow a slow drain-off of the wort while trying to match the flow level with hot water poured over the grains. Alternatively, you can *batch sparge*, which is (with the valve closed) pouring a quart (liter) or two of hot water over the grains, stirring, allowing it to rest a few minutes, and then stirring again. I've found I often do a combination of both. I usually pour in a quart or two of hot water to help raise the temperature of the grain bed and then open the spigot and proceed with continuous sparging. Your goal is to get about 6 to 7 gallons (24–28 L) of fermentable wort, which you will then boil down to a little over 5 gallons (20 L). During the boiling process, you will add flavoring ingredients such as hops, herbs, and spices at varying times, and will then proceed to cool the wort down and ferment it.

How exactly you go about brewing with all grain will depend on various factors that we'll cover when we get to brewing your first all-grain beer. Whichever route you decide to take, what's important to remember is that no method is the right method. If you can pull some degree of fermentable sugars from the grains (substituting with another sugar such as honey if you have to) and ferment it into a quaffable beer, you've done your job. Even if you go with simpler and quicker extract sessions most or all of the time, it doesn't hurt to fully understand the entire process so that you have a firm understanding of exactly how a field of grain can be turned into barrels of beer. Start small, and grow big only if you feel the need.

Making Your First All-Grain Brew

You'll want to set aside even more time for brew day when all-grain brewing than you do for extract brewing. Once you have your process down to a science, it shouldn't take more than a couple of hours, but always be prepared for contingencies. All-grain brewing can seem daunting at first, but just have at it a couple of times and you'll get it down. You may not reach your target gravity the first few times, but keeping a quart (liter) or so of honey on hand like I do will help you supplement some extra sugars with minimal (or at the very least, beneficial) impact on flavor. Once you've built a good all-grain system, the process itself is fairly simple. The technique covered here is known as the *single-infusion mash* technique. This is what most modern brewers use,

continued on page 198

Creating a Mash Tun

For modern all-grain brewing you'll first need to build or acquire equipment. You should already have everything you need for the boil, but all-grain brewing requires creating your wort from scratch, so you'll need to prepare to do that. There are all manner of DIY all-grain brewing setups on the Internet, and plenty of pricey ones that you can buy from homebrew stores. You can drive yourself crazy trying to find the perfect one for the right price, but there are only a few basic things your setup needs to accomplish. Some setups are more efficient, but in the end you should put together what works for you. It can be really fun (and really frustrating) to build your own setup, even if you're not of a technical mind-set. Research, experiment, and start brewing when you've put together something functional.

To create your own mash tun, you'll need a large well-insulated vessel (most homebrewers use coolers), a spigot, a few garden hose connectors and clamps, and a method for filtering the grain bed to keep small grain kernels from clogging the drain or getting into the wort. Do some image searches on the Web and you'll find all kinds of ingenious setups, some rather complicated and some simple and straightforward. I went with one that called for a flexible plumbing supply line (with the inside tubing pulled out) to serve as the grain filter. Later, I added a copper manifold, which is an option many brewers go with (minus the supply line). Others use various forms of false bottoms. For the cooler, I went with a 10-gallon cooler (about $60) with an easily removable spigot. Some brewers have luck running vinyl tubing snugly through the nonremovable spigots of more affordable rectangular coolers. To make one like mine, here's what you'll need:

EQUIPMENT

10-gallon (40 L) cylindrical or 50-quart (50 L) rectangular plastic cooler with removable spigot
24–36 inches (60–90 cm) of ½-inch (13 mm) diameter braided stainless-steel flexible supply line

½-inch (13 mm) stainless-steel ball valve and spigot (I ordered one
without a spigot and used a garden hose coupling and adapter to
make one, but you can also get one with a spigot)

1 or more hose clamps (depending on how you customize your setup)

½ × ¾-inch (13 × 19 mm) dual male pipe thread adapter

2 ½-inch (13 mm) faucet washers (sometimes sold as O-rings)

¾-inch (19 mm) GHT (garden hose thread) female garden hose-repair coupling with ⅝-inch (16 mm) barb (two if you purchased a
ball valve without a spigot)

Plumber's tape

3–5 feet of ⅜-inch (9.5 mm) OD (outer diameter) copper tubing (for
optional increased efficiency setup)

½-inch (13 mm) OD (outer diameter) vinyl tubing (for optional
increased efficiency setup; I cut a piece about ½ inch in length
from a hose I use for my wort chiller)

TOOLS

Hammer, small nails, slotted screwdriver, and needle-nose pliers

Hacksaw with blade for cutting metal and vise (optional)

Pipe cutter for cutting the copper tubing if you have one (or use your
hacksaw)

Tubing bender (optional for bending copper tubing without kinks; I
found I didn't need one)

Keep in mind that you may need to use materials of different diameter
or length, or use additional materials depending on how you go about
making your setup. Mine isn't the be-all and end-all of mash tuns. It
is, however, what I consider the simplest, most straightforward and
affordable setup (unless you can find a cheaper cooler than I did). It
took a lot of Internet browsing and several trips back and forth to the
local hardware store to eventually piece together this "quick, easy, and
cheap" setup, though. The folks in the plumbing section of my go-to
hardware store know me well, as I often buy multiple sizes and return
what I don't need once I've pieced things together. I'm confident that, if
you are able to find most or all of the supplies (some things may need to

be ordered from the Internet) in a trip or two to the hardware store, you can put together my exact setup with little problem. Otherwise, take note of the materials and piece together what you can with whatever works for you. Just be sure you have at least a spigot, a supply line for a

A finished mash tun decorated with stickers and old concert tickets.

filter, and hardware to connect the two. From there, it's up to how crazy you want to go with the additional options referenced here.

PROCESS

1. Remove the cooler's spigot and discard (or save to use for another project); then place ½-inch (13 mm) dual male pipe thread adapter into the hole, with the ¾-inch (19 mm) end on the *inside* and the ½-inch end on the *outside*.

2. Work one washer / O-ring over the inside-adapter thread, taking care to fit it snugly against the cooler wall. Although optional, adding a washer / O-ring to the outside thread is a good idea; I fit one against the ball valve thread to provide extra protection against both leakage and damaging the cooler plastic by overtightening.

3. Thread the ball valve tightly onto the outside end of the adapter, taking an extra turn or two to fit it tightly against the washer or cooler wall, but not overly tight (you can test for leaks later and adjust as needed). If you ordered one without a spigot, fashion your own spigot from a ½ × ¾-inch (13 × 19 mm) dual male pipe thread adapter and ¾-inch (19 mm) GHT (garden hose thread) female garden hose-repair coupling (any size barb will do).

4. Thread the female hose-repair coupling onto the inside ¾-inch (19 mm) of the adapter, tightening against the washer / O-ring but not overtightening.

5. Cut off both ends of the flexible supply line with a hacksaw and work the inside tubing out with a pair of needle-nose pliers, taking care to not squish the supply line closed. If you choose to go without the optional manifold, simply slide the sleeve over the barb and tighten it; otherwise, proceed to the next step.

6. Prepare the optional copper manifold. When I first built my mash tun, I simply used a 12-inch (30.5 cm) flexible supply line sleeve, which gave me decent efficiency and worked well as a filter but seemed like it could do better. Many brewers use the supply line only, but others use copper tubing to create a manifold with multiple openings. Some of these manifolds can be pretty elaborately designed. When I chose to upgrade my setup, I elected to combine the two while still keeping

things relatively simple. The concept of using a manifold is based on tests brewers have done that show it can increase efficiency by providing multiple entry points for the wort rather than just the one at the spigot. By punching multiple holes in the bottom of the manifold with a small nail and spiraling it so it covers as much bottom surface area as possible, you can theoretically draw in much more sugary wort, making it easier to hit your target gravity. I still used the supply line sleeve, but purchased some additional length to cover the manifold (which is why I have an extra hose clamp in the middle of mine). Not all brewers combine the two, but I figured this would help to avoid a stuck sparge from small grains working their way into the holes.

To prepare the manifold, start by cutting a length appropriate for your cooler bed. For my cylindrical cooler, I found that about 2½ feet (76 cm) was enough. Take the copper and bend it carefully into a spiral shape that covers as much of the bottom as possible while keeping enough of one end straight and centered that it will fit in the drain opening. Once you're satisfied with the shape, flatten the end on the inside of the spiral and bend the other end up slightly to fit it into the hose barb. You will also want to make sure the majority of the manifold is as flat against the bottom as possible. I found this a tad difficult to pull off, so I cut about an inch (2.5 cm) from my wort chiller's ½-inch (13 mm) OD vinyl tubing, then inserted one end tightly into the barb and the other over the copper tubing, providing a bit of extra flexibility.

Don't insert the manifold just yet, though. You'll want to note which part is the bottom and then punch holes about ½ inch (13 mm) apart all the way up to a little over an inch (2.5 cm) from the end at the drain opening (another option is to cut small slots with a hacksaw). Next, run the supply line sleeve over the manifold, leaving the drain-entrance end open and crimping shut the other end. Position the manifold on the cooler floor, taking care to place the holes on the bottom. Slip the hose clamp over the manifold opening, work the copper into the vinyl tubing, and tighten the clamp with a slotted screwdriver as tightly as possible over the end of the sleeve. You now officially have a mash tun!

The various pieces of my spigot arrangement laid out in order.

Cut off both ends of the flexible supply line with a hacksaw and work the inside tubing out with a pair of needle-nose pliers.

First, coil the manifold to cover as much surface area as possible.

Next, punch holes in it about ½ inch (13 mm) apart with a small nail.

Work the manifold into the supply line sleeve and attach to the inner spigot nipple with a short length of vinyl tubing (or whatever works best for you).

Alternatively, simply use the sleeve without the manifold. You can move it around with the mash paddle when stirring to cover more of the grain bed.

since today's well-modified malts require only a single temperature rest. In other words, the maltster has already done part of the job for you. Some homebrewers do choose to go with multistep mashes, but there isn't much reason to do this unless you're going with a very specialized recipe and intentionally using undermodified malts. You may also want to be prepared to do a mash pH adjustment (I usually don't do this), which is discussed in Adjusting Mash pH (chapter 4).

The first thing to do is line up all of your equipment. Along with the standard equipment you use for extract brewing (page 175), you'll need your mash tun, a large, deep spoon, a small pot or a pitcher for pouring sparge water, and something to stir the mash with. A long spoon will work, but you may want to eventually invest in a mash paddle—a wooden paddle with large holes in it to enable ease of movement through dense mash. A good thermometer is also important, preferably a digital one with a corded probe so that you can monitor the temperature of the mash without having to open the lid and minimize the benefit of the cooler's insulation. You'll likely pick up other equipment over time, but these are the essentials. The first thing you'll want to do is obtain your ingredients, which includes crushed malted grains. If you have them crushed for you, you can proceed to brewing. If not, it wouldn't hurt to revisit the section on milling grains (and the subsequent summary of the all-grain brewing process) starting on page 187.

PROCESS

Step 1: Mash in. Mix your brewing water (or *liquor*) with your crushed grains. The ratio of water to grains will vary based on your recipe, but some brewers like to adjust based on factors such as ambient temperature and the temperature of the grains on brew day. For most recipes, I simply add my grains and pour in enough hot water—or *strike water*—to cover the grains by a couple of inches (5 cm or so). You can add the water first (I usually add a bit and put the lid on the cover for a few minutes to preheat the cooler), but you'll need to be sure you have measured out the appropriate amount of brewing water in advance. Adding all of the grains and then pouring water presents the opportunity for clumped grains and air pockets, but if you pour slowly and mix thoroughly you should be fine. A happy medium is to add about a gallon (4 L) of hot water, pour in some mash and stir, pour in more water, and continue until your mash is thick enough to stir without congealing. This way you can monitor the temperature and, if you need some adjustments, heat the water more or add some cooler water until you reach optimal mash-in temperature. The target temperature for your mash will vary depending on your recipe and the style you're shooting for, but for most standard beers you'll want to stay in the range of 145 to 155°F (63–68°C). Generally I choose to heat my strike water to a bit more than this, usually to about 170°F (77°C), since it will inevitably cool down when it hits the grains.

Step 2: Temperature rest. After giving the mash a good stir and ensuring proper temperature, you can rest along with the mash. I usually let mine rest for 60 minutes, but sometimes go a bit over. Some brewers go as long as 90 minutes. Check the temperature once every 15 minutes or so (this is where a digital thermometer with a probe comes in handy). If it starts dropping too close to 145°F (63°C), particularly early on in the process, you'll need to add about a cup (250 mL) of hot water at a time, stir, and put the lid back on quickly to bring it back to optimal range. Some brewers use a combined brew kettle / mash tun so that they can provide direct heat to aid in keeping proper temperature. If you let the temperature drop too

After the mash-in, mash out by stirring with a mash paddle or long spoon.

low (145°F/60°C or below), you'll decrease your extract efficiency and possibly have a stuck sparge, as the mash will begin to gum up.

Step 3: Mash out. The mash-out (if you perform it) is considered part of the lautering process (separating the fermentable wort from the mash). In mashing out you are increasing the temperature of the grain bed, which makes for easier, more efficient lautering, and slows enzyme action. Your goal is to raise the temperature of the mash to about 170°F (77°C). This is an optional step but I recommend it for most batches. Prepare about a gallon (4 L) (you may not need it all) of hot water (about 200°F/93°C), pour a bit slowly over the grain, stir, check the temperature, and continue until you've reached 170°F.

Step 4: Vorlauf and sparge. Now that you've mashed out, it's time to complete the lautering process through the vorlauf (recirculating) and sparge (rinsing). The vorlauf is the first step, as recirculating the wort through the grain bed helps to set up the grain bed as a filter to keep the wort clear of grain husks. Drain a few quarts (liters) of wort from your mash tun's spigot into a pitcher or small pot and pour the wort slowly over the grain bed, repeating two or three times until

Sparging helps to draw more fermentables from the mash. Pour slowly and evenly across the grain bed.

the wort runs clear. Now you will sparge the grain bed to draw out as many fermentable sugars as possible. There are a couple of methods for doing this. Commercial breweries have the equipment to easily perform continuous sparging or fly sparging, which is sprinkling hot water (hot enough to keep your grain bed at about 170°F/77°C) slowly over the grain bed, covering as much of the surface as possible to capture an optimal amount of fermentable wort.

You can do this at home by opening the spigot of your mash tun slightly to create a small drain and then slowly pouring water over the grain bed to match the rate of the drain's flow. Or you can create a sparging device to connect to the top of your mash tun through a drilled hole. This usually consists of a series of connected PVC pipes or circular (or spiral) copper tubing with multiple holes through which the hot water drains onto the bed. A simpler, and still effective, method is to batch sparge, which is simply keeping the spigot closed, pouring a quart (liter) of sparge water over the grains, stirring, resting for a few minutes, and repeating two or three times. Either way, go ahead and fully open your spigot and

The vorlauf and lautering processes are both done by draining wort from the mash tun into the kettle.

collect your wort. To collect as much wort as possible, you'll need to slowly stir the grain bed, reaching the paddle as closely as possible to the bottom without disturbing your filter mechanism (although when I used only the supply line sleeve, I found that lifting it from time to time helped improve wort flow) to free up any wort that may still be residing in the grains. By now you should have collected around 6 to 6½ gallons (24–26 L) of wort. If you're short, or find that your specific gravity is unacceptably low, pour a bit more hot water over the grains, stir, and collect more wort. Sometimes you may need to pour some or all of the wort back over the grain bed, but I prefer not to do that. Once I've proceeded to boil my wort down to 5 gallons (20 L), I check the specific gravity and, if I don't like what I see, I simply pour in some honey (a bit of malt extract works, too). Generally you can expect to get about 6 gallons (24 L) of wort per 10 pounds (4.5 kg) of grain, or about 0.6 gallon per pound (5.1 L per kg). Don't overthink this; remember, you can always add more fermentable sugars. If you sparge excessively, you risk extracting too many tannins (which will lead to an unpleasant mouthfeel in the final product). You can always add a bit of water to the wort and make up for the lost fermentables by adding some sugars during the boil.

Step 5. Onward! From here, proceed to boiling, chilling, and fermenting your wort as with extract and BiaB brewing, and enjoy the satisfaction of having made beer from scratch!

Brewing All-Grain Beer in 1-Gallon (4 L) Batches

For most of my brewing life, I brewed 5-gallon (20 L) batches. My first brew kit was designed for 5-gallon batches. Pretty much every brewing recipe I read was for 5-gallon batches. Anything less just wasn't discussed. If you wanted to change your scale, it was usually to move up to 10-gallon (40 L) batches (or much larger if you planned on pursuing brewing professionally). I still brew plenty of 5-gallon batches, but I have always made mead and wine in 1-gallon (4 L) batches, so I began to think about doing the same with beer. Turns out I wasn't the only one. Thanks to the magic of the Internet, I found that there are a fair share of people who have been making 1-gallon batches for a while.

One-gallon (4 L) brewing kits have even begun to pop up in home-brewing stores. Personally I find the price of these kits to be barely worth the 12 or so bottles you get from them, but it does seem a good starting point for people who have never brewed before. When I brew 1-gallon batches, I simply use portions of the dry malt extracts and grains I have purchased to do smaller batches rather than buy a 1-gallon kit each time. I already have the equipment on hand, and it's easy to co-opt kitchenware for 1-gallon brewing. There are a few reasons I do 1-gallon batches. First, it's a great way to experiment with new flavor combinations (if I like a new recipe, I simply multiply all ingredient amounts by 5 when I'm ready to scale up). Second, it's a good method for using up excess malt from packages I've opened for larger batches; this also allows me to brew several 1-gallon batches at a time and have a variety of beers to sample rather than having 50 bottles of the same beer. Finally, it's a lot quicker and less cumbersome than a 5-gallon (20 L) batch. Brew days happen more often and take up less of my time now that I'm doing more 1-gallon batches. In short, I find I brew more when I brew with less!

The 1-gallon (4 L) extract process really isn't all that different from brewing 5-gallon (20 L) batches, only it's much simpler and less daunting. Simply follow the technique for brewing 1-gallon simple ales on page 166 and substitute extract for sugar or molasses.

For 1-gallon (4 L) all-grain brewing, the equipment is the same as for 1-gallon extract brewing, except that you'll need two 2- to 3-gallon (8–12 L) cooking pots and a fine-mesh strainer for holding the mash while it's being sparged (I use a colander with small enough holes to keep grains from falling through). Recipes will vary, but for most you'll have around 1 to 2 pounds of grains (0.5–1 kg) to 1 gallon of water.

PROCESS

1. Heat about 1 quart (1 L) of water to a bit above strike temperature (about 170°F/77°C).
2. Mash in the grains and keep the heat on (while continuously stirring) until the mash temperature reaches 145 to 155°F (63–68°C).
3. Place a lid on the pot and cut off the heat (if you're using a well-insulated pot), or keep the heat source on medium-low and monitor the temperature to ensure it stays at the appropriate range and doesn't

drop below 140°F (60°C). Another option is to wrap it well with a couple of towels. Stir the grains every 15 minutes and re-insulate.

4. After 1 hour place the pot back on the heat source and bring the temperature to 170°F (77°C) while stirring the mash.

5. In a separate pot, heat 1 gallon (4 L) of sparge water to 180°F (82°C).

6. Scoop or carefully pour the grains into a strainer or colander (which you can line with cheesecloth if you'd like to prevent small grain particles from making it into the wort).

7. Slowly pour the sparge water over the grains, covering as much of the grain bed as possible and avoiding creating channels that allow the water to flow too quickly through the grain and thus extract less sugar (a diffuser such as a fine-mesh screen will help with this). Repeat two or three times.

8. Once you've gathered your wort, proceed with boiling, cooling, and fermenting.

9. That's it! Less time and hassle dealing with large amounts of grain, less money spent, and you still have the satisfaction of having done everything from scratch (particularly if you malted the grains yourself).

When sparging a 1-gallon (4 L) all-grain beer, a diffuser such as a strainer or a fine-mesh screen will help distribute the water evenly across the grain bed.

Ancient All-Grain Brewing

In 2006 archaeologists uncovered strong evidence for a malting and brewing operation from a Late Bronze Age (1500–1200 BC) settlement at Tall Bazi in northern Syria. At the excavation site in the Euphrates Valley, they found 50 well-preserved houses that served as both residences and production facilities for a wide variety of materials before the city was suddenly destroyed for unknown reasons. One of the most tantalizing finds was that several houses featured a similar arrangement of three vessels, all located near ventilation, and nearly every house contained a thick-rimmed large vat with a wide opening able to hold up to 52 gallons (200 L) of liquid. In every house where it was found, this vat was partially buried in the ground and appeared to have never been moved. Often there was also a slightly smaller vessel (24 to 29 gallons/90–110 L) with a hole in the bottom. Additionally, storage jars were usually situated nearby, many containing remains of carbonized barley. Researchers ruled out the use of the large vessels for storing water or other liquids because of the potential for the growth of spoilage microbes in the warm environment (it would have been difficult to clean them thoroughly), and because storage jars generally contained smaller openings for easy sealing. Brewing and malting were considered to be their most likely purpose, and residue analysis was performed to test this hypothesis.

Both the large vessels and the vessels with the hole in the bottom contained residues of oxalate, which is formed when grain is saturated with water. While some of the other vessels contained tartrate, which would indicate that they contained wine, these vessels had none. Some starch grains and yeast were also found, although this wasn't necessarily evidence for beer since grains were also used for bread (which theoretically could then have been made into beer) and yeast would have been prevalent in the environment regardless of whether brewing was performed. Since the large vessels were partially sunk into the ground, it was theorized that they were used for cooling recently cooked beer wort. The researchers decided to test their theory by re-creating all phases of the brewing process using only instruments that would have been available during the time period. They proceeded to make what they termed a Bazi Beer. They found that the vessels with holes in them

Fun with Spent Grain

If you brew often with grain, you'll have a lot of spent grain you'll need to figure out what to do with. Unless you really plan ahead, a lot of it will end up in the compost, which isn't a bad place to put it, as it will provide your compost bed with all kinds of nutrients and other good stuff. There are plenty of other good uses for it, though. Despite your best efforts, you won't have sucked all of the sugars and nutrients out of it. Chickens and livestock love munching on spent grains. If you don't keep farm animals, consider saving grains to pass along to a local farmer. Be sure to either donate or freeze within a couple of days of brewing, or the grain will mold. Chickens and livestock aren't the only animals that enjoy spent grain, though. Many breweries sell spent-grain dog treats that are popular with patrons and their pets. You can easily make these at home with just some basic baking skills. A recipe I like is based on one my friend Amber "Pixie" Shehan blogged about on her website. She based hers on one from Deschutes Brewery, but many breweries offer similar recipes. You can tweak yours based on what you have available; just be sure to not use anything that would harm a dog, such as chocolate. Don't use grains that have had hops added during the mash-in, as hops are toxic to dogs.

Pig-Dog's Spent Grain Treats

Our pit-Lab mix, Miss Piggy (named for her voracious appetite after we saved her from the side of the road as a scrawny, mangy puppy), devours these treats when we make them for her.

INGREDIENTS

2 cups (428 mL) spent grain
1 cup (120 g) flour
1 egg
½ cup (125 g) natural, low-sugar peanut butter

DIRECTIONS

1. Preheat your oven to 350°F (180°C).

2. Mix all the ingredients in a large bowl. Be sure to really blend things together and get messy. Kids enjoy helping with this part almost as much as they enjoy making people cookies.

3. Sprinkle some flour on a clean cutting board, counter, or cookie sheet, plop the dough onto it, and roll it flat (around ¼ inch/6 mm thick). Cut the dough into several "biscuits" in whatever shape you desire, or use a biscuit or cookie cutter.

4. Place the treats on a lightly greased (with lard or meat gravy if you have it on hand) cookie sheet and bake them for 30 minutes.

5. Reduce the oven temperature to 225°F (107°C) and leave them in for an hour or two to dry out so they'll last longer.

6. Feed them to your canine friend as soon as they've cooled down and save the rest in the freezer in a plastic or paper baggie.

7. Feel free to let any stray kids taste them. I found them to be a little bland, but my two-year-old, Maisie, kept eating them instead of feeding them to the dog!

My daughter Sadie was the perfect assistant for making the treats.

were ideal for steeping and germinating grain to turn it into malt. They also theorized that the grain germination phase of malting would have been performed on reed mats, which is the method they chose in their re-creation, though these are rarely found preserved at archaeological sites due to their organic composition. After malting the grains, they kilned them in brick ovens to cut off germination. Next, they milled the stones on a saddle quern (essentially, a large flat rock and a smaller rock to use as a grinder).

Finally, they "cold" mashed (using the ambient temperatures of the environment and no external heat) the grains at 93°F (34°C) with a grist/water ratio of 1:8.3. For yeast, they added a mix of *Saccharomyces* and *Schizosaccharomyces* yeast and *Lactobacillus* bacteria. They then let the mix rest for 36 hours at about 75°F (24°C). The alcohol level of the resulting liquid isn't mentioned, but they do say that they intentionally diluted it to about 1.6 percent by volume since the liquid would have been used to sustain all members of the population throughout the day. Their conclusion was that this was a very drinkable beer that could last up to two months in modern storage conditions (43°F/6°C).[2]

In 2007 Billy Quinn and Declan Moore of Moore Environmental and Archaeological Consultants in Galway performed an experiment to test their theory that fulacht fiadh, ancient horseshoe-shaped mounds

An Early Neolithic (3700–3500 BC) saddle quern and rubbing stone found in Etton, Cambridgeshire, England. Courtesy of Claire H., Flickr.

in Ireland with troughs set into the ground and surrounded by stones, were actually early brewing sites. Archaeologists have theorized a wide range of potential uses for the sites, from cooking, to dye preparation, to saunas, to tanning—one thing they can agree on, though, is that the troughs at the site were likely used to heat water through the use of heated stones. Quinn and Moore proposed a use that their peers were skeptical of: They were used for brewing!

First, they sought out the ingredients and equipment that would have most likely been used during the Bronze Age. Their Bronze Age ale, they theorized, would have been made from crushed, malted grains with various herbs and, of course, yeast. For brewing equipment and facilities, they ascertained that they needed "a preparation area for malting, a heat source, grinding equipment, a mash tun (a sufficiently large vessel or pit), containers and a stirrer."[3] For a heat source, they used sandstone and granite stones heated in a fire. For the mash tun, they used a 60-year-old wooden trough "posthumously donated by Billy's granduncle." Next they dug a pit, lowered the trough into the ground, and added water. There was some initial leakage but they "eventually reached an equilibrium in the water level by simply flooding the immediate area."

Rather than malting their own barley, they chose malted barley provided by Aidan Murphy, master brewer with the Galway Hooker Brewing Company. After initially attempting to grind it using bottles on a hard surface, they eventually decided to go with "a very Bronze Age electrical food processor." Although they noted that Bronze Age brews were likely fermented with wild yeast or started with magic sticks, they chose to go with brewing yeast. They heated the stones in a fire for about two hours and then transferred the heated stones into the trough with a shovel. Then they placed a wicker basket into the water and began slowly adding in malted barley, keeping the water hot through the addition of more heated stones. After about 45 minutes they noticed the water had transformed into sweet, syrupy wort. From there they went the standard modern homebrewing route, boiling the wort (to which they added juniper, yarrow, and elderflower heads) and transferred it into plastic buckets with spigots for bottling. After letting it ferment for three days, they had what they described as a "relatively clear, copper-coloured brew with a distinctively sharp yet sweet taste. The hot rocks impart a slightly smoky caramelized character. A hard touch of sugar was evident with minimal bitterness and grainy flavour throughout. Overall, the taste was crisp, with a moderate to heavy body. In short it was nice!"[4] More proof that hops are not required for a refreshing, drinkable beer!

Cold Mashing, Cold Fermentation, and Raw Beer

Cold mashing and cold fermenting were completely foreign to me until I moved beyond modern brewing manuals and started researching older techniques. I always assumed that mashing at a high temperature and then boiling the wort were just how it was supposed to be done. Turns out our ancestors were pretty ingenious and came up with all kinds of ways to ferment beer. In traditional cold-fermentation practices, sometimes portions of the mash and wort are heated and other times they are not. Many of these techniques are still practiced today in places such as Finland and various regions of Africa, where a type of "raw" (uncooked) beer is made using techniques that have been passed down through generations. Anthropological research indicates that the heating of mash and wort and the time at which it takes place vary greatly depending on location. In Odd Nordland's survey of Norwegian brewing practices, he ascertained that there were seven common methods for extracting the wort from the mash:

> (1) both the mash and the wort were boiled, (2) the mash and the wort were boiled, and the wort was poured repeatedly over the mash, (3) the wort was boiled but not the mash, (4) the mash and some of the wort were boiled, (5) the mash was boiled but not the wort, (6) some of the wort was boiled but not the mash, and (7) neither the mash nor the wort was boiled.[5]

Beers traditionally brewed by the "raw" method were often wild-fermented or fermented with heirloom yeast, including sahti in Finland, *koduõlu* in Estonia, *gotlandsdricka* in Sweden, *maltøl* in Norway, gose in Germany (which is made with heated mash and boiled wort by most breweries today), and *kaimiškas* in Lithuania. All of these styles can also be considered farmhouse ales, since they originate from traditions in which the entire process was performed on a domestic scale, from malting, to ingredient selection, to brewing. With the variations in technique, you can perform a cold ferment in whichever manner works for you since there is no consensus as to what constitutes "proper" technique. What follows is the method I would recommend without having to procure equipment for making beer by truly authentic ancient processes. No matter what equipment you use, the process will lead to pretty much the same ancient brew. It's up to you as to how ancient you want to go in making it. You can also feel free to modify the ingredients to make whatever kind of brew you want.

INGREDIENTS

6 pounds (3 kg) malted uncrushed grain (pale malt or pilsner will work fine, but wheat, sorghum, oats, or other ancient grains are more historically authentic)

Enough water to fully submerge the grains (should be around 3–4 gallons/12–16 L)

Yarrow, meadowsweet, juniper, hawthorn or other berries, edible flower heads, or small amounts of whatever herb or wild-harvested plant you desire (ancient peoples didn't have specific measuring instruments; just use a fingerful of dry herbs or a sprig or two of fresh herbs and as many berries as you desire)

1–2 cups (250–500 mL) raw, unfiltered honey and any honeycomb, pollen, propolis, or other goodies from the hive you have available

EQUIPMENT

5-gallon (20 L) or larger ceramic crock, or other openmouthed nonmetal food-grade container (a plastic brewing bucket will work but take note that you may be inviting in some lactobacillus, which could stick around in any scratches)

Cloth cover for container

Secondary fermentation container(s); you can either filter this and drink it young—as likely would have happened historically—or transfer it into glass jugs with airlocks to fully ferment

A siphoning tube, sieve, funnel lined with cheesecloth, basket, or other type of filtering/liquid-transferring apparatus

Rocks—one large flat one and one smaller round one for a saddle quern (or use your preferred modern method of milling the grain)

Bottles with caps, corks, etc., if you wish to bottle and age it

PROCESS

While you can crush the grains by any means necessary and still make
the same beer, I like to be as hands-on as possible when making a primitive brew. It takes a bit longer than grinding with a grain mill, but I
like the tactile, meditative experience of grinding with a saddle quern.
Look up saddle quern images on the Web and you'll see all kinds of
variations, but all you really need to concern yourself with is finding
a large rock and a smaller one. The large rock should be large enough
to hold a handful or two of grain with space to keep too much of it
from falling off. If it has a curved surface, even better, but flat surfaces
work fine, too. The smaller rock is more effective if it's round enough
to roll across the grain, but it needn't be round. I like to use some rocks
full of fossils that I found in the woods of my childhood home (I hose
them down well and then pour boiling water over them to get rid of

Hand-crushed grain fermenting in the Kentucky summer heat with rocks used
for crushing grains.

any dirt and critters). My quern is thick and flat and shaped somewhat like Mjölnir (Thor's hammer in Norse mythology). I find that placing a handful of grain on the saddle rock and crushing it with the quern through a combination of rocking the wide end of the "hammer" back and forth and then laying it flat on the saddle and rubbing back and forth to create friction makes quick work of the grain. I'm able to crush it to a coarse consistency in under an hour.

Set your fermentation crock underneath the rock and scrape the ground grain into it, careful to lose only a little on the ground (you can place a ground cloth or newspapers underneath to catch any excess). You might also take a portion (around ½ pound/0.25 kg) of the grain and roast it over a fire beforehand. This will simulate how grains would have been dried after being malted—over a fire with varying degrees of heat and smokiness. I find that, even when I carefully control the fire, the grains range from slightly browned to charred (I leave out any that are completely burnt). Even a small amount of malt prepared this way will have an effect on the flavor of the final brew.

Once your grains are crushed and in your fermentation container, sprinkle in whichever herbs, berries, and other flavorings you've chosen. Next, take 4 gallons (20 L) of springwater or filtered tap water and heat it to a temperature based on the type of raw brewing you are interested in. If you're reproducing the Tall Bazi experiment, bring it to around 93°F (34°C). I did this, and left it out in the sun over two balmy Kentucky summer days of around 85 to 90°F (29–32°C), moving it inside to a room open to the outdoor air in the evenings to keep it away from critters. I found that I drew out enough sugars this way to reach around 1.050 (around 4 to 5 percent ABV) on my hydrometer for about 2 gallons (8 L) of wort. To keep things simple, I also didn't sparge. It's probably better to bring it to around 160°F (71°C), however, and then sparge with hot water to gather more fermentable wort. This certainly isn't the most efficient way to prepare wort, but it works, and proves that it would have been easy for ancient people to make a drinkable low- to medium-alcohol brew with rudimentary equipment.

Whatever temperature you decide to go with, don't add the honey until the wort has cooled down a bit. Once everything is in the mash, stir it well and cover it. I found that after three to four days, I achieved fermentation with nothing more than raw ingredients (and a bit of barm

Heating with Rocks (Safely)

Heating wort or mash water with rocks is as primitive as it gets, and is a fairly simple process. However, you need to take some precautions to ensure a safe, effective brew day. First, you'll need to gather the proper rocks, as not just any rock will do. You want dense, fine-textured rocks that aren't prone to shattering. Igneous rocks, which are formed from the solidification of molten rock from volcanoes, are ideal. Granite and basalt are good candidates, as is sandstone if you can find the kind that is metamorphic and heat-resistant. Avoid limestone, shale, or other sedimentary rocks, as they are more porous and prone to shattering, and can leach unwanted materials such as calcium hydroxide into the wort. Look for rocks that are about the size of a human head. They need to be large enough to retain a good amount of heat but also fit in your mash tun and brew kettle. Granite has worked well for me. I wasn't able to source any of the proper size from any of the local landscaping places, but one of them recommended a monument and headstone supplier. I called up and when I told the owner about my project he was happy to let me pick through some of his granite fragments. Some were pieces that had shattered from headstones before they were finished, initials and all—which means I now have to explain to people when they see pieces of gravestones by my fire pit that, no, I haven't been out robbing graveyards. I knew I had some solid rock when I attempted to break one of the larger ones in half with a sledgehammer and all I got was a bit of powder and a jarred arm. The stones have held up well so far, although one did split in half in the fire.

Take extra care when heating stones, even if you're working with something as solid as granite. Wear heavy clothing and gloves, and good eye protection. Bring the stones to heat slowly, either by preheating them in an oven on low heat or setting them close to the fire and working them in slowly. I like to dig a small pit that I line with rocks or bricks to retain heat and keep dirt off the stones. I place the stones on the bricks and build a fire over the stones, which I stoke for two to three hours, allowing coals to build over the rocks. When it's time to heat my mash water, I take some of the smaller rocks and use a shovel or some tongs to place them in the perforated metal basket that came with the turkey fryer that I use for a brew kettle. I generally warm the water some over the fire first, as rocks are most prone to shatter when there are extreme temperature differences. Then I slowly lower the basket into the water, raise and lift it a couple of times, and dump the rocks back in the fire once they're spent. Next I take a larger rock and repeat the process. Usually the first large rock brings me to my mash temperature, but sometimes I use a second or keep a propane burner on hand as a backup. I try to have at least four or five large rocks in the fire and a couple of small ones. Once I pour the mash water over the grains, I set a smaller rock directly on the grains to provide additional heat and to caramelize the grains.

I usually monitor with a thermometer but I don't worry too much about getting the perfect strike temperature, as hot rocks aren't the most precise of instruments. When it comes time to heat the wort, I try not to gather much more than 5 or 6 gallons (20–24 L), as the rapid heating and displacement from a large rock make for a likely boil-over. After putting on my protective gear, I take the largest rock I have, place it in my metal basket, and lower it *very* slowly into the wort, lifting up and down a couple of times as the wort begins to foam up. Once I feel

Set a hot rock carefully on the grains during the mash-in for additional caramelization and heat.

I've gotten enough from the rock, I set it aside and repeat with the rest of my rocks. Since I usually don't use hops for this type of beer, I don't worry about trying to get a full 60-minute boil. Heating it at a near boil for half an hour or so is usually enough, although you may want to consider using a propane burner to maintain a full 60-minute boil. The entire process can be done with hot rocks, but even if you only use one or two rocks, you'll still get the caramelized flavor the rocks impart (and go through a lot less trouble). Traditionally, one of the rocks was set aside and placed in the fermenter once cool to provide additional caramelization from the caramelized sugars that coated the rock upon its immersion into the wort. Be sure to set aside a good part of the day and procure some assistance. Heating beer wort with rocks causes all kinds of hissing, steaming, and foaming. It's a great spectator sport, and you may need some of those spectators to help with the heavy lifting.

from a previous batch), producing a cloudy liquid with a very grainy flavor and a definite lactic acid influence. Before drinking or racking it into jugs with airlocks, you could strain it through a basket, which is effective and historically authentic, but it does take some time and effort to pull off. I prefer to use a ladle and sieve, strain off the solids, and drink it as is. This is by no means a beer you'd have down in the local pub, but it is an authentic historical beer. Rough, raw, tangy, grainy, and low-alcohol, but very refreshing and nutritious. Drink it within a couple of days of visible fermentation, as it will sour quickly.

For a somewhat more refined and longer-lasting beer, I recommend heating the water and wort via the hot-rock method outlined in the sidebar on page 214, and drawing the wort from the mash to ferment rather than fermenting the mash. You can also keep some of the mash, ferment it, let it sour a bit, and add a bit of the sour mash to a larger batch to give it a bit of tang. There are many directions you can take these concepts to create your own unique ancient brew. Just be sure to not get wrapped up in the technicalities and appreciate the results—no matter what they are!

CHAPTER NINE

RECIPES

I t's time to get your hands dirty! Now that you've got a grasp on the history of beer, ale, gruit, and their many variations, you've got a strong foundation for moving forward with creating your own concoctions. For some of these recipes, it will be helpful to revisit the instructions on how to brew in chapter 8, as I will go into less detail on process here, but for some of the simpler ones, you can jump right in. Although I've loosely categorized each set of recipes by style, if you want to brew by historical methods and according to your own creativity and whims, it's worth keeping in mind that you needn't get hung up on style. Beer styles evolved over the years and in modern times have become somewhat regimented, particularly when it comes to competitive brewing. I have no problem with competitive brewing but I'm more interested in using styles as a guideline and starting point, understanding the effect of different ingredients and sugar ratios, and brewing with what ingredients I have managed to obtain locally (when possible) or grown or foraged myself. This is how styles developed—people brewed with what their local environment provided and developed unique styles that over time became associated with their region. Once brewing became commercialized, it became necessary to develop specific, repeatable recipes that could be easily reproduced on a large scale. That being said, it can help the brewing process to have some expectation as to what the final product should taste like. Hence, I have divided recipes into the following categories:

- Simple Ales
- Wheats and Farmhouse Ales
- Early European and British Beers
- Nordic Beers
- Indigenous American/South American and Corn-Based Beers
- Fruit and Vegetable Beers

Simple Ales

Something very close to our modern idea of beer can be made using simple household items and ingredients, with various types of processed sugar (cane sugar, brown sugar, molasses), or even honey serving in place of grains. The following recipes are my variations on traditional recipes, as well as some of my own creations.

Simple ales are a great drink for a hot summer afternoon.

Notes on Measurements

Water

For all 1-gallon (4 L) recipes, you may not end up with the full gallon due to displacement of water by the addition of ingredients, but you can always add a bit more during racking and bottling. For 5-gallon (20 L) recipes, I suggest starting with 5½ gallons (22 L) of water for extract recipes and 6 gallons (24 L) for all-grain recipes (this allows for additional water to be soaked up by grains and used in sparging). Remember that you will always lose some degree of volume throughout the boil and fermentation processes. Generally it's best to just accept that, but you can always increase volume by either adding a bit more water, or adding water blended with a sugar (which will boost alcohol level but also increase fermentation time) to keep from watering the brew down.

Yeast

For each recipe, I will recommend the ideal yeast first, along with a couple of other options. For the most part you can use whichever yeast you have on hand, but certain flavors will require certain yeasts. Unless I recommend otherwise (as in for higher-gravity beers such as bragots), the amount of yeast used for 1-gallon (4 L) batches should be approximately ½ teaspoon dried yeast, or ½ cup (125 mL) barm (from an actively fermenting batch or a wild yeast starter). For 5-gallon (20 L) batches, you can generally use the full packet of a commercial yeast, or use 3 to 4 teaspoons dried yeast or 1 to 2 cups (250–500 mL) barm. Note that dried yeast comes in packets of anywhere from 5 to around 11 grams. Generally, one packet will do. For any beer, erring on the side of a bit too much yeast is better than not adding enough, particularly for those with higher gravity / sugar content. If you don't have an active ferment within 24 hours of adding the yeast, add another couple of teaspoons and wait another 8 to 12 hours. If there is still no sign of fermentation, proceed to the troubleshooting section at the end of this book.

Ginger Beer

What follows is based on what I have found works best for a simple ginger beer. You may wish to adjust the amounts of ginger to taste. I like ginger, but it can easily become overpowering. I found that my early attempts were flavorful, but the ginger didn't really come through. The proportions for this recipe are what I recommend for a beer with a pronounced but not overwhelming ginger flavor.

INGREDIENTS FOR 1 GALLON (4 L)

1 gallon (4 L) springwater or filtered tap water
1 pound (0.5 kg) brown sugar, light brown sugar, or cane sugar
2–3 ounces (57–85 g) fresh gingerroot, chopped or bruised (double, triple, or even quadruple if you like a strong ginger flavor)
Juice of ½ small lemon, 2 ounces (60 mL) lemon juice, or 1 ounce (28 g) cream of tartar (a common substitute for citric acid)
Brewing yeast, ale yeast, bread yeast, or barm

PROCESS

1. Bring the water just to a boil in a stockpot.
2. Stir in the sugar until fully dissolved.
3. Bruise the ginger lightly by squeezing it with your finger or pressing with a spoon or butter knife and drop it into the pot. Add the lemon juice or cream of tartar.
4. Reduce the heat to medium-low and shut it off after half an hour.
5. Let the liquid cool to milk-warm (warm to the back of your hand) and add the yeast; then leave overnight with a cloth covering the pot (I should note that sometimes I just sprinkle the yeast directly into the jug during the next step with similar results).
6. Strain the solids out and pour into a 1-gallon (4 L) jug or other container with an airlock.
7. Allow to ferment fully, prime with sugar or honey, and bottle.

Many early recipes call for bottling this shortly after it begins fermenting, making for a carbonated, low-to-no-alcohol "soda" more akin to a modern ginger ale. If you prefer to do this, use about a quarter of the sugar, skip step 6, and go straight to bottling. Just be extra vigilant that you open, vent, or refrigerate the bottle within *no longer* than 24 hours. The built-up CO_2 can cause anything from light fizzing, to gushing, to exploding bottles if left too long unattended. Refrigeration will slow fermentation significantly. You can safely keep this in the refrigerator for weeks or months if you want but it's best drunk young. If you bottle in plastic soda or water bottles, you can gauge carbonation by monitoring the expansion of the plastic. When the bottle is firm it's ready.

Ginger Beer Variations

In perusing old brewing recipes, I often find ginger referenced as the sole root in a beer, but many other roots and flavorings were used in traditional brewing, often along with ginger, including burdock, dandelion, sarsaparilla, and sassafras. Additional flavoring ingredients included allspice, birch bark (and many other barks), coriander, juniper, wintergreen, and vanilla beans. You can use as many or as few if you want, provided you use small quantities of each. One combination I particularly enjoy is ginger and coriander. The idea for this recipe came from my friend Devon Young, who writes the blog *Nitty Gritty Life* (nittygrittylife.com). A homesteader and trained herbalist, Devon blogs on subjects such as farming, gardening, cooking, and fermentation while running a holistic health care practice and farming 10 acres (4 ha) in Oregon's Willamette Valley with her husband and children. Devon is well versed in the history of brewsters and alewives and considers herself a brewster.

Although she learned winemaking from a modern, technical standpoint, she doesn't consider herself to be very technical when she's making wine, beer, and mead. "I am very untraditional, as I like to work with various herbs and spices to craft my ferments," she explained. "There are wonderful bitter, tannic, and pungent herbs that make for really delicious brews, meads, and wines. I am particularly fond of mugwort and sages for lighter-style brews and various sweeter and spicier herbs and spices to craft super-unique ales." Her take on cleanliness and attention to detail is that clean equipment and moderate temperatures are crucial for a good ferment. She stores her fermentation equipment in its own well-cleaned area, and works to minimize cross-contamination, as she also ferments many food products through lactic fermentation.

I enjoy a cold glass of ginger-coriander ale on a hot summer day, and my kids love it when I prepare it for them as a natural soda. Here is Devon's recipe with my slight variations.

INGREDIENTS FOR 1 GALLON (4 L)

1 gallon (4 L) springwater or filtered tap water
1 pound (0.5 kg) cane sugar
8 ounces (227 g) fresh gingerroot, chopped or bruised
1 ounce (28 g) lightly crushed dried coriander seed
2 tablespoons dried orange peel granules (I sometimes use 2 wedges of a freshly sliced orange instead)
Brewing yeast, ale yeast, bread yeast, or barm

PROCESS

1. Bring the water just to a boil in a stockpot.
2. Stir in the sugar until fully dissolved.
3. Add all the other ingredients (except the yeast).
4. Reduce the heat to medium-low and shut it off after half an hour.
5. Let the wort cool, strain into a fermenter, add the yeast, ferment for about 2 weeks, prime, bottle, and begin sampling in about a week.

Herbal and Wild Simple Ales

The recipes here are barely the tip of the iceberg of what is possible with a little bit of herbalism and foraging knowledge. Just be sure you fully understand what you are brewing with and that your ingredients have been ethically harvested and are free of pesticides or other human-made contaminants. For any of these, you can substitute sugar with 1 pound (0.5 kg) to 1½ pounds (0.75 kg) of light-to-dark dry malt extract to make a grain-based beer.

Note: Unless specified otherwise, all herbal measurements are for dried herbs. Double measurement for fresh herbs, as dried herbs have more concentrated flavors.

Juniper Simple Ale/Digestif

I like to use this mix of ingredients for grain-based beers and meads as well. It reminds me of Scandinavian liqueurs and schnapps that balance bitter with sweet. These drinks work well as a digestif, as they contain carminative herbs, which have chemical properties that aid with digestion. Not everyone likes the bitterness, but I find it's well worth developing a taste for, particularly since it's balanced well with a sweet, fruity flavor.

INGREDIENTS FOR 1 GALLON (4 L)

1 gallon (4 L) springwater or filtered tap water
½ pound (0.25 kg) cane sugar
½ pound (0.25 kg) light brown sugar
1 teaspoon dried wormwood
1 teaspoon dried mugwort
1 teaspoon caraway seeds
1 tablespoon juniper berries
Brewing yeast, ale yeast, bread yeast, or barm

PROCESS

1. Bring the water just to a boil in a stockpot.
2. Stir in the sugar until fully dissolved.
3. Add all the other ingredients (except the yeast), reduce the heat to medium-low, and shut it off after half an hour.
4. Let the wort cool, strain into a fermenter, add the yeast, ferment for about 2 weeks, prime, bottle, and begin sampling in about a week.

Spruce Simple Ale

Spruce was a common flavoring and preservative ingredient used along with or instead of hops, and often brewed with molasses. I provide grain-based recipes for spruce beer later on in this chapter, but for now, here is a simple ale version. As with any simple ales, you can use molasses, brown sugar, cane sugar, honey, or any combination. Most traditional recipes call only for molasses, but I find molasses to be a bit much when used exclusively, so I usually go with brown sugar or half brown sugar / half molasses.

INGREDIENTS FOR 1 GALLON (4 L)

1 gallon (4 L) springwater or filtered tap water
½ pound (0.25 kg) cane sugar

Spruce or pine needles can be added during the boil, during fermentation as a tea or extract, or just before bottling.

½ pound (0.25 kg) molasses
½ ounce (14 g) low-alpha hops (optional)
2–4 spruce tips (more or less depending on the intensity of their smell/flavor)
½ teaspoon brewing yeast, ale yeast, or bread yeast, or ½ cup (125 mL) barm

PROCESS

1. Bring the water just to a boil in a stockpot.
2. Stir in the sugar and molasses until fully dissolved.
3. Add the hops (optional).
4. Heat at a low, rolling boil, shut off the heat after half an hour, and add the spruce.
5. Let the wort cool, strain into a fermenter, add the yeast, ferment for about 2 weeks, prime, bottle, and begin sampling in about a week.

Oak Bark and Mushroom Beer

For details on brewing with bark and mushrooms, see chapter 7.

INGREDIENTS FOR 1 GALLON (4 L)

1 gallon (4 L) springwater or filtered tap water
1 pound (0.5 kg) cane sugar

Recently harvested oak bark cambium.

1 ounce (28 g) fresh or ½ ounce (14 g) dried shiitake, wine cap
    stropharia, or other mushrooms
Juice of ½ small lemon, 2 ounces (60 mL) lemon juice, or 1 ounce
    (28 g) cream of tartar
1 small handful (about ½ ounce/14 g) oak bark (or substitute other
    hardwood bark)
Brewing yeast, ale yeast, bread yeast, or barm

PROCESS
1. Bring the water just to a boil in a stockpot.
2. Stir in the sugar until fully dissolved.
3. Add all the ingredients except the oak bark and yeast.
4. Reduce the heat to medium-low and shut it off after half
    an hour.
5. Add the bark, let the wort cool, strain into a fermenter, add the
    yeast, ferment for about 2 weeks, prime, bottle, and begin
    sampling in about a week.

Yarrow and Meadowsweet Simple Ale

You don't necessarily have to use both herbs in this recipe, but can
double the amount of one if that's all you have. Adding in some of the
leaves will help provide some bittering/herbal flavor.

INGREDIENTS FOR 1 GALLON (4 L)

1 gallon (4 L) springwater or filtered tap water

1 pound (0.5 kg) cane or brown sugar, or 1 pound (0.5 kg) dry malt extract

1 ounce (28 g) fresh or ½ ounce (14 g) dried yarrow flowers

1 ounce (28 g) fresh or ½ ounce (14 g) dried meadowsweet flowers

½ ounce (14 g) fresh or ¼ ounce (7 g) dried meadowsweet and yarrow leaves

Juice of ½ small lemon, 2 ounces (60 mL) lemon juice, or 1 ounce (28 g) cream of tartar

Brewing yeast, ale yeast, bread yeast, or barm

PROCESS

1. Bring the water just to a boil in a stockpot.
2. Stir in the sugar until fully dissolved.
3. Add all the ingredients except the yeast.
4. Reduce the heat to medium-low and shut it off after half an hour.
5. Let the wort cool, strain into a fermenter, add the yeast, ferment for about 2 weeks, prime, bottle, and begin sampling in about a week.

Wormwood and Meadowsweet Simple Ale

This beer can be made to taste very much like a hopped grain beer brewed by modern methods, with or without the hops and grain. I've noted a few variations you can try, so you can adjust this recipe to your tastes. The wormwood definitely provides bittering, but not everyone can handle it. I personally prefer just a hint of it over the flavor of most super-hoppy beers, but you'll need to try it for yourself and decide.

INGREDIENTS FOR 1 GALLON (4 L)

1 gallon (4 L) springwater or filtered tap water

1 pound (0.5 kg) cane or brown sugar (or substitute 1 pound/0.5 kg dry malt extract)

½ ounce (14 g) fresh or ¼ ounce (7 g) dried wormwood

Optional substitute for wormwood: 1 ounce (28 g) Fuggle or other low-alpha hops

1 ounce (28 g) fresh or ½ ounce (14 g) dried meadowsweet flowers

½ ounce (14 g) fresh or ¼ ounce (7 g) dried meadowsweet leaves

Juice of ½ small lemon, 2 ounces (60 mL) lemon juice, or 1 ounce
   (28 g) cream of tartar
Brewing yeast, ale yeast, bread yeast, or barm

PROCESS

1. Bring the water just to a boil in a stockpot.
2. Stir in the sugar until fully dissolved.
3. Add all the ingredients except the yeast.
4. Reduce the heat to medium-low and shut it off after half an hour.
5. Let the wort cool, strain into a fermenter, add the yeast, ferment for about 2 weeks, prime, bottle, and begin sampling in about a week.

Small Mead

Technically drinks derived from fermented honey are considered mead. Depending on how much honey you use, mead can vary in alcohol content from 2 percent ABV to as much as 18 percent. Meads with 10 percent ABV or higher can take several months to fully ferment, and longer to age for drinkability, although the use of a strong yeast and the addition of nutrients can speed up the process. Small mead, sometimes called *short mead* (or marketed by meaderies as "session mead" or "craft mead"), can be ready to drink within weeks of starting fermentation. It's basically simple ale made with honey instead of sugar.

   Small meads made the traditional way (without the use of store-bought nutrients or other additives) should employ some sort of spice or fruit to cover up off flavors. Straight honey-water meads (known in mead-competition circles as a *show meads*) with no more additives than minimal flavor and fermentation enhancers (acids, tannins, and nutrients) often require several months of bottle aging to mellow out harsh or off flavors. Adding spices and larger amounts of citrus, and using a smaller ratio of honey to water, can make for a quicker drinkable mead. One popular citrus-and-spice combination is orange wedges with cinnamon, allspice, cloves, and ginger. This nearly fool-proof recipe makes for refreshing mead that drinks very much like a simple ale. Provided you keep to a similar honey-to-water ratio, you can experiment with all kinds of spices and citrus fruits. Think of the following as a blueprint that you can use to experiment to your heart's desire. Note that you can use any honey, but lighter varieties—such as wildflower honeys—work best. In place of the suggested spices, you can also visit your herb garden or go on a hike and collect whatever edible plants call out to you; flowers such as violets, dandelions, and rose of Sharon/hibiscus work well.

INGREDIENTS FOR 1 GALLON (4 L)

1½–2 pounds (0.75–1 kg) honey

1 gallon (4 L) springwater or filtered tap water

Brewing yeast, ale yeast, bread yeast, or barm

10–12 raisins or equivalent amount of other dried fruit

½ orange or lemon, cut into wedges, or ½ cup (125 mL) orange juice, or ¼ cup (60 mL) lemon juice

Suggested flavoring additions (use as many as you dare): 1 cinnamon stick, 2 cloves, 1 whole nutmeg, 2–4 thin slices ginger, 2 cardamom pods, ½ star anise pod

PROCESS

1. Mix the honey and warm water (60–70°F/15–21°C) in a 1-gallon (4 L) jug.
2. Place a lid (tightly) on the jug and shake it vigorously to aerate the *must*, or use a thin stirring implement such as a chopstick to stir it while carefully swirling the jug.
3. Add the flavoring ingredients.
4. Add the yeast or barm.
5. Place an airlock in the vessel and leave it in a warm, dark area to ferment for 2 to 3 weeks.

You can rack it halfway through the process and filter out the solids if you want. I usually give this mead 3 to 4 weeks and then start tasting it by carefully pouring a small glass. When I like it, I filter the solids out and pour the liquid into a container with a spigot, making sure to finish it off over the next week or two before it turns to vinegar. Another option is to transfer it to flip-top bottles while there is still some residual fermentation, adding just a bit of honey or sugar to ensure carbonation. Refrigerate after 24 hours and open carefully. Small meads are good to drink carbonated in the summer, or warmed as a mulled mead with additional spices and a slice or two of orange or lemon in the winter.

Juniper Small Mead/Digestif

This is a small mead clone of the Juniper Simple Ale/Digestif recipe if you would rather use honey instead of sugar.

INGREDIENTS FOR 1 GALLON (4 L)

1½–2 pounds (0.75–1 kg) wildflower honey or other light honey
1 gallon (4 L) springwater or filtered tap water
10–12 raisins or equivalent amount of other dried fruit
1 teaspoon dried wormwood
1 teaspoon dried mugwort
1 teaspoon caraway seeds
1 tablespoon juniper berries
Brewing yeast, ale yeast, bread yeast, or barm

A small mead in the works resting among several other meads.

PROCESS

1. Mix the honey and warm water (60–70°F/15–21°C) in a 1-gallon (4 L) jug.
2. Place a lid (tightly) on the jug and shake it vigorously to aerate the must, or use a thin stirring implement such as a chopstick to stir it while carefully swirling the jug.
3. Add the flavoring ingredients.
4. Add the yeast or barm.
5. Place an airlock in the vessel and leave it in a warm, dark area to ferment for 2 to 3 weeks.
6. Rack and filter, wait another week or two (sneaking samples to check its progress), bottle (if desired), and enjoy after a good meal.

Grain-Based Beers

Be sure to visit the sections on brewing with extract and all-grain brewing before tackling these. If you already know how to brew with grain, then have at it! Because I have already provided details on process in the techniques sections of chapter 8, I'll simply provide basic recipes here and note where anything varies from standard.

Wheats and Farmhouse Ales

> In order to brew authentic farmhouse ale, it may become necessary to depart from some deeply ingrained practices. . . . If we don't make the effort to experiment with a variety of brewing methods, we can get boxed in by habit and inflexibility.
>
> —*Phil Markowski,* Farmhouse Ales: Culture and Craftsmanship in the Belgian Tradition[1]

Farmhouse ales are a persnickety bunch. Belonging to Belgian and French traditions, their brewing processes stray from what is generally accepted for British and German beers. From fermentation temperatures, to ingredient selection and treatment, to using multi-strain yeast and bacteria cultures—brewing farmhouse ales is about finding the proper balance among art, creativity, and technicality. While brewers have come up with a somewhat clear definition of what exactly makes a farmhouse ale, if we want to be truly authentic, we can ignore it for the most part. This is because historic farmhouse ale was pretty much what it sounds like: a rustic ale brewed in a farmhouse as an extension of the harvest within a particular region. Recipes and resultant flavors varied both by season and by each farmer-brewer's unique approach. Due to the fact that these were "peasant ales" brewed in rural areas and weren't well documented, we know little about precisely how they were brewed. This isn't to say that there isn't a basic blueprint we can start with, but farmhouse ales brewed in your own home (whether or not you live in a farmhouse) should be about experimentation and working with local and seasonal ingredients to the best of your ability.

Farmhouse brews were usually made in the winter to store up a provision of beer for the busy sowing and harvesting seasons. For this reason, they needed to last through the following winter. Two primary ways of doing this were to increase the alcohol content and to boost the hopping rate. While hop-heavy beer was more refreshing, high-malt beer provided more nourishment.[2] Originating in the Flanders region of Belgium, these ales would eventually come to comprise two styles: the French *bière de garde* (beer for keeping) and the Belgian *saison* (season). Given the vast range of ingredients and flavoring characteristics that make up ales made in even these narrowed-down style definitions, the recipes I've experimented with may or may not approximate either. Think of it as brewing "in the spirit of the thing." Note that all of these recipes feature wheat, and all feature some amount of kettle or mash adjuncts. These were often characteristics of farmhouse brews, since wheat was a common grain to grow and harvest, and adjunct sugars were often added, for economic reasons if nothing else.

Spiced Saison

This brew drinks crisp and refreshing, with just the right amount of maltiness. The banana aroma typical of wheat beer is present but not overpowering, and everything is nicely balanced by the spice additions. Note: As with other recipes, I have truncated descriptions of the brewing process unless any of the steps differ from the description of the all-grain brewing process in chapter 8.

INGREDIENTS FOR 5 GALLONS (20 L)

Grains

6 pounds (3 kg) pilsner malt

2 pounds (1 kg) wheat malt

Extract Alternative

3 pounds (1.5 kg) plain light dry malt extract

3 pounds (1.5 kg) wheat dry malt extract

½ pound (0.25 kg) pilsner malt (steep for half an hour before the boil)

Flavoring Ingredients

1 ounce (28 g) Hallertau hops at 60 minutes

2 ounces (57 g) Indian sarsaparilla at 20 minutes

1 star anise pod at 20 minutes

Water, Yeast, and Kettle Adjuncts

6½ gallons (26 L) springwater or filtered tap water

Wheat or Belgian ale yeast, or barm

PROCESS

1. **All-grain:** Mash the grains for 1 hour at 145 to 155°F (63–68°C). Mash out, vorlauf, sparge, and gather 6 to 6½ gallons (24–26 L) of wort.

2. **All-grain and extract:** Boil the wort for 60 minutes, add ingredients according to the schedule, cool, add the yeast, ferment, prime, and bottle.

Wheat beer looks and tastes beautiful in a fluted glass.

Saison Spices

You can vary the spice additions for this brew to produce a wide range of flavors, with results that range from subtle to bold. As with hops, spices should be added so that their character is barely noticeable, with a result that is well balanced and teases you as to what exactly it is you taste with each drink. However, any ingredient can be increased by a couple of ounces (grams) if you would like that flavor to be the star. Remember, strongly flavored spices such as star anise, cloves, and ginger can easily become overpowering. You can use some or all of these ingredients depending on your preferences, and in whatever quantity you desire. And remember that the later you add them, the more pronounced their effect will be. Note that the amounts I recommend are for subtle effect in a 5-gallon (20 L) batch. Also, except where stated otherwise, the quantities are for amounts in powdered form (for best effect, they should be purchased whole and ground or crushed just before using).

Table 9.1. Spices for Saisons and Other Wheats

Spice	Notes and Recommended Amounts per 5 Gallons
Allspice	⅛ ounce (6 g) or 3–4 crushed seeds
Cardamom	2–3 whole pods
Cinnamon	1 ounce (28 g) or a 2- to 3-inch (5–7.5 cm) stick
Cloves	⅛ ounce (6 g) or 3–4 crushed seeds
Coriander	½ ounce (14 g); use Indian coriander if you can find it
Cumin	¼ ounce (7 g)
Curaçao (bitter orange)	½ ounce (14 g)
Ginger	2 ounces (57 g) usually does it for a subtle effect, but you can double or even triple if you want a more pronounced ginger flavor (note that this is for whole, fresh ginger; use about ½ teaspoon in powdered form)
Grains of paradise	¼ ounce (7 g)
Licorice root	½ ounce (14 g)
Nutmeg	⅛ ounce (6 g) or 1–2 crushed seeds
Star anise	1–2 pods coarsely crushed
Sweet orange peel	1 ounce (28 g)

Spiced Orange Wheat (Partial Mash)

This simple wheat uses mostly extract for those who want to play around with wheat flavors but don't want to invest in the time and effort of brewing an all-grain wheat. Oatmeal or unmalted wheat is often used in this type of brew for flavor and to provide a thick mouthfeel. You'll get more of this effect when brewing with all grain, but I've found that they still impart some pleasant notes when done as a partial mash. Take care to only use the zest (outer skin) of the orange, as including the white pith can make for a rather . . . challenging drink. Some of the juice can be used if you feel it needs a stronger orange flavor, but I recommend adding it in small amounts at bottling until you're satisfied with the taste.

INGREDIENTS FOR 5 GALLONS (20 L)

Grains

6 pounds (3 kg) wheat DME
1 pound (0.5 kg) pilsner malt
1 pound (0.5 kg) oatmeal (I usually use thick-rolled—because that's
    what I have on hand for my breakfast—but instant can impart
    more oatmeal character)

Flavoring Ingredients

½ ounce (14 g) Hallertau hops at 30 minutes
1 ounce (14 g) Tettnanger hops (or another low-alpha variety
    such as Saaz) at 30 minutes
½ ounce (14 g) Hallertau hops at 5 minutes
Zest of 2 oranges (or ½ ounce/14 g Curaçao) at 5 minutes
¼ ounce (7 g) grains of paradise at 5 minutes
2 ounces (57 g) fresh ginger at 5 minutes

Water, Yeast, and Kettle Adjuncts

6 gallons (24 L) springwater or filtered tap water
Wheat or Belgian ale yeast, or barm

PROCESS

1. Mash the grains and oatmeal in 2 gallons (8 L) of water for
    1 hour at 145 to 155°F (63–68°C). Remove the grain bag and let

any excess liquid drain back into the wort without excessively squeezing the grains.

2. Add another 4 gallons (16 L) of water, bring to a boil, cut off the heat, add in the extract grains, and bring the mixture back to a low boil while continuously stirring.

3. Boil the wort for 60 minutes, add ingredients according to the schedule, cool, add the yeast, ferment, prime, and bottle.

Juniper Herbal Wheat

This recipe employs some traditional flavors common to Scandinavian and other early ales. It's a good candidate for what early herbal beers would have tasted like. When first testing this recipe, I used wheat simply because I had a bag of it I needed to finish off, and because it was a common grain in early ales. I also added a bit of flaked barley to give it some heft, and some honey for extra fermentables.

INGREDIENTS FOR 1 GALLON (4 L)

Grains

1½ pounds (0.75 kg) wheat pale malt (or substitute 1½ pounds wheat or other DME)

1 pound (0.5 kg) flaked barley

Flavoring Ingredients

1 teaspoon dried yarrow at 30 minutes

2 teaspoons dried meadowsweet at 55 minutes

½ tablespoon juniper berries

1 cup (250 mL) raw honey (any variety; as close to from-the-hive as possible) at 60 minutes

Water, Yeast, and Kettle Adjuncts

2 gallons (8 L) springwater or filtered tap water (or 1 gallon/4 L for extract alternative)

English or Belgian ale yeast, or barm

ALL-GRAIN PROCESS

1. Steep the grains in a grain bag in 2 gallons (8 L) of water for 1 hour at 152 to 156°F (67–69°C). Remove the grain bag and let any

excess wort drain back into the pot without excessively squeezing the grains.

2. Open the bag and slowly pour in sparge water heated to 180°F (82°C), through a mesh screen if possible. Work the grains around with a spoon in between pours to break up the goop created by the flaked barley.

3. Set the bag in another pot, pouring whatever else drains into the extra pot into the boil kettle after it sits for a bit.

4. Bring the wort to a low boil while continuously stirring.

5. Boil for 60 minutes, adding ingredients according to the schedule, cool, rack into a fermenter, add the yeast, and ferment.

6. Drink this while it's still fermenting and cloudy (preferably with a meal) for the most authentic experience, or fully ferment, prime, and bottle.

EXTRACT PROCESS

1. Steep the flaked barley in a grain bag in 1 gallon (4 L) of water for half an hour at 152 to 156°F (67–69°C). Remove the grain bag and let any excess liquid drain back into the wort without excessively squeezing the grains.

2. Add the extract and stir until fully dissolved and settled into a gently rolling boil.

3. Boil the wort for 60 minutes, add ingredients according to the schedule, cool, add the yeast, ferment, prime, and bottle.

Sassafras Forest Wheat (Extract)

Sassafras has been used traditionally for medicinal and flavoring purposes for millennia. You can use sassafras flavoring if you prefer, but I like to use the real thing. I also like to add little bits of the forest when making this, such as spruce tips and oak bark. Sometimes I add ½ teaspoon of dried orange peel for flavoring, but the spruce usually provides enough citrus if you want to go with a true forest beer. A low-alpha hops (about ¼ ounce/7 g) can also be added 30 minutes into the boil if you desire. You can really take this basic formula and substitute various flavoring ingredients, malts, and yeasts to make what sounds good.

INGREDIENTS FOR 1 GALLON (4 L)

Grains

1 pound (0.5 kg) wheat DME (or substitute the same amount of pale malt for a pale ale, or cane sugar for a simple ale)

Flavoring Ingredients

1 teaspoon chipped sassafras root or bark
2 teaspoons oak bark cadmium at end of boil
1 spruce tip at end of boil
½ teaspoon dried orange peel (optional)

Water, Yeast, and Kettle Adjuncts

1 gallon (4 L) springwater or filtered tap water
Brewing, wheat, ale, or bread yeast, or barm

PROCESS

1. Bring the water just to a boil in a stockpot.
2. Stir in the DME or sugar until fully dissolved.
3. Add the sassafras.
4. Reduce the heat to maintain a slight boil.
5. If you're using hops, add about ¼ ounce (7 g) of a low-alpha hops such as Golding at 30 minutes.
6. After 60 minutes, cut off the heat, and add the remainder of the ingredients.
7. Cover, let cool, strain into a fermenter, add the yeast, ferment, prime, and bottle.

Early European and British Beers

To some degree all of the beers in this section are based on recipes that were common throughout Europe, but particularly in Britain, from the 18th century going back into the mists of time. Their common thread is that they are all malty, grain-based beers. Many feature adjuncts such as honey or molasses, and many are flavored with herbs and spices. Try a couple of them and sit back while you're sipping and mulling over the flavor, transporting yourself to a time when these beers nourished and brought enjoyment to many a person, whether in the home, while socializing in an alehouse, or in the cabin of a ship bound for distant lands.

Spruce Pale Ale (Extract/Mini Mash)

Although molasses and brown sugar are the core ingredients of simple ales, you can make excellent beers more suited to modern tastes using malted grains and malt extract (I do like to add a bit of molasses for a degree of authenticity, though). Nearly any style can be brewed with spruce, but lighter, malty styles such as pales and browns complement the flavor of spruce the best. You won't need to add hops, as spruce has its own preservative qualities, but a small amount to provide just a bit of hoppy bitterness and aroma isn't a bad idea. The proper time at which to add spruce tips is up for debate. Many modern spruce recipes call for adding them during the boil, just as with hops. I've made flavorful spruce beers this way with milder-flavored spruce, but subjecting them to the rigors of boiling can bring out strong, overly resinous flavors. Generally, it's best to add them after cutting off the boil and waiting around half an hour before cooling the wort. Or make a tea from the tips, taste the tea to determine its strength, and add it to the secondary fermentation.

INGREDIENTS FOR 5 GALLONS (20 L)

3 pounds (1.5 kg) dry light pale malt extract
1 pound (0.5 kg) crushed pilsner malt grains
2 pounds (1 kg) crushed pale malt grains
½ pound (0.25 kg) crushed Carapils malt grains
¼ pound (113 g) crushed caramel malt grains
1 pound (0.5 kg) blackstrap molasses
6 gallons (24 L) springwater or filtered tap water
1 ounce (28 g) low-alpha hops such as Saaz (optional)
4–6 spruce tips (more or less depending on the intensity of their smell/flavor)
British ale yeast, brewer's yeast, or barm

PROCESS

1. Steep the crushed grains in a grain bag or cheesecloth in 1½ gallons (6 L) of water at 145 to 155°F (63–68°C) for 1 hour. Remove the bag and set it in a strainer over the pot. Rinse the grain by pouring 2 quarts (2 L) of 180°F (82°C) water over it.

Drain the bag for 10 minutes, pressing gently with a spoon from time to time.

2. About halfway through the steeping process, start boiling 4 gallons (16 L) of water in a large brewpot. Stir in the extract until you have a low rolling boil with no foaming.

3. If you're adding hops, add ½ ounce (14 g) at 30 minutes.

4. At 60 minutes, add the remaining hops and spruce.

5. Give it 20 to 30 minutes before chilling to give the spruce flavor time to infuse into the wort. Alternatively, add 1 cup (250 mL) of spruce tea now or to the primary fermentation along with your yeast (or rehydrate your yeast in the spruce tea).

6. Cool, add the yeast, ferment, prime, and bottle.

Spiced Dark Ale

This beer comes close to being a porter, but I think of it more as a dark ale. You can vary its level of thickness by using a bit less or a bit more Blackprinz, or trying out some different adjunct dark malts. Keep in mind that Blackprinz was developed to be a dark malt with no bitterness, so other dark malts will impart more bitterness. Black Patent Malt (sometimes just "Black Malt") can be a good alternative. Its flavor is often described as "sharp" or "acrid," but I've only found it to be subtly so. Even in the amounts recommended here, the spices come through fairly strongly. In my mind they balance well with the bitterness of the dark grains, and the hops provide a nice counterbalance. Use less spices or add more hops if you don't want the spice flavor to come through as strong. This is the perfect ale to use for wassail (see chapter 2).

INGREDIENTS FOR 5 GALLONS (20 L)

Grains

10 pounds (5 kg) Light Munich malt
1 pound (0.5 kg) Blackprinz malt
1 pound (0.5 kg) beechwood smoked malt

Extract Alternative

8 pounds (4 kg) plain amber DME; steep remaining adjunct grains for half an hour before the boil

Flavoring Ingredients

1 ounce (28 g) East Kent Golding hops at 30 minutes

¼ ounce (7 g) grains of paradise at 5 minutes

¼ ounce (7 g) fenugreek at 5 minutes

3 pods cardamom at 5 minutes

¼ ounce (7 g) orange peel at 5 minutes

3 whole cloves at 5 minutes

4 whole allspice seeds at 5 minutes

1 cinnamon stick (about 2 inches/5 cm in length) at 5 minutes

Water, Yeast, and Kettle Adjuncts

6 gallons (24 L) springwater or filtered tap water

1 quart (1 L) wildflower honey (this beer can also handle a darker honey) at end of boil

1 pint (500 mL) molasses

British ale yeast, brewing yeast, or barm

PROCESS

1. **All grain:** Mash the grains for 1 hour at 145 to 155°F (63–68°C). Mash out, vorlauf, sparge, and gather 6 to 6½ gallons (24–26 L) of wort.

2. **All grain and extract:** Boil the wort for 60 minutes, add ingredients according to the schedule, cool, add the yeast, ferment, prime, and bottle.

A spiced dark ale ready to be drunk or warmed and made into a wassail . . . and then drunk.

Heather Ale

Although you can make ales with all manner of edible flowers, heather ale has its own special place in history and legend, covered in detail in chapter 2. You can make a pretty tasty version of this legendary ale, although it's hard to say if it has the same kick as the mind-altering heather ales supposedly made by the Picts, Scots, and Vikings. Wearing a kilt or Viking tunic, or covering yourself in blue paint and tattoos like the Picts while drinking it, may add to the effect. I've found that some dried heather can add a strong herbal flavor. Try to find the freshest heather you can, or consider making a tea from the flowers first to add before bottling and adjust to taste.

INGREDIENTS FOR 5 GALLONS (20 L)

Grains

8 pounds (4 kg) pale malt
¾ pound (0.4 kg) Briess Carapils malt
¾ pound (0.4 kg) caramel malt

Extract Alternative

6 pounds (3 kg) pale DME; steep remaining adjunct grains for half an
   hour before the boil

Flavoring Ingredients

¼ pound (113 g) dried heather tips at 55 minutes
1 ounce (28 g) Fuggle or other low-alpha hops (optional) at 30 minutes

Water, Yeast, and Kettle Adjuncts

6 gallons (24 L) springwater or filtered tap water
1 pound (0.5 kg) wildflower honey (heather if possible) at 60 minutes
British ale yeast, brewing yeast, or barm

PROCESS

1. **All grain:** Mash the grains for 1 hour at 145 to 155°F (63–68°C). Mash out, vorlauf, sparge, and gather 6 to 6½ gallons (24–26 L) of wort.
2. **All grain and extract:** Boil the wort for 60 minutes, add ingredients according to the schedule, cool, add the yeast, ferment, prime, and bottle.

Brewing with Honey:
Welsh Ales and Bragots

Honey-based beers, including bragots and Welsh ales, enjoy a long-standing tradition in the British Isles. Bragots have substantially more honey and can technically be considered mead as much as beer. Pegging down exactly what constitutes a Welsh ale can be difficult, but in later records it was shown to contain less honey than bragot, and by the 1800s it was brewed with no honey (or occasionally with brown sugar or molasses in place of honey).[3] It is almost definitely a direct ancestor of bragot, and is often referred to in Anglo-Saxon texts as sweet, strong, dark, or in one case as "glutinous, heady and soporific."[4] It was likely a high-malt brew, lending it strength, but also sweetness due to fermentation completing before the malt sugars were fully converted. Like bragot, honey may have been used in the initial fermentation, or as a sweetener before drinking. In addition, it may have had a smoky flavor, as the malt was often kilned over a fire.[5] Both bragot and Welsh ale were highly esteemed in Wales and Ireland, and often show up as payment for land rent, being worth more than standard ale and less than mead.[6] I've hunted down echoes of recipes in older texts, and have come across some more modern attempts at emulating them. The recipes included here are a combination of the two. The core ingredients in my Welsh-style ales and bragots are: brown malt (sometimes with a bit of roasted malt thrown in), smoked malt, honey, molasses or brown sugar, grains of paradise, and a few additional spices such as ginger, cinnamon, licorice root, or cloves. As with any style, use these recipes as starting points to modify as you please since there are no hard-and-fast rules. I will differentiate each type of Welsh ale with a name that most accurately resembles its overall coloring and flavor profile.

Welsh Brown Ale

Brown ales were originally an all-malt British style of ale, although their strength, flavoring, and many other factors varied. Because this recipe produces a brown, almost copper-colored ale I thought this was the best designation for it.

INGREDIENTS FOR 5 GALLONS (20 L)

Grains

10 pounds (5 kg) Muntons Maris Otter malt (or other pale malt)
1 pound (0.5 kg) cherrywood-smoked malt
1 pound (0.5 kg) Briess Carapils malt
1 pound (0.5 kg) caramel malt

Extract Alternative

8 pounds (4 kg) plain amber DME; steep remaining adjunct grains for
   half an hour before the boil

Flavoring Ingredients

1 ounce (28 g) Fuggle hops at 60 minutes
¼ ounce (7 g) grains of paradise at 5 minutes
¼ ounce (7 g) licorice root at 5 minutes
3 pods cardamom at 5 minutes
¼ ounce (7 g) coriander at 5 minutes
2 whole cloves at 5 minutes
2 whole nutmeg seeds at 5 minutes
1 ounce (28 g) fresh ginger at 5 minutes

Water, Yeast, and Kettle Adjuncts

6 gallons (24 L) springwater or filtered tap water
1 quart (1 L) wildflower or other light honey at end of boil
British ale yeast, brewing yeast, or barm

PROCESS

1. **All grain:** Mash the grains for 1 hour at 145 to 155°F (63–68°C). Mash out, vorlauf, sparge, and gather 6 to 6½ gallons (24–26 L) of wort.
2. **All grain and extract:** Boil the wort for 60 minutes, add ingredients according to the schedule, cool, add the yeast, ferment, prime, and bottle.

Welsh Porter

This one always gets rave reviews from tasters. It's definitely a meal of a beer. Very dark and thick, it lies somewhere between a porter and a stout. The combination of chocolate malt with cherry wood malt gives it a strong, smooth flavor without being overwhelming. Even though it feels like a meal-and-a-half going down, I find myself immediately craving another.

INGREDIENTS FOR 5 GALLONS (20 L)

Grains

10 pounds (5 kg) pale ale malt

1 pound (0.5 kg) cherrywood-smoked malt

1 pound (0.5 kg) chocolate malt

Extract Alternative

6 pounds (3 kg) plain amber DME; steep remaining adjunct grains for half an hour before the boil

Flavoring Ingredients

1 ounce (28 g) Fuggle hops at 60 minutes

¼ ounce (7 g) grains of paradise at 5 minutes

¼ ounce (7 g) licorice root at 5 minutes

Water, Yeast, and Kettle Adjuncts

6 gallons (24 L) springwater or filtered tap water

1 quart (1 L) wildflower or other light honey at end of boil

British ale yeast, brewing yeast, or barm

PROCESS

1. **All grain:** Mash the grains for 1 hour at 145 to 155°F (63–68°C). Mash out, vorlauf, sparge, and gather 6 to 6½ gallons (24–26 L) of wort.
2. **All grain and extract:** Boil the wort for 60 minutes, add ingredients according to the schedule, cool, add the yeast, ferment, prime, and bottle.

Spiced Bragot (Extract)

This basic, pale ale extract bragot can be modified as you desire with different extracts, honeys, herbs and spices, and hops. You can pretty much add this same amount of honey to any beer to make it a bragot. Just be sure to use a yeast that can handle the high alcohol content (usually around 10 to 14 percent ABV). Since bragots were traditionally spiced, this recipe calls for only spices. Hops were eventually added, though, and modern bragots often contain hops. Most bragots can handle a high level of mid- to high-alpha hops, but will need to be aged six months to a year for the hop bitterness to mellow out. Consider experimenting with additional spices, but go light.

INGREDIENTS FOR 5 GALLONS (20L)

Grains

6 pounds (3 kg) plain amber DME
2 pounds (1 kg) pale DME

Flavoring Ingredients

½ ounce (14 g) grains of paradise at 5 minutes
½ ounce (14 g) chopped fresh or candied ginger at 5 minutes
2 whole cloves at 5 minutes
1 cinnamon stick (about 2 inches/5 cm in length) at 5 minutes
1 cup raisins at 60 minutes

Water, Yeast, and Kettle Adjuncts

6 gallons (24 L) springwater or filtered tap water
9–12 pounds (4.5–6 kg) light- to medium-bodied honey such as sourwood or wildflower at 60 minutes
2 packets (10 g) Lalvin ICV D47 wine yeast or Safale US-05 ale yeast (you can also use 2 cups/500 mL barm, but keep in mind this will require a high-alcohol-tolerant yeast)

PROCESS

1. Bring the water to a boil, carefully add the extract, and stir constantly to keep the wort from sticking to the bottom.
2. Once you have a steady boil and are past the danger of overboil, set a timer for 60 minutes.
3. Add ingredients according to the schedule.
4. Cut off the heat, chill the liquid to pitching temperature, and rack into a 5- to 6-gallon (20–24 L) fermentation vessel (preferably a bucket), being sure to splash as much as possible to aerate the wort.
5. Add the yeast and place a cloth over the bucket, leaving in an open fermenter for 12 to 24 hours to ensure sufficient aeration.

6. Once it starts fermenting, monitor it and clean up any messes (these can produce a lot of krausen).
7. When fermentation slows down after about a week, rack to a secondary fermenter and monitor until fermentation is complete (a clarified, still beer, or a steady reading on a hydrometer for a couple of days).
8. Rack into a bottling bucket and prime with ½ cup (125 mL) of honey (you can also leave out priming and drink this still like a wine).
9. Bottle and try to age for at least a few months, if not longer.
10. Drink it like a Viking . . . or a Yeti.

Nordic Beers

This section is woefully deficient in fully embracing the gamut of styles and variations on styles in what is an extremely rich history of brewing in Northern Europe. Like French and Belgian farmhouse brewing, what makes each style presented here "proper" is elusive, as each region and each brewer had a unique style, brewing technique, and heirloom yeast strain. I'll cover the basics of what most of these brews have in common and then provide some information and recipes on how you can work to emulate variations on each style in your own "farmhouse."

The best-known traditional Northern European beer is Finnish sahti, but other related beers exist in Nordic and Baltic countries (Scandinavian and Baltic countries are connected by the Baltic Sea and have experienced much cross-migration and integration throughout history), including: koduõlu in Estonia, gotlandsdricka in Sweden, maltøl in Norway, and kaimiškas in Lithuania.[7] In addition, Germany has traditional beers that are more like farmhouse brews than they are the regimented Reinheitsgebot beers. These include *rauchbier* (smoked beer) and gose (which was traditionally a spontaneously fermented, cold-mashed beer).

Appalachian Sahti

Since I live at the foothills of the Appalachian mountain range, I prefer to think of my sahtis as Appalachian variants on Finnish brews. I can procure pretty much all of the ingredients locally—including herbs—and bread yeast, wild yeast, and barm are no problem, so really the only thing missing is my not being in Finland. Since eastern red cedar is actually a type of juniper, I can procure it locally, although I prefer to use spruce tips for flavoring, as the flavor of North American juniper isn't quite the same as the Scandinavian variant. I'm not always able to obtain my grains locally, but while there may be some differences in the way they're grown and roasted in Finland, I'm still using pretty much the same types of grains that a Finn would use. Note that much of what makes a "proper" sahti is the process of brewing with all grains and whole ingredients; you can come close to the flavor with extract but I recommend going as all-grain as possible if you want it to feel and taste more authentic.

INGREDIENTS FOR 5 GALLONS (20 L)

Grains

5 pounds (2.5 kg) pilsner malt
4 pounds (2 kg) light Munich malt
1 pound (0.5 kg) rye malt

Extract Alternative

6 pounds (3 kg) plain amber DME; steep remaining adjunct grains
    for half an hour before the boil
1 pound (0.5 kg) rye malt

Flavoring Ingredients

Several juniper branches, 2–4 feet in length (0.6–1.2 m); use eastern
    red cedar in the eastern US, Rocky Mountain juniper in the
    western US, or spruce if you can't locate either
1 ounce (28 g) crushed dried juniper berries (or substitute
    hawthorn berries)
¼ ounce (7 g) meadowsweet flowers at end of boil
¼ ounce (7 g) yarrow flowers at end of boil
1 ounce (28 g) Saaz or other low-alpha hops (optional) at 60 minutes
Optional (for stone-beer method): 4–5 solid, non-porous rocks
    (see sidebar in chapter 8), such as granite, that will fit with ease
    into your mash tun and kettle

Water, Yeast, and Kettle Adjuncts

6 gallons (24 L) springwater or filtered tap water

Sahti

To enjoy a "true" sahti, you'll probably have to travel to Finland. Beer produced in this style is so tied to the land and regional yeast strains that it would be very difficult to reproduce it authentically. On top of that, it's not known for its ability to keep and is usually drunk young. As Petteri Lähdeniemi of Finlandia Sahti (one of the few commercial sahti breweries) noted in a 2016 interview, "You can travel across Finland and find all different kinds of sahti. Some would argue that sahti has many sub-categories and prefer to call it just 'ancient beer' rather than sahti because of the various styles."[8]

Ales in the sahti vein are often made of both malted and unmalted grains. Barley is most common, but rye, oats, and wheat are also sometimes used as adjuncts. One thing that seems near universal is the use of juniper (the branches are used as a grain-bed filter, and berries are sometimes used as well). A sort of poor man's sahti was sometimes produced by boiling juniper twigs and berries down to an extract, or blending sugar, water, and juniper twigs, and fermenting the mixture with baker's yeast. No malt was used other than sometimes very small amounts for flavor.[9] In some cases alder twigs were used, or alder bark shavings added to the brew to improve its flavor or act as a preservative.[10] While the yeast used for sahti was traditionally an heirloom strain unique to each brewer, these days it is usually bread yeast (the same yeast was traditionally used for both brewing and baking). While you may get close with a standard ale yeast, you'd get a better approximation of true sahti by using a Finnish baker's yeast. I have read on homebrewing forums that the difference in flavor between sahti brewed with Finnish baker's yeast and that brewed

Bread or wheat yeast, or barm
1 quart (1 L) wildflower or other light honey at end of boil

PROCESS (ALL-GRAIN, STEINBIER METHOD)

1. Prepare a pit, line it with rocks or bricks to retain heat and keep dirt off your heating stones, and place the stones on the bricks.

with other strains is so minimal that there isn't much reason to go to the effort unless you want to be truly authentic. One characteristic that Finnish yeast produces is high levels of phenol, which imparts a banana-like aroma akin to what is found in Hefeweizens and some Belgian brews, so you could probably get away with using a Hefeweizen or Belgian yeast strain. Or create a yeast starter and ferment it with your own house strain!

While some sahti brewers today use hops to make sahti more palatable to modern tastes, they weren't traditionally used (except sometimes in very small amounts for their antiseptic effects). Many of the same herbs we find in herbal beers were used, although the actual evidence of which herbs were used, how much, when they were gathered, and when they were added to the boil (or even to the malt) is frustratingly lacking. I tend to just go with the herbs that work for my other herbal brews and hope I'm at least being somewhat respectful of tradition. Some herbs that we can say with a fair bit of confidence were used include Saint-John's-wort (*Hypericum maculatum*), bog myrtle (*Myrica gale*), yarrow (*Achillea millefolium*), tansy (*Tanacetum vulgare*), and caraway (*Carum carvi*).[11]

Traditionally, sahti—and all Finnish brews for that matter—was made at home in two large wooden vessels; one served as a mash tun, and the other was a troughlike vessel (*kuurna*) used for lautering. Since it would be a fire hazard to heat a wooden vessel from the outside, brewers would use the hot-rock method to heat the mash. The only heat came from the rock. Some modern sahti brewers boil the mash rather than the wort as a nod to this tradition, while others boil the wort (anywhere from one minute to five hours). This results in a beer with a short shelf life, but it also has an interesting grainy texture and flavor, and a wholesome, nutritious body much like the fabled "beer as food" of yore.[12]

Build a fire and stoke it for 2 to 3 hours, allowing coals to build over the rocks.

2. Grind the malt, lay some juniper or spruce branches at the bottom of the mash tun, pour in about one-quarter of the grain, set more branches in the mash tun vertically, and pour in the rest of the grain.

3. Start heating 3 gallons (12 L) of water in a pot over the fire around an hour before mashing the grains.

4. Slowly lower one of the larger rocks into the strike water, preferably with a perforated metal basket.

5. Place the rock back in the fire and pour enough of the water over the grains to just cover them. Then place one of your smaller rocks in the center of the mash tun using tongs, taking care to avoid touching the sides.

6. Quickly place a lid on the mash tun and provide additional insulation by whatever means you can (such as by wrapping it with a blanket). You may need up to 2 hours to get sufficient enzyme conversion. Resist the urge to be scientific. I have monitored my mash with a thermometer and, while at times I barely reached 140°F (60°C), I still drew off a wort that produced a tasty (albeit cloudy and grainy) beer of around 3 to 5 percent ABV. To raise the temperature, you can place the rock back in the fire and substitute

I like to drink my sahti and other ancient cloudy beers in a stein or mug, as glasses were used more once people learned to appreciate the look of a clarified beer.

one of the other rocks, but try to approach this from an ancient perspective and don't stress the technical details.

7. Alternatively, perform a multiple-step infusion mash using whichever heating method you desire, including rocks. First, heat your strike water to 134°F (57°C) and blend with the grains in your mash tun. Every 15 to 20 minutes, pour small amounts of near-boiling (200°F/93°C) water over the mash to slowly raise the temperature. Do this four or five times until you reach a mash-out temperature of about 160°F (71°C).

8. Once you're comfortable that you've received a full-enough conversion (remember, this isn't the most efficient method for achieving full conversion), mash out, vorlauf, sparge, and gather 5½ to 6 gallons (22–24 L) of wort.

9. To boil the wort with rocks, place hot rocks carefully in the water (it doesn't hurt to wear protective clothing and goggles in case they shatter). Prepare for lots of hissing and steaming. You're not going to get a long boil this way, and may not even quite reach the boiling point, but you'll definitely be cooking the wort. Feel free to stoke the fire some more and cook the wort over a grate (or on a large, flat rock in the fire).

10. If you're doing a standard boil, add the flavoring ingredients at the end, or steep them for 15 minutes to half an hour if you're heating the old-fashioned way. Add honey (optional) after the boil or just before adding the yeast.

11. Allow the wort to cool until it's warm to the back of your hand (or speed it up with a wort chiller), rack and filter out the solids, add the yeast, and ferment.

DRINKING AND BOTTLING

Sahti is traditionally drunk young, either flat or while still fermenting. I begin sampling mine about three days after initiating fermentation. It has a malty and not-at-all-cloying sweetness with just a hint of bitterness. I find it very refreshing at this stage. The grain flavor is definitely present—it really does feel like you're drinking a meal. I still like it when it goes flat, but usually reserve a couple of gallons to bottle-carbonate. With the preservative power of the honey and herbs, it keeps as long as a standard beer, although sometimes it picks up a hint of sourness.

Gotlandsdricka and Rauchbier

Rauchbier is German for "smoked beer" and hence is more of a process description than an actual style. Gotlandsdricka is a Swedish ale made with smoked malt. It also sometimes incorporates honey, making it similar to Welsh ale. Prior to the industrial revolution, most beers were smoked beers, as malt was smoked as part of the process of drying and roasting it over a fire. In some regions of Germany and Sweden, the tradition of smoking malt stuck around, hence we have some smoked beer styles. Pretty much any style of beer can be a rauchbier, although traditionally they were barley-based lagers like Helles and Märzen.

Gotlandsdricka's name comes from the remote island of Gotland off the southeast coast of Sweden in the Baltic Sea. *Gotland* means "good land" and *dricka* means "drink." So, essentially, this is "Gotland's drink." One of its primary flavoring components is juniper branches, which also

Smoking malt using indirect heat to avoid overly charring the malt. I smoke my Scandinavian brews with a bit of soaked juniper or spruce branch along with the wood chips.

serve as a mash tun filter as with Finnish sahti. Also like sahti, this is a farmhouse brew, and has been brewed in various forms for generations, with each farmhouse/family having its own recipe. Some say this style dates as far back as the Vikings, although I haven't seen any direct evidence for this. We can assume that the methods and recipes that have been passed down had their roots in Viking times, but until I see direct archaeological evidence for this I'll just go with "this is probably how the Vikings did it." The methods and ingredients are fairly similar to those of sahti, with some variations.

The first step for any smoked beer is to of course smoke the malt. You can purchase smoked malt, but the commercial versions I've used have never been very smoky. I smoke my own in my smoker via the indirect-heat method by placing the malt in a metal pan on one side and heating a couple of pieces of charcoal on the other. I then take juniper or red cedar branches and chunks of wood such as hickory or mesquite that I soak thoroughly in water beforehand, and drop a couple on the coals every hour or so. Traditionally (and still today in Gotland), the malt was smoked over a fire for about a week. Beechwood is often referenced in brewing literature but people likely used whatever wood was available. I find that smoking my malt for four to five hours and then leaving it in the smoker overnight once the coals have died down imparts enough smoky flavor. I usually let it get hot enough for some of the grains to roast as well. The following recipe is my own take on the brew.

INGREDIENTS FOR 5 GALLONS (20 L)

Grains

6 pounds (3 kg) pale barley malt
4 pounds (2 kg) rye malt (smoke all or a portion of it, or replace
    1 pound/0.5 kg of it with 1 pound of any commercial smoked malt)
1 pound (0.5 kg) unmalted flaked wheat
½ pound (0.25 kg) rice hulls (optional; for extra filtering due to
    the wheat)

Extract Alternative

6 pounds (3 kg) plain amber DME
1 pound (0.5 kg) rye malt, smoked (steep for half an hour before
    the boil)

Flavoring Ingredients

Several juniper branches, 2–4 feet (0.6–1.2 m) in length; use eastern
red cedar in the eastern US, Rocky Mountain juniper in the
western US, or spruce/pine if you can't locate either

1 ounce (28 g) crushed dried juniper berries (or substitute
hawthorn berries)

¼ ounce (7 g) meadowsweet flowers at end of boil

¼ ounce (7 g) yarrow flowers at end of boil

1 ounce (28 g) Saaz or other low-alpha hops (optional) at 60 minutes

Optional (for stone-beer method): 4–5 solid, nonporous rocks (see
sidebar in chapter 8), such as granite, that will fit with ease into
your mash tun and kettle

Water, Yeast, and Kettle Adjuncts

6 gallons (24 L) springwater or filtered tap water

Bread or wheat yeast, or barm

1 quart (1 L) wildflower or other light honey at end of boil

PROCESS (ALL-GRAIN, STEINBIER METHOD)

1. Prepare a pit, line it with rocks or bricks to retain heat and keep
   dirt off your heating stones, and place the stones on the bricks.
   Build a fire and stoke it for 2 to 3 hours, allowing coals to build
   over the rocks.

2. Make a porridge from the malted wheat while you're waiting,
   cooking over low heat for at least half an hour, stirring regularly.

3. Smoke and grind the malt, lay some juniper branches at the bottom
   of the mash tun, pour in about one-quarter of the grain, set more
   branches in the mash tun vertically, add the wheat porridge and
   rice hulls, and pour in the rest of the grain.

4. Start heating 3 gallons (12 L) of water in a pot over the fire around
   an hour before mashing the grains.

5. Slowly lower one of the larger rocks into the strike water, preferably with a perforated metal basket.

6. Place the rock back in the fire and pour enough of the water over
   the grains to just cover them. Then place one of your smaller rocks
   in the center of the mash tun using tongs, taking care to avoid
   touching the sides.

7. Quickly place a lid on the mash tun and provide additional insulation by whatever means you can (such as by wrapping it with a blanket). Give it 2 hours to get as much enzyme conversion as possible if you're able.

8. Once you're comfortable that you've received as full a conversion as you can, mash out, vorlauf, sparge, and gather 5½ to 6 gallons (22–24 L) of wort. The gravity for this can vary, but I usually get around 1.030 to 1.050. Remember, it can always be increased with additional honey or sugar.

9. To boil the wort with rocks, place hot rocks carefully in the water (it doesn't hurt to wear protective clothing and goggles should they shatter). Prepare for lots of hissing and steaming. You're not going to get a long boil this way, and may not even quite reach the boiling point, but you'll definitely be cooking the wort. Feel free to stoke the fire some more and cook the wort over a grate (or on a large, flat rock in the fire).

10. If you're doing a standard boil, add the flavoring ingredients at the end, or steep them for 15 minutes to half an hour if you're heating the old-fashioned way. Add honey (optional) after the boil or just before adding the yeast.

11. Allow the wort to cool until it's warm to the back of your hand (or speed it up with a wort chiller), rack and filter out the solids, add the yeast, and ferment.

DRINKING AND BOTTLING

This drinks very similarly to sahti, depending on which yeast you use, how much wort extraction you managed, and other factors. Drink it slowly with a meal, or make a tea of whichever herbs you have on hand with a bit of honey just before drinking if you feel the flavor isn't quite to your liking. This can sometimes be a rather tasty brew and other times it can be . . . unique, due to the many difficult-to-control factors that come with traditional heating methods. However, you can adjust any of the factors you desire by using the rocks for heating only one portion of the process (I recommend the wort in this case), skipping the juniper branches, using spruce instead, and so on. Remember, this is farmhouse brewing. Come up with your own recipe and technique and save the yeast for future batches if you like it. Start your own tradition!

Indigenous American / South American and Corn-Based Beers

There are various ways to brew with corn, and chicha is as good a place as any to start. This is a purely corn-based brew, although it is often flavored with fruit such as pineapple or berries (which technically makes it a *fruitillada*). It can be served sweet, young, and barely fermented, or fermented into alcohol and drunk dry with just a bit of sweetness (and varying degrees of sour). I prefer the traditional way of drawing out the enzymes and sugars through the introduction of saliva, but it's not always easy to convince people to join you in a chewing and spitting party, let alone convince them to drink the final product. Hence I make 1-gallon batches, which means I don't have to chew as much and can keep it all to myself, except for my braver acquaintances. Really, though, if you can get past the squeamishness of the initial chewing, there's nothing to be concerned about, as any germs in the saliva are long gone by the time the chicha is boiled and fermented.

Chicha de Muko

When made with the spit method, you are making *Chicha de Muko* (*muko* is the term for the spitballs of corn). For a more modern (but still ancient) interpretation of chicha complete with barley grains, I recommend the book *Ancient Brews Rediscovered and Re-Created* by Patrick McGovern, which has a homebrew recipe that he and Sam Calagione of Dogfish Head Brewery created.

INGREDIENTS FOR 1 GALLON (4 L)

1 pound (0.5 kg) whole organic purple corn kernels, plus an extra ½ pound (0.25 kg) or so, as you will lose some during the chewing process; or use 1 pound (0.5 kg) malted corn for chicha without spittle

2¾ gallons (11 L) springwater or filtered tap water

1 cup (150 g) grits or polenta, ¼ pound (113 g) flaked corn, or ¼ pound (113 g) feed corn

½ pound (0.25 kg) piloncillo or light brown sugar

Cinnamon, cloves, Curaçao, coriander, etc. (optional)

¼ pineapple, 2 slices (no peel) of an orange, 1 pint (220 g) straw-
berries or any other berry, and 1 pint (220 g) mango chunks or
any other fruit to make a fruitillada, a delicious traditional South
American corn beer with fruit (optional)
Brewing yeast or ale yeast (Belgian yeast is good for this), or barm

PROCESS (SKIP TO STEP 5 IF USING MALTED CORN)

1. Rinse and then cook the corn on low heat in just enough water to
   cover it for 1 to 2 hours, or until it is soft enough to chew; or soak it
   in warm water overnight. An alternative method is to coarsely grind
   the corn in a blender first, though I've found this creates a powdery
   mess that is even more unpleasant than chewing whole corn.
2. Chew, chew, chew and spit, spit, spit. Try to keep the saliva from
   dispersing too much into the corn and causing it to liquefy. The
   best way to do this is to form a ball from it by placing it between
   your tongue and the top of your mouth. This also keeps it from the
   back of your mouth, preventing you from swallowing it or gagging.
   Keep in mind throughout the process that moistened purple corn
   creates purple liquid and splattering is inevitable. Be prepared to
   clean up or blame someone else if you forget to.
3. Place the spitballs/muko on a cookie sheet or dehydrator drying rack
   and dry them in an oven, in a dehydrator, or out in the sun. Once
   they're fully dry, keep them in a cool, dry area until you've accumulated
   enough. Give yourself several days, or even weeks, to do this. Even
   with the help of friends, this is a slow process and will drive you nuts
   with its jaw-numbing repetition if you try to do it all in one sitting.
4. When you're finally ready for brew day, start by heating 2 quarts
   (2 L) of water. Add the grits, polenta, or flaked/feed corn to the
   water and stir well. Heat the mixture on medium-low heat, stirring
   regularly to keep the corn from sticking to the bottom.
5. Next, heat 2 gallons (8 L) of water to 160°F (71°C) in a large
   stockpot. Place the muko and corn porridge in a grain bag, breaking
   apart any stuck-together corn into small chunks. Steep the bag in
   the pot for 1 hour at 150 to 155°F (66–68°C). Take care to not let
   the bottom of the bag stick to the bottom and burn by using a false
   bottom or metal spoons, and raise the bag up and down a few times
   every 15 minutes to help disperse the wort sugars.

6. Lift the bag, sparge with 1 quart (1 L) of 180°F (82°C) water, and allow to fully drain. It doesn't hurt to have an extra pot on hand to minimize the mess. Drain about 1 quart into the extra pot and then have a helper pour it back over the grain bag to draw out any extra sugars.
7. Add the piloncillo or brown sugar, and stir to dissolve.
8. Boil the mixture for an hour, stirring occasionally.
9. Add the optional spices in a spice bag at the end of the boil.
10. Remove from the heat, cool for half an hour, and add the flavoring fruit. If you're using fruit for wild yeast, save some or all for the transfer to the fermentation vessel.
11. Transfer to an openmouthed crock or jar, cover with a cloth, and stir a couple of times daily for about a week.
12. Ladle into cups straight from the crock/jar and drink while still fermenting, or proceed to the next step.
13. Rack into a 1-gallon (4 L) glass jug and allow it to clarify and further ferment for 3 to 4 days. Either way, it should reach around 3 to 4 percent ABV.
14. Prime with ½ cup (100 g) of cane sugar, and bottle.
15. Whether you're drinking straight from the fermenter or bottling, drink it as soon as possible, as it will sour with age due to the lack of antibacterial ingredients. I prefer this the traditional way, straight from the fermenter while still fermenting. It's sweet, delicious, and mildly alcoholic.

Modernized Chicha BiaB

For those who can't handle the thought of saliva beer, you can malt the corn as detailed in "Malt Your Own Grain at Home," a sidebar in chapter 3.

INGREDIENTS FOR 3 GALLONS (12 L)

3 pounds (1.5 kg) purple corn kernels
5 gallons (20 L) springwater or filtered tap water (approximate; you'll lose some in the mash)
1 pound (0.5 kg) flaked corn, or 4 cups (600 g) precooked grits or polenta
4 pounds (2 kg) pale malt
1 pound (0.5 kg) piloncillo or light brown sugar

Muko balls soaked with saliva and ready for drying.

A 1-gallon (4 L) batch of chicha being brewed.

Corn can also be malted as an alternative to the chew-and-spit method.

¼ ounce (7 g) coriander at 5 minutes (feel free to add similar amounts of spices such as cinnamon, cloves, or Curaçao)
1 ounce (28 g) low-alpha hops such as Willamette or Fuggle at 60 minutes
Varying amounts of fruit for flavoring or wild yeast (optional)
Brewing yeast or Belgian ale yeast (any ale yeast will do), or barm

PROCESS

1. Malt the corn a couple of days in advance (see the sidebar in chapter 3).
2. Bring 3 gallons (12 L) of water to 180°F (82°C). Add the flaked corn, grits, or polenta, the malted ground purple corn, and the

ground malt to a bag, lower it into the water, and let it steep at 150 to 155°F (66–68°C) for 1 hour.

3. Lift the bag and sparge with 1 gallon (4 L) of 180°F/82°C water. Drain the bag, set it aside in an extra pot, and add whatever drains out of it to the boil.

4. Add the piloncillo or brown sugar, and stir to dissolve.

5. Boil the wort for 60 minutes, and add ingredients according to the schedule.

6. Remove from the heat, cool for half an hour, and add optional flavoring fruit.

7. Cool, add the yeast, ferment, prime, and bottle. This will hold up longer than traditional chicha due to the hops but it still has a short shelf life (try to drink it all within a month or two).

The traditional way to drink chicha, fruitillada, or any of its variants is to first pour some on the ground to give the earth its share, then offer some to the *apus* (mountain spirits) by blowing a bit from your glass into the wind. Next, greet your fellow drinkers with whatever greeting or toast you desire and clink your glasses together. While drinking it, be sure to exclaim "Chichitaaaaaa, chicherooooo!" after every couple of sips.[13]

Fruit and Vegetable Beers

I've outlined the technique for brewing with fruits and vegetables in chapter 7, so I won't go into too much detail here. I've included two recipes for you to try, and suggest substitutions of similar ingredients if you want to experiment further or don't have access to some of the ingredients.

Pawpaw Wheat (Extract)/Simple Ale

If you're not familiar with the pawpaw (*Asimina triloba*), I highly recommend the book *Pawpaw: In Search of America's Forgotten Fruit* by Andrew Moore. It's a well-informed and engaging love song to this all-American fruit as well as a travelogue through the regions of North America where the pawpaw is prevalent. Although sometimes found in outlying areas, it tends to grow as far south as Louisiana and Alabama, as far north as

Slice each pawpaw in half (or peel the skin off), deseed, lick your fingers clean, add to the wort after cutting off the boil, and drink when ready.

Michigan and Illinois, as far west as Kansas, and it spreads nearly to the Atlantic on the East Coast. "Pawpaws are a river fruit," says Moore. "They grow under many conditions and in many climates, but they're most abundant and reliably found growing in the deep alluvial soil of American bottomlands, along creeks, streams, and great rivers from the mighty Mississippi to the Wabash, Susquehanna, Missouri, and Potomac."[14] I'm lucky enough to live in a region (eastern Kentucky) where they are prevalent.

To be honest, I was only vaguely aware of pawpaws when I was growing up. After I read Andy's book and met him, his passion for the pawpaw rubbed off and I began to seek out pawpaw trees. Turns out I didn't have to go much farther than my front door to find groves of pawpaw trees along creeksides and even in public fruit tree groves. During their peak season (around mid-August to early September in my region) I watch for them to fall to the ground and snatch them up before someone else does, freezing them until I have enough for beer. Admittedly, it's difficult not to eat them right from the ground. Opinions vary as to what constitutes a perfectly ripe pawpaw, but they're a persnickety fruit and have no interest in ripening on the tree. Rock-hard until just before falling, they go through a period of soft ripeness with a bright yellow, custardlike filling. I prefer them at this stage for brewing, but letting them turn brown—which some people like to do—works fine, too. For this recipe you can swap out pawpaws for the same amounts of mango or banana, which are as close as it gets to similar-tasting fruits. I've also used persimmons in similar recipes. This beer can reach a level of sourness that doesn't appeal to everyone. You can minimize this by adding a bit of hops or another preservative/bittering herb such as mugwort or yarrow. Or drink it within a couple of days of fermenting for a low-alcohol, sweet, and very refreshing lightly fermented ale.

INGREDIENTS FOR 1 GALLON (4 L)

2 pounds (1 kg) pawpaws, mangoes, bananas, or persimmons
1 gallon (4 L) springwater or filtered tap water
1 pound (0.5 kg) wheat DME (or substitute cane sugar for a simple ale)
½ ounce (15 g) low-alpha hops such as Willamette or Fuggle (optional)
½ ounce (15 g) fresh or ¼ ounce (7 g) dried mugwort or yarrow leaves
   (optional)

Pawpaw or mango beer makes for a refreshing summer drink, particularly with a slice of orange.

½ teaspoon crushed coriander
Juice of ½ small lemon, or 2 ounces (60 mL) lemon juice
Wheat, Belgian or bread yeast, or barm

PROCESS (SKIP TO STEP 5 IF USING MALTED CORN)

1. Peel and deseed (if you're using pawpaws or mangoes) the fruit and set aside.
2. Bring the water to a barely rolling boil and stir in the extract or sugar.
3. Add the optional bittering herbs and boil for half an hour.
4. Cut off the heat and add the coriander, lemon juice, and fruit.
5. Let the mixture cool, then transfer everything, fruit and all, to a bucket, crock, or other widemouthed fermenter (this can produce a lot of krausen) and sprinkle the yeast over the surface.
6. Place the fermenter in a warm area with a cloth over it for 24 hours or until fermentation slows down.
7. Filter out the solids and rack to a 1-gallon (4 L) jug with airlock.
8. Prime with 2 tablespoons of cane sugar, and bottle.

Rhubarb Ginger/Simple Ale

I planted some rhubarb in a corner of the garden on a whim one year, primarily to use for brewing. If you plant it, be aware that it's a hardy perennial and will stick around for quite a while. I tend to harvest mine in late spring and freeze it if I don't use it right away. I've made rhubarb wine so I figured I may as well give beer a try. You can make a fairly authentic Belgian ale with rhubarb, as it will give the ale that characteristic Belgian tang due to its high level of tartness. As with pawpaw beer, bittering herbs or hops can be used to counteract any souring.

INGREDIENTS FOR 1 GALLON (4 L)

6–7 stalks rhubarb
1 gallon (4 L) springwater or filtered tap water
1 pound (0.5 kg) dark DME (or substitute brown sugar for a simple ale)
8 ounces (227 g) fresh gingerroot, chopped or bruised
½ ounce (14 g) low-alpha hops such as Willamette or Fuggle (optional)
½ ounce (14 g) fresh or ¼ ounce (7 g) dried mugwort or yarrow leaves (optional)

Juice of ½ small lemon, or 2 ounces (60 mL) lemon juice
Belgian or brewer's yeast, or barm

PROCESS

1. Clean the rhubarb thoroughly and remove all traces of leaves (which are toxic).
2. Bring the water to a barely rolling boil and stir in the extract or sugar.
3. Add the ginger and optional bittering herbs and boil for half an hour.
4. Cut off the heat and add the lemon juice and rhubarb.
5. Let the mixture cool, then transfer it to a fermentation jug (sliding the rhubarb in lengthwise) or bucket, and sprinkle the yeast over the surface.
6. Place a lid (if you're using a bucket) and airlock on the fermenter and let the mixture fully ferment.
7. Prime with 2 tablespoons of cane sugar, and bottle.

Grog

Once you've made some successful brews and have a good idea of what amounts, ratios, and combinations of ingredients tend to work, you're ready to cut loose, throw a bunch of stuff in a bucket or crock, and hope for the best. I'm not advising you to haphazardly mix random ingredients, but you can make some pretty interesting brews just by loosening up and having some fun. We know from archaeological evidence that the ingredients of what we now consider beer, mead, or wine would often be either brewed together or blended after fermentation into a type of grog. These grogs would often contain a large number of herbs. Once you've got enough brews going at once, or have various brews bottled, give grog a try. Sometimes when I'm racking multiple brews I'll take a bit of each from various stages of fermentation and pour them all in a fermentation bucket, jug, or carboy together. More often than not, the result is plenty drinkable. This is a good way to remove yourself from the restrictions of styles and categorization. Your grog may not taste quite like a beer, quite like a mead, quite like a wine, or quite like a cider, but if it's tasty, it's tasty . . . and it may just give you an idea for a recipe to repeat.

CHAPTER TEN

BUILD YOUR OWN BEER

ow that you know all about the history of beer, the plethora of stories and myths surrounding this most noble of beverages, and the wide variety of possible flavors and styles, it's time to get creative and build your own recipes (if you haven't already by substituting,

Feel free to personalize your equipment as well as your beer. I covered my mash tun in stickers and some old concert tickets. Yes, I have diverse taste (and am a bit of a metalhead and a product of the 1990s).

improvising, and experimenting with the recipes in chapter 9). It's best to not go overboard with improvisation initially, but a little tweaking here and there doesn't hurt if you don't have access to some of the ingredients or want to add or substitute sugars to adjust your brew's gravity. It's fun to go beyond this, but it's important to do so with the right mind-set. With a strong understanding of the proper ratio of sugar sources and flavoring/preservation herbs, you can consistently make flavorful beers with only the occasional bump in the road. Prepare your taste buds before traveling this route, though. When you start doing more than just tweaking, the results may vary wildly. It's not too often that I make a beer that goes into the compost pile, but sometimes something goes wrong or I learn not to overdo a particular ingredient. I could easily make the same excellent beers time and again, but I prefer to continually push the boundaries. Often I end up with beers that are very enjoyable, but sometimes I learn that I need to make some adjustments the next time around. Or one will be close but not quite there, so I blend it with another beer, ale, or mead that has a complementary flavor profile. Sometimes I don't care much for a beer (such as when it's a bit too sour, tart, or bitter for my palate), so I have someone else try it and find that they enjoy it.

You may find, as I have, that brewers who only follow the rote modern homebrewing practices give you looks of concern or even derision when you explain that you made a beer without hops, drank your beer while it was still fermenting, used little to no malt, didn't boil your wort, didn't bother with sanitizing chemicals, and so on, but as my friend Amber "Pixie" Shehan says: "Don't let the hyper-science-minded brewfolk intimidate you into thinking you have to have a degree to make a decent beer. . . . Just take the time to be thorough and really clean your fermentation and transfer gear well. Don't stress out, and I've found it helps for a very happy fermentation if you sing, laugh, or dance during the process!"

The Grain Bill: The Nitty-Gritty of Malt and Grain Selection

While there are many subtleties when it comes to grain selection, by following a fairly loose set of parameters you can be assured of a drinkable beer, even if it doesn't always quite come out the way you planned.

As you experiment with different grains, you'll become better tuned in as to how to manipulate your grain bill to meet specific goals for flavor profile, ABV, clarity, and other elements of a quality beer.

When putting together a grain bill—whether all grain or partial mash—the most critical element is ensuring you have a high degree of fermentable sugars. The majority of your grain bill should consist of either crushed grains, extract, or a sugar source such as cane sugar, honey, sorghum, or molasses. Your goal is to have enough sugars to ferment the starches into alcohol; otherwise you're just making a cereal gruel. Secondary to this are adjunct grains and other ingredients, which provide a degree of sugar content, but are primarily for flavoring and sometimes for other subtle effects, such as body and coloring. Your main fermentable malt is your base malt, and can sometimes be the only malt in the bill. Not all malts can be used as a sole base malt—only the ones that have the right amount of enzymes to convert starches to sugars. In most cases you will be using at least some adjuncts and/or extra sugar sources along with your base malt. If you're the scientific, detail-oriented type, there are mathematical formulas that can be found in many brewing books and online to help you calculate a highly efficient grain bill. If you're just starting out, or if you're like me and would rather work more through intuition, trial and error, and an understanding of the ingredients you're using, you can get away with not being super-efficient and mathematical and still make quality beer. A good way to start is to work from someone else's recipe or one of your own that you've found to be successful, and make small modifications to achieve subtly different flavor profiles. This is a good way to get a feel for how different levels of grain and other fermentables affect the final product. From there you can use your new-found knowledge to develop and fine-tune your own recipes. Keep in mind that all recipes will need to be adjusted somewhat, as each brewer's brewing system and other environmental parameters differ.

Here are the targets you will need to plan for in developing your grain bill, how most brewers approach planning for those targets, and how I find I operate when planning my own brews.

Gravity: This is one area where most brewing recipes stress getting as close to target as possible. The more sugars, the higher the gravity, and thus the higher the alcohol level. Personally, I'm not obsessed with brewing to style. I have a general idea of what types of flavors I want in the final product and sometimes a traditional style that I'm shooting for. If you want to brew to style, particularly if you're brewing for a competition, consider this factor strongly when calculating your grain bill.

Finished volume: This is the amount of final product you will have in your fermenter. For most homebrewers, this is 5 gallons (20 L), although amounts may vary. Remember that water will dilute the sugars, so the more you add, the lower the gravity. Also, you should always have at least ½ gallon (2 L) more water than your intended final volume pre-boil, as you will lose water due to evaporation. So when I'm calculating the grain bill for a 5-gallon recipe, I usually factor in 5½ gallons (22 L) of wort volume.

Fermentables: After selecting your grains based on the flavor profile you want, separate the fermentables from the flavoring adjuncts and determine how much you'll need to reach your target gravity (or thereabouts). I usually go by a previous recipe of my own or someone else's and choose base malts that I know have similar flavor profiles and starch-conversion potential. Sometimes, if I check the gravity level during the brewing process and feel I would like something with a bit higher gravity, I'll add some honey, molasses, or another sugar, usually while the wort is still hot to sterilize the new ingredient and ensure that it fully dissolves. Honey is sometimes an exception to this rule if I'm making a drink more akin to a mead and want the natural aroma and fermentation-enhancing properties of the honey.

Efficiency: When determining the amount of your fermentables—if you want to get specific rather than use your intuition—shoot for 100 percent of the amount of ingredients you need for your target gravity, and then add a bit. This can be up to 10 to 20 percent more, because unless you're working with extract only, you will never get the full sugar potential from your mashed grains. Different systems have differing efficiencies. Some brewers determine the level of efficiency for their system by dividing the total gravity they get from their mash runoff (wort) by the potential gravity of the grains used. However, these calculations can vary with each batch based on factors such as type of grain, environmental factors, accuracy of readings, and more. If you're a true math geek and enjoy this sort of sleuthing, there are plenty of sources for how to calculate efficiency as accurately as possible (*Designing Great Beers* by Ray Daniels is one). If you're willing to work with approximates (I warrant most of us are), the vast majority of homebrewers and professional craft brewers generally reach between 65 and 80 percent efficiency.[1] Start out by calculating 65 to 70 percent efficiency and go from there. I break out in hives when I see a mathematical formula, even a simple one, and have thus never calculated my efficiency. The beer doesn't seem to mind.

Flavor, color, and body: While choosing the appropriate malt and adjuncts for fermentability is key to determining alcohol level and, to a degree, flavor, adjunct grains are where the real art comes in. Even a difference of ¼ pound (113 g) in the amount of adjunct grains can have a significant effect on the final flavor, color, and body of the beer. Understand the basics of each adjunct and experiment (carefully) from there. Keep in mind that two similarly named malts from two malt manufacturers can give fairly different results. Unless you're really looking to fine-tune a specific, repeatable recipe, and have the time, money, and resources to access and experiment with malts from multiple manufacturers, don't drive yourself crazy over this. Just do your best and jump in!

Art, Science, and Intuition

When it comes down to it, brewers all employ their own individual ratio of art to science; some fall more on the art and intuition side, while others fall more on the science and math side. Brewers from both ends of the spectrum and everywhere in between make great beers. Talk to other brewers or read brewing books, articles, or blogs for different perspectives. It's great to learn how others go about brewing but in the end, go with what works best for you. Many of my early batches of beer were brewed from extract kits, but rarely did I use only what was in the kit; instead I would experiment with additional flavoring adjuncts and fermentables, and turned out plenty of great beers (and a few that required adjustments the next time around). With only extract and adjunct grains, you really don't need to worry about efficiency. When you start working with mash, it helps to have an understanding of fermentables and their potential gravity, but don't worry about shooting for precise targets unless you're aiming for a very specific style or flavor profile.

Whether you're brewing to your own flavor preferences, to re-create a historical recipe and see what happens, or to create something for which your friends and loved ones will worship you, you'll want to come up with an overarching goal for brewing that includes not only flavor but also body, visual appeal, distinctiveness, alcohol effect (not the effect after one too many, but the effect alcohol content has on individual sips), and overall experience. That may sound like a lot (I could definitely add more to the list), but you don't need to consider each of these individually when creating a recipe. Just think about the overall experience you would like from the beer and work backward from there. For instance, if you want a smooth, well-balanced beer that is thick, rich, and drinks like a meal, these are the types of ingredients you may want to consider for a 5-gallon (20 L) batch:

Primary grain: 8 to 10 pounds (4–5 kg) of a pale German or British malt.
Adjunct grain 1: ½ to ¾ pound (0.25–0.4 kg) of a dark, low-astringency malt such as Briess Blackprinz or a chocolate malt, or ¼ pound (113 g) of Muntons Black malt or another coffee-like malt if you want a bit of astringent bitterness for balance.
Adjunct grain 2: ¾ to 1 pound (0.4–0.5 kg) caramel malt.
Adjunct grain 3: ½ to ¾ pound (0.25–0.4 kg) cherrywood-smoked malt.
Adjunct grain 4: ¾ to 1 pound (0.4–0.5 kg) Carapils malt for increased head retention and body.
Adjunct sugar: 1 pound (0.5 kg) honey.
Flavoring ingredients: ½ to 1 ounce (14–28 g) maximum for any herb or spice. Double or triple any you want to be at the forefront.

For a lighter but still smooth ale, simply leave out the darker grains and perhaps include some additional light grains. Or if you want a strongly flavored, robust pale ale, use pale malt with some caramel, smoked, and maybe Carapils. Pick at least one flavor (perhaps hops or a strong bittering herb such as mugwort) to stand out from the rest. As you can see, even the slightest changes in ingredients other than the pale malt base can result in a drastically different beer. Be sure to take note of ingredients you plan on adding and how they might counteract with or be overwhelmed by another ingredient. If you're adding something for a reason other than flavoring (such as to increase the gravity or serve as a preservative), this may not matter. As in cooking, variation in ingredients can create a layered flavor and impart depth. However, if you throw in a whole lot of chili pepper (in cooking or brewing), you may end up with something that will make you sweat but any flavor nuances will be lost. It's often a good idea to use more than one malt, even for the base malt. If you're just employing malts to reach a certain gravity, the varieties you use don't matter too much, but if you're looking to add depth of flavor, pay attention. Adding a small amount of Munich to a pale beer will add a degree of maltiness and nuttiness, but the effect will be diminished (or unnoticeable) in beer with high levels of dark adjuncts.

Even subtle adjustments to how you use malted grains, extract, and other sugars can make a big difference in the final product, sometimes unintentionally unless you're the type of brewer who is extremely precise with measurements, temperatures, and other factors. For instance, when you're brewing with all grain, changes in mash temperature can lead to alterations in the beer's body and flavor. During mash-in, temperatures at the lower end of the spectrum (148°F/64°C) will lead to a lighter-bodied beer, whereas temperatures closer to the high end (156°F/69°C) will lead to a full-bodied beer. Staying between the two (152°F/67°C) will lead to a more medium-bodied beer. When brewing with extract, be sure to consider steeping specialty grains before adding the extract, as you can make some significant adjustments to flavor this way. Additionally, you can start the boil with only about one-quarter of the extract and save the rest for the last 10 to 15 minutes. This technique is known as late-extract addition, and is intended to result in a lighter-colored wort or to produce interesting new flavors.[2]

Letting Loose and Getting Funky

Even armed with basic knowledge and understanding of ingredient flavors and fermentability, there's nothing wrong with throwing caution to the wind. Practice witchcraft! Be an alchemist! Get medieval! Go Neolithic!

Of course you'll need to be prepared for some challenges to your taste buds, but this is where you can have the most fun. It's best to do 1-gallon (4 L) batches when you're going this wild, and to use ingredients that you haven't invested a lot of money or time into. Using up some of your malted grains or a couple of pounds of extract won't break the bank, and chances are good you'll create something plenty drinkable. Following are some suggestions on how to make an "informal" brew day quick, easy, and relaxing.

Sugar/malt selection: Use only cane sugar or brown sugar, or combine the two (or use extract for a more modern beer-like experience); or use a small amount of malted grains or extract blended with various other sugar sources to provide a bit of that grainy flavor and impart some other subtleties.

Flavoring and adjunct ingredients: Drop in bits of honey, molasses, sorghum, or even maple syrup for subtle adjustments to flavor and increased gravity. Also try various botanicals and spices, taking care to first understand flavor compatibility, bitterness levels, and medicinal properties/contraindications. Add fruit, berries, or fruit juice.

Yeast and fermentation: Don't be afraid to use bread yeast or wild ferment. Use the krausen of a new batch of beer or the lees of a recently racked or bottled batch of beer (or mead, cider, or other ferment) for yeast and nutrients. Experiment with fermenting at different temperatures to see if there is a flavor difference between similar recipes.

Cleanliness and preparation: Be clean but don't worry. That should be your mantra in general, but when you're brewing willy-nilly, just make sure you use equipment that has been cleaned recently or give it a quick rinse in hot water. I've thrown together some very quick, last-minute brews this way. It took very little time or thought and practically no preparation. I just heat some water, dissolve whatever sugars I have on hand, drop in some herbs and other ingredients, add whatever yeast is convenient, and plop it in a fermenter. Most times I turn out something drinkable; other times it's not bad but needs to be blended with something else. Or I use it for cooking.

Brewing process: Once you understand the different types of brewing processes available to the homebrewer, it's a great time to try out different variations. Try cold fermenting, low to no boil, long boils, varying mash temperatures, and any other variation you can think of. While ingredients will definitely play a part in the final flavor, how you brew with those ingredients will have an effect entirely its own.

Judging, Tasting, and Enjoying Your Beer

The final step in brewing your own beer is probably the best one—tasting it! I always feel a tingle of excitement and just a hint of trepidation upon tasting a new batch of beer. I know there's always the chance that something didn't turn out quite right, or that it didn't turn out right at all. Regardless, true to my personal philosophy of "I don't have to do it this way just because you say I do," I don't really follow any of the standard rules when it comes to tasting and judging beer. I know what works for me and that's all I'm concerned about. If you want to know how to really taste a beer to judge it for flavor characteristics, body, mouthfeel, and other factors, there are plenty of books and websites that will tell you how to do so properly. Or take a test to become a certified beer judge through the American Homebrewers Association's (AHA) Beer Judge Certification Program (BJCP) or a similar program. Just be sure to take into account when you're tasting historical or experimental beers that the flavor may not be what you'll expect, or necessarily like. If the latter is the case, take note of what you didn't like about it and make some adjustments next time.

In general, what I look for when I first taste a new beer is something along these lines:

- How does it pour? Does it seem kind of flat or does it fizz just the right amount? Does it gush and have too much of a head, or does it produce a nice, foamy head? Does this really matter if it tastes good?
- Once it's in the glass and I've allowed any head to dissipate, I look to see how the coloring turned out. This is only somewhat important in my mind, but it is good to take note of. I then hold it up to my nose and check the aroma. If CO_2 tickles my nose hairs, I give the carbonation a bit more time to die down. Aroma definitely has an effect on flavor, but I've had beers that didn't smell good yet went down just fine.
- Once I take a sip, I start with the overall effect. Does it initially hit me with a sense of satisfaction, or does the enjoyment sneak up on me? Does it start out "challenging" but then move on to "interesting" to eventually "not bad for what it is"? Or does it just plain not work for me?

- Whatever I come up with after the initial taste, I give it a moment, maybe take a sip of water, and then take a long, lingering sip, allowing it to flow across my tongue and hit all of my taste receptors. This is where I work to determine the factors that led to my initial thoughts. Can I taste too much of an ingredient? Not enough? Is it well balanced or not so well balanced? Does it taste like it picked up something during fermentation that has nothing to do with the ingredients or brewing process? Can I determine if any of the factors from the brewing methods I employed directly affected the flavor outcome?
- From here, hopefully it's good enough that I finish the glass and decide whether I'm desirous of another or if it makes me want something else. Truthfully, some beers are enjoyable enough after one glass but aren't really meant for more than one in a sitting. Some work better when paired with food. In general, though, I'm interested in the overall effect. Did it give me a sense of satisfaction or do I feel it needs something different next time? Was the alcohol level apparent? Would it have been better during a different season (light, refreshing beers work best in the summer and dark, heavy beers tend to drink better in the winter)? Finally, does it have a warming alcohol effect, does it have little perceivable alcohol, or is it a bit hot (too much booziness)?

Although I'm not a super-social person, I do try to get together with others and have them sample a new brew on occasion. This doesn't happen often, but when I have a brew I particularly like or one I'm not quite sure about I try to save some bottles to share with friends or bring to a get-together so I can get the opinion of an acquaintance or even a complete stranger. Sometimes the beers I like don't get the best reception from others, and sometimes beers I don't care for are well liked by more . . . sophisticated . . . palates. I try to take into account each person's overall personality and what I know about their taste preferences. Some people are very accustomed to modern beers or are really into hops, meaning most of what I produce won't be to their liking or they'll be just plain confused as to why anyone would want to make something like this. Others I know to be more adventurous or at least somewhat knowledgeable about brewing and fermentation history and the many nuances possible in fermented products. This is why I *always* brew for myself in the end. Why not please yourself and hope some like-minded folks will come along for the ride?

⟫⟶ ACKNOWLEDGMENTS ⟵⟪

There is no way I can thank everyone who helped this book come together, inspired portions of it, or just plain put up with me every time I had to say (or strongly imply), "Leave me alone; I'm working on a book." Not only did I take up vast amounts of time writing, rewriting, researching, and fact-checking, but the countless hours I spent brewing, racking, bottling, and cleaning (and cleaning, and cleaning . . .) made me into an even more reclusive recalcitrant than I already was. I can never show enough gratitude to my wife, Jenna, for taking care of dinner and kid-wrangling (and saving the dishes for me since it's usually mostly my mess anyway) while I worked late to finish portions of this book or had a brew or three I needed to focus on. And I must thank my daughters, Sadie and Maisie, for helping me realize that there's always time to let them sit on my lap and "help" me write my "Papa Drink" book. Then there are the countless friends and family whom I dare not mention for fear of leaving someone out (or be tempted to try to list them all since I've already given my editor a much longer manuscript than I had initially proposed).

And then there's my extended family: the many event organizers, vendors, speakers, publisher representatives, and other writers I mingle with as I travel to speak and teach. I wouldn't dare forget the attendees of my workshops and presentations, and folks whom I converse with as I'm roaming the grounds of events such as the Mother Earth News Fair. I always feel enlivened (and a bit exhausted) when I return from my travels, having been reminded that it's good to leave my Hobbit-hole once in a while for good friends, good food, and good brew. My immense gratitude goes to Susan Verberg for her assistance in digging up obscure historical information and brewing recipes, and to Amber "Pixie" Shehan and Devon Young for agreeing to be profiled. This book couldn't have happened without all of the good folks at Chelsea Green. Thanks to my editor, Michael Metivier, for keeping me from rambling too much, and to everyone else who helps design and distribute so many amazing books. I'm honored to be in your company. Finally, to those fortunate (?) few (namely Steven Cole and my brothers Nate and Zach) who taste tested my brews (including the not-so-good ones), I give my hearty thanks and a Viking *skål*!

TROUBLESHOOTING

Nothing ever goes as planned. Or at least that's how it sometimes seems in brewing. For the most part, with proper planning and attention to process, your brews will turn out as expected. However, things can go wrong, or sometimes they just go . . . different. Part of the fun of brewing is learning to understand and appreciate that not all of your troubles are necessarily a bad thing. Occasionally I'll have a brew that just turns out undrinkable, but often it's just different than I expected, or something that others like more than I do. This section is meant to help you troubleshoot some of the more common problems in brewing. There are many other subtle surprises that may or may not be problems. Read up, visit forums, and talk to other brewers when something problematic comes up that you don't find the answer for here.

Ferment Is Slow or "Stuck"

There are various factors that can cause a slow or weak fermentation. The usual suspects are: aeration, temperature, and water. Be sure to "splash" your wort by pouring it vigorously into the fermentation container, as this will help introduce oxygen important for yeast to thrive. You can also stir it vigorously with a long spoon. If there is no visible fermentation 24 hours after you've added yeast, try aerating again either by stirring or by pouring into a clean bucket and back into your fermenter. If you still get no fermentation, it could be because you either didn't use a viable yeast or didn't pay enough attention to the other two factors.

Temperature is a vital factor. Most yeasts, particularly ale yeasts, ferment best in a warm area, preferably no cooler than 70°F (21°C) and not much hotter. Fermentation will proceed faster in hotter temperatures, but this can also produce additional qualities you may or may not appreciate. Typical flavor "qualities" of a hot ferment are fruity, solvent-like (fingernail polish—yum!), and wine-like flavors. Use whatever method works best for you in a home environment to ensure a warm, but not too warm, environment. In cooler seasons, set the fermentation container near a heat source (but not too near) and rotate it occasionally to ensure even heating. Don't set the container directly on a cold floor, and wrap it with a blanket or sleeping bag to keep it cozy. In the summer position it where it won't cook. If you don't use air-conditioning, this can be tough. You may need to move it to different locations during different times of the day, but don't stress this too much. Just be sure it's kept from overly cool temperatures.

The final culprit, which can be the most frustrating, is water. Generally if you use tap water, all chlorine will dissipate with boiling. Some ferments, though, don't require boiling. Be sure to boil your tap water (even if it's filtered) before using it for a low-to-no-heat ferment, or be safe and use springwater. Also, take care that your water source doesn't have chloramine (see chapter 4). If you just can't get your wort to ferment, let it sit for a day or two (or as a last resort, bring it to a brief boil and cool it to the *proper* temperature), and pitch more yeast.

Poor Mash Yield or Set Mash (Slow Wort Runoff)

Unless you're an ultra-super-awesome brewer, you're rarely going to get much more than 80 to 90 percent efficiency in your mash yield. You want to draw as many sugars as you can from the malt without over-sparging, which can potentially lead to a husky, astringent flavor. I always keep honey, malt extract, or in some cases cane sugar on hand to help bring my gravity up if I don't get a great yield. Some possible culprits of poor mash yield are:

- Grain is ground too coarse. Try to achieve finely ground grains with the husk mostly intact without going as far as making flour.
- Incorrect temperature. This is unavoidable when you're brewing by ancient methods or by the cold-mash method. This is one reason early beers often contained high levels of honey as an additional fermentable.

Possible culprits of set mash are:

- Grains ground too fine, or not enough husks are intact. Sometimes patience and a lot of stirring will take care of this. For my setup, I sometimes carefully lift the filter a bit while moving the mash at the bottom around, or move mash away from the spigot. For grain bills that have a lot of sticky (wheat or unmalted) grains, be sure to add some rice husks. Adding some more hot water doesn't hurt, but don't add too much or you risk diluting the runoff. After you add it, try removing any fine flour that has turned into a sticky paste.

- Incorrect temperature. Again, this is unavoidable when you're brewing by ancient methods or by the cold-mash method. For conventional, modern recipes, try to keep things in the proper temperature range. Plan on taking more time for older recipes. Much of this time can simply be spent waiting. Give it a longer temperature rest, maybe 90 minutes to two hours. Many older and modern-traditional recipes call for soaking the grains overnight. This is where the true experimentalist/historical re-enactor in you comes out.

When you're working with all-grain recipes, you can only do the best you can do. Whether you're just starting out or have a few batches under your belt, try not to get frustrated. There are a lot of rewards to all-grain brewing, but there are also a lot more avenues by which things can fail to go as expected. This is coming from someone who often gets frustrated (likely unnecessarily) because I simply can't control things as much as I'd like. Practice lots of patience, and don't be afraid to cheat to make sure you end up with your ultimate goal, a tasty batch of brew.

Funky Flavors

The list of possible off flavors or aromas is fairly long and, as referenced previously, depends partially on individual taste preferences. I highlight a few here. Research further if there is a flavor you just can't figure out, or simply enjoy the idiosyncrasies of your brew.

SOUR

The most obvious culprit is lactobacillus contamination, but it's often hard to pin down exactly how it occurred. Cleanliness problems are the first place to check. Modern brewing dogma would tell you that you didn't *sanitize* well enough, but I would say that perhaps some of your equipment wasn't *cleaned* well enough. Again, it's hard to say with this one. Some of my brews where I've avoided using hops or other preservative botanicals go sour if not drunk fairly quick, as do some of my fruit and vegetable brews. Wish I could offer you a more clear solution for this one. Enjoy it as best you can, blend it with something else, and take extra care the next time around.

GOATY, BARNYARD, OR SWEATY SOCKS

None of these flavors sound particularly appealing, but in small amounts they can actually add to the complexity of a good brew. If it's just too much, this is another likely victim of lactobacillus contamination.

BUTTERY

Diacetyl is a chemical that is used to imitate butter flavors in processed foods. It can occur naturally in brewing and is an expected flavor for some styles. If you get it and don't mind it, don't worry about it. If you don't like it, give it some time before opening another bottle and it may dissipate. Some yeast strains and even malts will naturally produce this flavor, as will fermenting at warmer temperatures.

SKUNKY OR RUBBERY

Anyone who has traveled to Europe and enjoyed a beer there and then had the same beer at home (usually bottled in a green or clear bottle) knows this flavor. For instance, I enjoyed Heineken a great deal when I visited Holland but just can't get into it in the States. You will experience the same disparity in your brews if you let them become exposed to sunlight or even fluorescent lights after bottling. I haven't noticed any problems from brief exposure to fluorescents, but the best solution is to bottle primarily in dark brown bottles.

CIDERY

Not really a problem in my book but maybe a flavor you don't want in all of your brews. The common modern homebrewing maxim is that too much corn sugar or cane sugar will impart a cidery flavor, which is true. That's no reason to not use sugar as an adjunct, or the primary sugar source, though. Most simple ales will produce this flavor, I suppose, though I'm not sure I would describe a lot of my simple ales as cidery (although I have received comments that some of them have a nice fruity profile, even though I used no fruits). I've made grain-based beers where I got poor mash yield and used a substantial amount of sugar to compensate that turned out to be unique, quite flavorful beers.

Priming Problems (Under- or Over-Carbonation)

See Bottling and Priming for Carbonation in chapter 8 for information on priming. Priming problems are pretty simple to identify, and can in most cases be corrected, or at least put up with. Keep in mind first that many traditional beers, sahti for example, are drunk flat or very lightly carbonated. You may want to intentionally drink them this way to be authentic—or if a beer comes out a little flat, congratulate yourself on drinking a historically authentic beer. Overpriming and underpriming essentially come down to problems with too much or too little priming sugar, but this isn't always the case.

If you open a beer and it gushes or foams excessively, you likely either used too much sugar for the style and gravity level of the beer, bottled before fermentation was complete, or both. There's no real solution to this, other than opening each bottle very carefully, preferably outside (I would say over a sink were it not for the gusher I had once that shot straight to the ceiling), and with a glass on hand to carefully pour the brew into. If all of the bottles gush, try to finish them up as soon as possible, opening each with a towel wrapped around in case of explosion. If only some of the bottles gush, you likely had some residue in your bottle. When saving bottles for reuse, always be sure to clean them thoroughly directly after use, as dried residue can be tough to get out.

If your beer is flat or nearly flat, there are a few likely culprits:

- Not enough priming sugar. Use more next time, give the bottles time to ferment a bit more, or open the bottles, add ½ teaspoon of sugar to each, recap, and give them a few more weeks to carbonate.
- Not enough yeast left for bottle carbonation (for beers that have been left in the secondary fermenter for a long period). Repeat the above process, except with yeast rather than sugar.
- Yeast has become cold-shocked. While most beers and ales are best aged at cellar temperature (50 to 55°F/10–13°C), they should be left at a warmer temperature for 24 to 48 hours before being moved to cellar temperature if possible. You can move them to a

warmer temperature for a week or two and then back to the cellar in the hope of initiating carbonation.

I'm fully aware that most of these solutions sound like a real pain when working with, say, 50 or so bottles of beer—particularly when it's hard to tell which of the above issues is the culprit. I generally don't worry about it and take steps to avoid similar issues with future brews. One thing I'll often do if a beer doesn't have the level of carbonation I desire is to take a similar beer or one with a complementary flavor that has strong carbonation and simply blend them in a glass.

Haze

If the beer is a bit hazy and that bothers you, don't look at it or drink it from an opaque vessel. In rare cases haze may affect flavor, but there are likely other issues involved. When judging beers, haze is considered an issue depending on the style, but I don't concern myself with it. Most homebrews will have some degree of haze due to various factors. You can add gelatin or isinglass when priming to avoid this, or invest in a beer-filtration system. Or just have a drink and enjoy the haze.

Mold or Other Growths

Generally, if you follow strict cleanliness procedures, you won't experience any actual mold, particularly if you're fermenting primarily in an anaerobic/closed-container environment. Fermentation foam (krausen) forms a protective layer that keeps out contaminants during early stages of fermentation. As fermentation progresses, particularly if you have left the beer in its fermenter for several weeks, you may see a thin white film, or pellicle, form on the surface. This is a good sign, and should be left alone. This is a strain of yeast, *Brettanomyces* (see chapter 5), referred to by beer brewers as "the Brett" and by vintners as "Flor" (flower). Leave it alone and simply stir it in when priming. Although *Brettanomyces* can be intentionally added for a souring effect, I've had pellicle show up in a few beers and meads, and none have gone sour that I didn't intend to go sour.

BREWING GLOSSARY

Acetic acid: The acid that is produced when a fermentation turns to vinegar. Not to be confused with citric, malic, and tartaric acids, which can be used for balance.

Acetobacter: A ubiquitous airborne bacteria that can cause any alcohol ferment to metabolize into acetic acid given enough contact with oxygen.

Adjunct: Ingredients added to a mead, wine, or beer that aren't absolutely necessary, but will aid fermentation or provide a more complex flavor profile.

Aeration: The process of stirring the liquid in a vessel, swirling the vessel, or racking into another vessel to incorporate large amounts of oxygen. Necessary for initiating a wild fermentation or ensuring an active fermentation once fermentation commences. Also a technique for restarting a "stuck" fermentation.

Aerobic bacteria: Bacteria (such as acetobacter) that require oxygen to survive.

Airlock: A simple mechanism that allows carbon dioxide to escape a fermentation vessel while preventing outside air or flies, ants, and other bugs from entering.

Alcohol by volume (ABV): Percentage volume of alcohol per volume in mead, beer, or wine.

Ale: Depending on what era of history you're talking about, it's tough to find a definitive definition, but generally ales are top-fermented beers that ferment best in warmer temperatures.

All-grain beer: Beer that is brewed entirely from malted grains (sometimes along with some adjuncts), as opposed to malt-extract beers.

Alpha acid: A hop resin that imparts bitterness into beer when converted into iso-alpha acids through boiling (isomerization).

Anaerobic bacteria: Bacteria that do not require oxygen to survive.

Attenuation: Often referenced as a percentage, the degree to which yeast ferments the sugars in wort during fermentation, causing it to drop in specific gravity.

Backslopping: The process of initiating fermentation by incorporating a small amount of a previous active ferment into a new batch. See *barm, bug,* and *starter.*

Barm: A sample of actively fermenting beer that can be added to wort to initiate fermentation in a new brew, or saved for a future brew. See *backslopping, bug,* and *starter.*

Beer: See this book.

Bottle conditioning: Bottling beer or other alcoholic ferments before fermentation is complete (or, more commonly, by *priming* through the addition of a small amount of sugar, honey, or malt extract) to allow secondary fermentation in the bottle if carbonation is desired.

Bragot (also braggot, brag, bragio, brakkatt, or bracket): A mead-beer hybrid made with honey and malt. It was traditionally flavored with herbs and spices, and occasionally with hops.

Bug: Similar to *barm* or *backslop* in that a bug is an active ferment used to initiate future ferments. A bug is created intentionally as a starter using a small amount of liquid rather than being taken from a larger volume of an active ferment.

Carbonation: Carbon dioxide that is created by adding sugar or honey to a fermented liquid prior to bottling to initiate bubbling or "sparkle." Can also be created by cutting an active ferment off completely from outside air contact. Potentially dangerous if proper precautions aren't taken.

Carboy: A large glass or plastic vessel (5 gallons/20 L or larger) with a narrow neck designed specifically for brewing and winemaking. Similarly shaped smaller vessels can also be referred to as carboys, but more accurately as jugs.

Closed fermentation: Fermenting by cutting the beer off from outside air through an airlock so that only non-souring bacteria and yeast can thrive. See *anaerobic bacteria*.

Doughing in (or mashing in): The first step in all-grain brewing, in which ground malt is mixed with hot water.

Dry malt extract (sometimes dried malt extract): Usually referred to as DME, this is malt extract that has been dried into a powdered form and can be reconstituted by adding it to hot water.

Extract brewing: Brewing with liquid or dried extract rather than whole grains (although sometimes small amounts of grains are added for flavoring).

Fermentation: For alcohol-production purposes, the process by which sugar is broken down into carbon dioxide and alcohol through the addition of yeast. Other types of fermentation don't necessarily produce alcohol.

Flocculation: The process by which single yeast cells aggregate into clumps of thousands and drop to the bottom of the fermenter near the end of fermentation, resulting in clarified final product.

Grist: Crushed malt and adjuncts that have been blended with hot water for mashing.

Head (and head retention): Foam that rises at the top of a poured beer. Head retention is when some of the foam sticks around after most of the rest dissipates. This tends to happen more with thicker beers such as porters and stouts, but can be achieved with lighter beers as well.

Hulled/unhulled seeds: Unhulled grain seeds are required for sprouting/malting/germination of grains for grain-based ferments. Hulled seeds are those that have had the outer layers removed.

Hydrometer: A glass instrument that is used to measure the specific gravity of beer at the beginning of brewing and then again at the end. The difference between the two measurements can help you calculate the final product's alcohol level.

IBU (International Bittering Unit): A unit of measurement used to express a beer's bitterness by measuring the concentration of iso-alpha acids provided by hops in a finished volume of beer. In practical use it's really just a marketing term.

Krausen: The thick, puffy head of foam that forms on the surface of wort during the first few days of fermentation.

Lactic acid: An acid produced by bacteria (such as *Lactobacillus*) that can potentially "contaminate" and sour a beer during fermentation without proper cleaning of equipment and through extended open fermentation. Can be used intentionally in small amounts to provide various degrees of souring.

Lautering: The process of separating wort from spent grains produced during the mashing process.

Lauter tun: A vessel with a false bottom or straining mechanism and spigot used to strain sweet wort from spent grains after mashing.

Lees: Dead yeast cells that fall to the bottom of the brewing vessel as yeast devours sugar and enzymes to produce alcohol in mead or wine. For beer, it is called *trub*.

Liquid malt extract (LME): Wort that has been reduced to a sugary syrup that can be used for extract brewing.

Malt: Barley or other grains that have been germinated or sprouted, releasing enzymes that break down complex carbohydrates into simple carbohydrates, which can then be fermented into alcohol.

Malt extract: Liquid wort that has been condensed into a syrup or powder for reconstitution by homebrewers. The process requires less time and equipment than all-grain brewing, but is also less flexible in regard to recipe fine-tuning.

Mead: Any alcoholic beverage fermented primarily from honey. Bragot is a possible exception, as it is both a mead and a beer.

Mouthfeel: The sensation of consistency or viscosity when tasting an alcoholic beverage.

Must: Unfermented wine or mead, or "new wine."

Open fermentation: Sometimes confused with wild fermentation, the process of fermenting in a large-mouthed vessel covered by a porous cloth to provide aeration. Can be done with both wild and commercial yeast fermentations.

Pasteurization: Sterilization through heating. Commonly applied in modern times to remove most or all bacteria from honey, milk, or other substances.

Racking: Transferring (by siphoning or pouring through a funnel and strainer) beer and other alcoholic ferments between primary and secondary fermentation vessels, leaving behind *lees* (also *yeast cake*, or *trub*) gathered at the bottom of the fermenter and any solids. Stems from the Provençal (a dialect of Provence in southern France) *arracar*, which in turn stems from *raca*, meaning "stems and husks of grapes," or "dregs."

Reinheitsgebot: The purity law instituted in Bavaria in 1516 that subsequently was extended to all German brewers making beer that was to be consumed in Germany. The law requires the use of malted grains, hops, yeast, and water only.

Saccharification: The chemical process that occurs in converting the starches in malt into fermentable sugars.

Sanitization: Not to be confused with *sterilization*, the process of cleaning food and beverage preparation equipment to reduce the amount of microbial life. In homebrewing this is usually done with cleaning agents such as natural or human-made chemicals, but can also be accomplished with heat.

Sparge: The process of spraying spent grains with hot water to extract the remaining sugars from the husks.

Starter: A small amount of an actively fermenting liquid used to initiate fermentation. See *backslopping, barm,* and *bug.*

Sterilization: The use of high temperatures to eliminate bacteria from the surfaces of equipment used in the brewing process. It is near impossible to fully sterilize in a home environment, but we can eliminate the majority of "problem" bacteria via high heat such as the use of boiling or very hot water or air (including washing and drying equipment in a dishwasher). See *sanitization.*

Trub: The sediment at the bottom of a newly fermented batch of beer. See *lees.*

Vorlauf: The process of recirculating wort through the grain bed to draw out any remaining sugars.

Wild fermentation: A process for initiating a ferment solely through use of wild yeasts present in the air, or in a substrate such as organic botanicals or raw honey.

Wort: Unfermented beer, or more specifically the liquid created by drawing sugars from malt and adding hops, herbs, and other ingredients. In conventional brewing, wort is boiled before fermenting it, but traditionally this was not always the case. High in sugar and thus high in gravity, it will ferment into alcohol when yeast is added.

Yeast: Eukaryotic, single-celled fungal microorganisms that are catalysts for fermentation.

Zymurgy (or zymology): The scientific study of fermentation. A branch of applied chemistry, it is most often used in reference to brewing. *Zymurgy* is the name of the official magazine of the American Homebrewers Association (AHA).

INTERNET RESOURCES AND FUN STUFF

alehorn.com: Offering "Viking Drinking Horn Vessels and Accessories," this is a great site to visit if you want to drink your homebrewed ales and meads in an authentic historical vessel. They also have a blog covering topics such as homebrewing and life as a modern Viking. Most of their products can be custom-engraved. For the bearded brewer they also offer shaving and beard-care products made primarily from natural horn materials.

www.pixiespocket.com: This is my friend Amber Shehan's (profiled in chapter 1) website and blog. Amber, or "Pixie," blogs on brewing, cooking, foraging, natural health, tarot reading, and other pixie-like subjects. She also offers items for sale such as bulk herbs and infused honey.

nittygrittylife.com: As described in chapter 9, Devon is a homesteader and trained herbalist who blogs on various subjects including brewing, herbalism, food preservation, and fermentation.

www.growforagecookferment.com: Colleen Codekas, along with her husband, Joel, manages this blog. The name pretty much covers it all. I've picked up some great fermentation recipes and techniques here.

www.folkherbalism.com: The home of *Plant Healer* magazine and its associated Good Medicine Confluence festival. The subscription-based magazine (along with some free online content) provides a wealth of information on herbalism, combining folk knowledge with modern science. Magazine writers and festival presenters (including myself) also discuss fermentation and natural, plant-based brewing.

www.garshol.priv.no/blog: Also known as Larsblog, the blog is authored by Lars Marius Garshol, who travels extensively throughout Scandinavia to research Scandinavian farmhouse brewing. It's a top-notch and well-researched source on resurrecting ancient Nordic brewing traditions (which are still alive and well in parts of Scandinavia); I can't recommend it highly enough. Garshol is also the author of two books: *Gårdsøl—Det Norske ølet* (*Gårdsøl—the Norwegian Beer*) and *Lithuanian Beer—a Rough Guide*.

www.brewingnordic.com: Another great resource on traditional Nordic (and Baltic) brewing, the site's author, Mika Laitinen, is Finnish, and focuses his research on Finnish farmhouse brewing and related subjects. Laitinen is also the co-author of two books in Finnish: *Sahti: Elävä Muinaisolut* (*Sahti: Ancient Ale with a Living Tradition*) and *Rakkaudella Pantua: Kotioluen Uusi Tuleminen* (*Brewed with Passion: The Revival of the Homebrew*).

merryn.dineley.com: A great resource for information on re-creating ancient brewing and malting practices, it is run by experimental archaeologist Merryn Dineley, and brew-checked by her husband, Graham, a veteran brewer with 30 years under his belt.

www.witteklavervier.nl/us: A great resource on the history of beer and gruit from a Dutch perspective that is much more fact-based than much of the information out there. Many myths, particularly in regard to gruit, are debunked. The main website is in Dutch, but this link will take you to the English-language version.

www.milkthefunk.com: Initially starting as a Facebook group in March 2013 devoted to advanced and "funky" homebrewing topics, Milk the Funk (MTF) is now a "communal authority on alternative yeast and bacteria fermentation with an emphasis in alternative brewing techniques." A large portion of the website is a wiki devoted to brewing, and they offer a podcast and forum.

www.theyeastbay.com: Offering "artisanal yeast for the innovative brewer," this website is an impressive repository of all manner of rare and atypical yeast strains and bacteria. They offer their strains to homebrewers and craft brewers in a high-quality liquid culture.

brewingclassical.wordpress.com: The *Brewing Classical Styles* beer blog is "dedicated to everything associated with beer in ancient Greece and Rome" with a stated goal of cataloging "all Greek and Roman literary references to beer and beer-related things." Although this is primarily a historical and archaeological blog, the authors re-create recipes based on their translations of ancient Greek and Roman texts and offer tasting notes. They also review beers that have some sort of a classical bent. The main author and translator is Kyle A. Jazwa, while Kimberley van den Bergis serves as co-author and social media manager. Kyle has a PhD in archaeology and Kimberly was working toward her own as of the writing of this book. Both participate in regular digs in Greece, Italy, and the US.

www.themadfermentationist.com: Michael Tonsmeire's (aka "The Mad Fermentationist") website and blog *Experimental Homebrewing | Mad Science in the Pursuit of Great Beer* is a great resource for tips and ideas on brewing beyond the boundaries. Although Tonsmeire is a self-professed hop lover, his website is a great source for detailed descriptions of experimental homebrews. He is also a sour beer aficionado, and is author of the book *American Sour Beers* (Brewers Publications, 2014).

www.experimentalbrew.com: Drew Beechum and Denny Conn are authors of the book *Experimental Homebrewing: Mad Science in the Pursuit of Great Beer* (Voyageur

Press, 2014). The title pretty much sums up their website and podcast, in which they "yammer on about the wackiness of beer science and the science of beer wackiness!" The website has write-ups on their brewing experiments, recipes, a forum, and other resources. They are also authors of the book *Homebrew All-Stars* (Voyageur Press, 2016).

www.wildfermentation.com: An invaluable resource for information on fermenting food and beverages through the use of wild yeast and bacteria and natural ingredients. The site also has several forums for tips and troubleshooting. It is the companion site to Sandor Katz's book *Wild Fermentation* and his follow-up, *The Art of Fermentation.*

www.spruceontap.com: Sells spruce tips harvested sustainably from trees in the San Juan Mountain Range of southern Colorado, as well as yarrow, juniper berries, and other wild-harvested ingredients common to traditional Scandinavian and early American ales and meads. Additionally provides recipes and tips for brewing with these ingredients.

www.mountainroseherbs.com: Although there are many reputable websites that offer herbs for sale (and some not-so-reputable ones), this is the one I use. I like how dedicated they are to ethical, sustainable harvesting, organics, and fair trade.

www.beeradvocate.com: An online community with articles, forums, and other resources for all things beer and brewing. As described on the site, "Beer-Advocate (BA) is a global, grassroots network, powered by an independent community of enthusiasts and professionals dedicated to supporting and promoting better beer."

byo.com: The online home of *Brew Your Own* magazine. Like the magazine, it is chock-full of recipes, brewing tips, and information on the craft-beer industry.

zythophile.co.uk: British beer writer Martyn Cornell's website and blog. Full of information on beer and beer history, it's particularly useful for debunking beer myths.

www.jereme-zimmerman.com: My personal website, it *should* have regularly updated blogs and information on brewing, fermentation, and all kinds of other stuff. At least that was my plan when I started it. I've found that I'm terribly inconsistent at blogging. However, you will find a portfolio that I update as regularly as possible that contains links to my writings on brewing, fermentation, and the modern-homesteading, sustainability, and craft malting, brewing, and distilling movements. I also have a page with links to my videos and podcast/radio interviews, and other media. You can order my books through this site, and can contact me with questions or to arrange to have me speak. I can respond to inquiries as well, but please understand I may not always have time to respond, and there's only so much I can do to troubleshoot or explain process by email!

www.facebook.com/JeremeZimmYeti: My official Facebook page. I post events and share information that I hope will be useful to my followers here. My personal page (which I don't use much) is for my, well, personal stuff. If you try to friend me or contact me through that page you may very well never hear from me.

www.facebook.com/vikingnerds: A fun little page I run with my good friend Dave Brown. We share goofy (and sometimes serious) Viking- and brewing-related stuff and sell our tabletop game Don't Fall in the Mead Hall, which lets you emulate a bunch of Vikings drinking, throwing chairs, and doing other Viking stuff.

www.youtube.com/vikingnerds: Lots of goofy, strange videos but also some brewing videos. As of the writing of this book, we have been focusing on mead but there very well may be some beer-brewing videos in the future.

www.thegamecrafter.com/designers/viking-nerds: At present, the best place to purchase Don't Fall in the Mead Hall, along with any accessories, expansions, and other games we publish. There's nothing like drinking a homebrewed ancient beer from a drinking horn or tankard while pretending to be a Viking.

steader.com: A subscription-based skill-sharing website with videos filmed by professional videographers of in-depth homesteading-related courses presented by experts in their field. I may even have some videos on there!

⟫⟶ NOTES ⟵⟪

Introduction: Zen and the Art of Yeti Brewing

1. John Bickerdyke, *The Curiosities of Ale & Beer* (London: Springer, first published in 1889; republished in 1965), 2.

Chapter One: A History of Ale and Beer

1. Andrew Boorde, *The fyrst boke of the introduction of knowledge made by Andrew Borde, of physycke doctor. A compendyous regyment; or, A dyetary of helth made in Mountpyllier* (London: The Early English Text Society, 1995), 256.
2. Christine P. Rhodes, ed., *The Encyclopedia of Beer* (New York: Henry Holt, 1995), 71.
3. Rhodes, *The Encyclopedia of Beer*, 30.
4. John Bickerdyke, *The Curiosities of Ale & Beer* (London: Springer, first published in 1889: republished in 1965), 6–7.
5. Ann Hagen, *A Second Handbook of Anglo-Saxon Food and Drink: Production and Distribution* (Norfolk, UK: Anglo-Saxon Books, 1995), 205.
6. Hagen, *A Second Handbook of Anglo-Saxon Food and Drink*, 206–07.
7. Hagen, *A Second Handbook of Anglo-Saxon Food and Drink*, 207.
8. Iain Gately, *Drink: A Cultural History of Alcohol* (London: Gotham Books, a member of the Penguin Group, 2008), 3–6.
9. Patrick E. McGovern, *Uncorking the Past: The Quest for Wine, Beer, and Other Alcoholic Beverages* (Berkeley, Los Angeles, and London: University of California Press, 2009), 141–42.
10. Solomon H. Katz and Mary M. Voigt, "Bread and Beer: The Early Use of Cereals in the Human Diet," *Expedition* 28, no. 2 (1986): 27.
11. Katz and Voigt, "Bread and Beer," 27.
12. Dane Hucklebridge, *The United States of Beer: A Freewheeling History of the All-American Drink* (New York: HarperCollins, 2016), 192–94.
13. Patrick E. McGovern, *Ancient Brews: Rediscovered and Re-Created* (New York: W. W. Norton & Company, 2017), 210.
14. McGovern, *Ancient Brews*, 212.
15. Jack Lazor, *The Organic Grain Grower* (White River Junction, VT: Chelsea Green, 2013), 113.
16. Neil MacGregor, *A History of the World in 100 Objects* (New York: Viking Penguin, a member of the Penguin Group, 2011), 51.
17. MacGregor, *A History of the World in 100 Objects*, 37.
18. McGovern, *Uncorking the Past*, 146.
19. Gately, *Drink: A Cultural History of Alcohol*, 38–40.
20. Gately, *Drink: A Cultural History of Alcohol*, 51–54.

21. McGovern, *Uncorking the Past*, 144–45, 152–53.

22. Gregg Smith, *Beer: A History of Suds and Civilization from Mesopotamia to Microbreweries* (New York: Avon, 1995), 21–23.

23. Hucklebridge, *The United States of Beer*, 26.

24. Ian Spencer Hornsey, *A History of Beer and Brewing* (Cambridge, UK: Royal Society of Chemistry, 2003), 534–36.

25. Roel Mulder, "Further Notes on the Essence of Gruit: An Alternative View," *Brewery History: The Journal of the Brewery History Society* 169 (2017): 73.

26. Frederik Ruis, "A Note on the Essence of Gruit," *Brewery History: The Journal of the Brewery History Society* 166 (2016): 51.

27. Mulder, "Further Notes on the Essence of Gruit," 74.

28. Ruis, "A Note on the Essence of Gruit," 52.

29. Ruis, "A Note on the Essence of Gruit," 50.

30. Justyna Wubs-Mrozewicz, "Hopped Beer as an Innovation: The Bergen Beer Market around 1200–1600 in the European Context," in *Trade, Diplomacy and Cultural Exchange*, ed. Hanno Brand (Hilversum, Netherlands: Uitgeverij Verloren, 2005), 155–56.

31. Hucklebridge, *The United States of Beer*, 28–30.

32. Hucklebridge, *The United States of Beer*, 30.

33. Frederik Ruis, "True gruitbeer," Witte Klavervier, www.witteklavervier.nl/us/history/myths-about-beer/true-gruitbeer.

34. Gavin D. Smith, *Beer: A Global History* (London: Reaktion Books, 2014), 54.

35. Hucklebridge, *The United States of Beer*, 30.

36. Hucklebridge, *The United States of Beer*, 21–22.

37. Judith M. Bennett, *Ale, Beer, and Brewsters in England: Women's Work in a Changing World, 1300–1600* (New York: Oxford University Press, 1996), 34–36.

38. Hucklebridge, *The United States of Beer*, 51–65.

39. D. Peris, et al., "Complex Ancestries of Lager-Brewing Hybrids Were Shaped by Standing Variation in the Wild Yeast *Saccharomyces eubayanus*," *PLOS Genetics* 12, no. 7 (2016).

40. Gately, *Drink: A Cultural History of Alcohol*, 315.

41. Gately, *Drink: A Cultural History of Alcohol*, 247–48.

42. Gately, *Drink: A Cultural History of Alcohol*, 317–18.

43. Kat Eschner, "How Some Breweries Survived Prohibition," *Smithsonian*, April 7, 2017, www.smithsonianmag.com/smart-news/how-some-breweries-survived-prohibition.

44. Hucklebridge, *The United States of Beer*, 254–57.

45. Steve Hindy, *The Craft Beer Revolution: How a Band of Microbrewers Is Transforming the World's Favorite Drink* (Basingstoke, UK: Palgrave Macmillan, a division of St. Martin's Press, 2014), 9.

46. Hindy, *The Craft Beer Revolution*, 33.

Chapter Two: Stories, Folklore, and Feasting Traditions

1. Ian Spencer Hornsey, *A History of Beer and Brewing* (Cambridge, UK: Royal Society of Chemistry, 2003), 75–76.

2. Hornsey, *A History of Beer and Brewing*, 81–82.

3. Black, Cunningham, Robson, and Zólyomi, *The Literature of Ancient Sumer* (Oxford, UK: Oxford University Press, 2004), 297.

4. Johanna Stucky, "Nin-Kasi: Mesopotamian Goddess of Beer," *Cross-Quarterly for the Goddess Woman* 6, no. 1 (Samhain 2006).

5. Samuel Noah Kramer, ed., *Mythologies of the Ancient World* (Garden City, NY: Anchor Books, 1961), 115–16.

6. Peter Damerow, trans., from "Sumerian Beer: The Origins of Brewing Technology in Ancient Mesopotamia," *Cuneiform Digital Library Journal* 2 (2012).

7. Black, Cunningham, Robson, and Zólyomi, *The Literature of Ancient Sumer*, 330–33.

8. Joshua J. Mark, "Beer in Ancient Egypt," *Ancient History Encyclopedia*, March 16, 2017, www.ancient.eu/article/1033/beer-in-ancient-egypt.

9. Mark, "Beer in Ancient Egypt."

10. Bo Almqvist, *Viking Ale: Studies on Folklore Contacts Between the Northern and the Western Worlds* (Aberystwyth, Wales, UK: Boethius Press, 1991), 66–67.

11. Almqvist, *Viking Ale*, 65–67.

12. Almqvist, *Viking Ale*, 67.

13. Robert Louis Stevenson, *Ballads* (London: Chatto & Windus, 1895).

14. David MacRitchie, "Memories of the Picts," *The Scottish Antiquary; or, Northern Notes and Queries* 14, no. 55 (1900): 121–22.

15. MacRitchie, "Memories of the Picts," 124.

16. MacRitchie, "Memories of the Picts," 128.

17. Almqvist, *Viking Ale*, 80.

18. Almqvist, *Viking Ale*, 8.

19. Stephen Harrod Buhner, *Sacred and Herbal Healing Beers* (Boulder, CO: Brewers Publications, 1998), 28.

20. "Heather Honey," *Honey Traveler* (blog), www.honeytraveler.com/single-flower-honey/heather-honey.

21. Gwyn Jones and Thomas Jones, tr., *The Mabinogion* (London: Dent, 1949; reprinted in 1966), 115.

22. Andrew Breeze, "What Was 'Welsh Ale' in Anglo-Saxon England?," *Neophilologus* 88, no. 2 (2004): 300–301.

23. W. F. Kirby, trans., *Kalevala: The Land of Heroes* (London: J. M. Dent & Sons 1907; reprinted, New York: E. P. Dutton, 1961), 228–29.

24. Kirby, *Kalevala*, 229.

25. John Martin Crawford, trans., *The Kalevala: The Epic Poem of Finland* (New York: John B. Alden, 1888), 312.

26. John Bickerdyke, *The Curiosities of Ale & Beer* (London: Springer, first published in 1889; republished in 1965), 232.

27. *Online Etymology Dictionary*, www.etymonline.com.

28. Martyn Cornell, "Bride Ale—Too Many of You Are Getting This Wrong," *Zythophile*, November 17, 2010, zythophile.co.uk/2010/11/17/bride-ale-too-many-of-you-are-getting-this-wrong.

29. Bickerdyke, *The Curiosities of Ale & Beer*, 280–81.

Chapter Three: Grain

1. Merryn Dineley, "Who Were the First Maltsters?: The Archaeological Evidence for Floor Malting," *Brewer and Distiller International*, February 2016: 36.

2. Jack Lazor, *The Organic Grain Grower* (White River Junction, VT: Chelsea Green, 2013), 237–38.

3. Gene Logsdon, *Small-Scale Grain Raising* (White River Junction, VT: Chelsea Green, 2009), 157.

4. Dave Thomas, *The Craft Maltsters' Handbook* (Hayward, CA: White Mule Press, a division of the American Distilling Association, 2014), 15–17.
5. Lazor, *The Organic Grain Grower*, 276–77.
6. Thomas, *The Craft Maltsters' Handbook*, 2.
7. William Harrison, Description of Elizabethan England, 1577 (from Holinshed's Chronicles), chapter 6: "Of the Food and Diet of the English," from Modern History Sourcebook, Fordham University, sourcebooks.fordham.edu/mod/1577harrison-england.asp.
8. John Bickerdyke, *The Curiosities of Ale & Beer* (London: Springer, first published in 1889; republished in 1965), 49.
9. John Mallett, *Malt: A Practical Guide from Field to Brewhouse* (Boulder, CO: Brewers Publications), 31.
10. Amy Halloran, *The New Bread Basket* (White River Junction, VT: Chelsea Green, 2015), 175–88. Additional information procured during a phone interview with Andrea on November 30, 2017, and through subsequent email conversations.

Chapter Four: Water

1. William Ellis, *The London and Country Brewer* (London: Half Moon and Seven Stars, 1736), 24.
2. Seth C. Rasmussen, *The Quest for Aqua Vitae: The History and Chemistry of Alcohol from Antiquity to the Middle Ages* (Fargo, ND: Springer, 2014), 2.
3. John Palmer and Colin Kaminski, *Water: A Comprehensive Guide for Brewers* (Boulder, CO: Brewers Publications, 2013), 146.
4. Ann Hagen, *A Second Handbook of Anglo-Saxon Food and Drink: Production and Distribution* (Norfolk, UK: Anglo-Saxon Books, 1995), 205.
5. Pete Brown, *Miracle Brew* (White River Junction, VT: Chelsea Green, 2017), 104.
6. Brown, *Miracle Brew*, 105–6.
7. Brown, *Miracle Brew*, 106–7.
8. Gregg Smith, *Beer in America: The Early Years—1587–1840* (Boulder, CO: Siris Books, an imprint of Brewers Publications, 1998), 39.
9. Iain Gately, *Drink: A Cultural History of Alcohol* (London: Gotham Books, a member of the Penguin Group, 2008), 232.
10. Gately, *Drink: A Cultural History of Alcohol*, 231.
11. Gately, *Drink: A Cultural History of Alcohol*, 301–02.
12. Brown, *Miracle Brew*, 24–27.
13. Brown, *Miracle Brew*, 192–93.
14. "Water Treatment Using Carbon Filters: GAC Filter Information," Minnesota Department of Health, www.health.state.mn.us/divs/eh/hazardous/topics/gac.html.
15. Randy Mosher, *Radical Brewing: Recipes, Tales & World-Altering Meditations in a Glass* (Boulder, CO: Brewers Publications, 2004), 56.
16. Charlie Papazian, *The New Complete Joy of Homebrewing* (New York: Avon Books, 1991), 111.
17. Mosher, *Radical Brewing*, 26–27.
18. Ray Daniels, *Designing Great Beers* (Boulder, CO: Brewers Publications, 1996 and 2000), 66.
19. Mosher, *Radical Brewing*, 55.

Chapter 5: Yeast

1. Pete Brown, *Miracle Brew* (White River Junction, VT: Chelsea Green, 2017), 188–89.
2. Jennifer McDowall, "Enzymes of Glycolysis," InterPro, www.ebi.ac.uk/interpro/potm/2004_2/Page1.htm.

3. Charles Darwin, *The Descent of Man, and Selection in Relation to Sex* (New York: D. Appleton, 1896), 7.

4. Patrick E. McGovern, *Ancient Brews: Re-Discovered and Re-Created* (New York: W. W. Norton & Company, 2017), 10–11.

5. "barm (n.)," *Online Etymology Dictionary*, www.etymonline.com/word/barm.

6. Odd Nordland, *Brewing and Beer Traditions in Norway: The Social Anthropological Background of the Brewing Industry* (Gjovik, Norway: Mariendals Boktrykkeri, 1969), 252–54.

7. Merryn Dineley and Graham Dineley, "Neolithic Ale: Barley as a Source of Malt Sugars for Fermentation," chapter 13 in Andrew S. Fairbairn, *Plants in Neolithic Britain and Beyond* (Oxford, UK: Oxbow Books, 2000).

8. Merryn Dineley, "Big Pots: Fermentation and Storage," *Ancient Malt and Ale: An Archaeologist, a Brewer and a Blog About How the Ale Was Made* (blog), July 17, 2016, merryn.dineley.com/2016 /07/big-pots-fermentation-and-storage.html.

9. Jeff Sparrow, *Wild Brews: Beer Beyond the Influence of Brewer's Yeast* (Boulder, CO: Brewers Publications, 2005), 105.

10. Sparrow, *Wild Brews*, 108.

11. Sparrow, *Wild Brews*, 109.

12. Sandor Katz, *The Art of Fermentation* (White River Junction, VT: Chelsea Green, 2012), 249.

13. Ray Daniels, *Designing Great Beers* (Boulder, CO: Brewers Publications, 1996 and 2000), 112.

14. Charlie Papazian, *The New Complete Joy of Homebrewing* (New York: Avon Books, 1984 and 1991).

Chapter Six: Hops

1. Gavin D. Smith, *Beer: A Global History* (London: Reaktion Books, 2014), 13.

2. Laura Ten Eyck and Dietrich Gehring, *The Hop Grower's Handbook* (White River Junction, VT: Chelsea Green, 2015), 15.

3. Ten Eyck and Gehring, *The Hop Grower's Handbook*, 16–17.

4. Ann Hagen, *A Second Handbook of Anglo-Saxon Food and Drink: Production and Distribution* (Norfolk, UK: Anglo-Saxon Books, 1995), 210.

5. Dr. Gay Wilson, "Plant Remains from the Graveney Boat and the Early History of *Humulus Lupulus* L. in W. Europe," *New Philologist* 75, no. 3 (1975): 637–38.

6. Mika Rissanen (author), Juha Tahvanainen (author), and Ruth Urbom (translator), *Down Beer Street: History in a Pint Glass* (London: Souvenir Press, 2016), 38.

7. Martyn Cornell, "A Short History of Hops," *Zythophile*, November 20, 2009.

8. "The Letters of John Wesley," Wesley Center Online, wesley.nnu.edu/john-wesley/the -letters-of-john-wesley/wesleys-letters-1789b.

9. Ten Eyck and Gehring, *The Hop Grower's Handbook*, 93.

10. Ten Eyck and Gehring, *The Hop Grower's Handbook*, 94–95.

11. Ten Eyck and Gehring, *The Hop Grower's Handbook*, 22.

12. Ten Eyck and Gehring, *The Hop Grower's Handbook*, 22.

13. *New Crops and Organics*, North Carolina State Extension, newcropsorganics.ces.ncsu.edu /specialty-crops/nc-hops.

14. Ten Eyck and Gehring, *The Hop Grower's Handbook*, 37.

Chapter Seven: Flavoring Ingredients and Adjuncts

1. John Hull Brown, *Early American Beverages* (New York: Bonanza Books by arrangement with Charles E. Tuttle, 1966), 29.

2. William Ellis, *The London and Country Brewer, The Seventh Edition* (London: Printed for T. Astley and sold by R. Baldwin, 1759), 37–38.

3. "St. John's Wort," National Center for Complementary and Integrative Health, nccih.nih .gov/health/stjohnswort/ataglance.htm.

4. Kate Cummings, "Sassafras Tea: Using a Traditional Method of Preparation to Reduce the Carcinogenic Compound Safrole" (master's thesis, Clemson University, 2012), 1.

5. Mika Laitinen, January 31, 2018, comment on "Sahti Recipe and Farmhouse Brewing Tips," *Brewing Nordic*, https://www.brewingnordic.com/farmhouse-ales/sahti-recipe/ #comment-740.

6. Patrick E. McGovern, *Uncorking the Past: The Quest for Wine, Beer, and Other Alcoholic Beverages* (Berkeley, Los Angeles, and London: University of California Press, 2009), 144–45.

7. McGovern, *Uncorking the Past*, 37.

8. Gregg Smith, *Beer in America: The Early Years—1587–1840* (Boulder, CO: Siris Books, an imprint of Brewers Publications, 1998), 132–33.

9. Stanley Baron, *Brewed in America: A History of Beer and Ale in the United States* (Boston: Little, Brown, 1962), 17.

10. Baron, *Brewed in America*, 95.

11. Iain Gately, *Drink: A Cultural History of Alcohol* (London: Gotham Books, a member of the Penguin Group, 2008), 142–43.

12. Sandor Katz, *The Art of Fermentation* (White River Junction, VT: Chelsea Green, 2012), 253.

13. McGovern, *Uncorking the Past*, 253.

14. Morris J. Bitzer, Extension Specialist, "Sweet Sorghum for Syrup" (Cooperative Extension Service, University of Kentucky College of Agriculture); reviewed by Morris Bitzer, Extension Specialist (issued 2002, revised 2005, revised 2009); reviewed by Todd Pfeiffer, Professor (revised 2013), www2.ca.uky.edu/agcomm/pubs/agr/agr122/agr122.pdf.

Chapter Eight: Brewing Techniques

1. Pascal Baudar, *The Wildcrafting Brewer: Creating Unique Drinks and Boozy Concoctions from Nature's Ingredients* (White River Junction, VT: Chelsea Green, 2018), 37.

2. Wulf Schiefenhövel and Helen M. Macbeth, *Liquid Bread: Beer and Brewing in Cross-Cultural Perspective* (New York: Berghahn Books, 2011), 47–54.

3. Billy Quinn and Declan Moore, "Ale, Brewing and Fulacht Fiadh," *Archaeology Ireland* (Winter 2007).

4. Quinn and Moore, "Ale, Brewing and Fulacht Fiadh."

5. Odd Nordland, *Brewing and Beer Traditions in Norway: The Social Anthropological Background of the Brewing Industry* (Gjovik, Norway: Mariendals Boktrykkeri, 1969), 173.

Chapter Nine: Recipes

1. Phil Markowski, *Farmhouse Ales: Culture and Craftsmanship in the Belgian Tradition* (Boulder, CO: Brewers Publications, 2004), 8.

2. Markowski, *Farmhouse Ales*, 11.

3. Randy Mosher, *Radical Brewing: Recipes, Tales & World-Altering Meditations in a Glass* (Boulder, CO: Brewers Publications, 2004), 274.

4. Ann Hagen, *A Second Handbook of Anglo-Saxon Food and Drink: Production and Distribution* (Norfolk, UK: Anglo-Saxon Books, 1995), 216.

5. Hagen, *A Second Handbook of Anglo-Saxon Food and Drink*, 216.

6. Andrew Breeze, "What Was 'Welsh Ale' in Anglo-Saxon England?," *Neophilologus* 88, no. 2 (2004): 299–301.

7. Mika Laitinen, "Sahti and Related Ancient Farmhouse Ales," *Brewing Nordic*, August 2016, www.brewingnordic.com/farmhouse-ales/ancient-homebrew-sahti.

8. Ilkka Sirén, "Sahti, the Ancient Beer of Finland, Is Not for Beginners," *Vice Munchies*, August 10, 2016, munchies.vice.com/en_us/article/xymvnj/sahti-the-ancient-beer-of-finland-is-not-for-beginners.

9. Odd Nordland, *Brewing and Beer Traditions in Norway: The Social Anthropological Background of the Brewing Industry* (Gjovik, Norway: Mariendals Boktrykkeri, 1969), 130–31.

10. Nordland, *Brewing and Beer Traditions in Norway*, 134.

11. Nordland, *Brewing and Beer Traditions in Norway*, 216–19.

12. Laitinen, "Sahti and Related Ancient Farmhouse Ales."

13. Walter Coraza Morveli, "Frutillada, the Special Drink of Cuzco's Carnival," *Cuzco Eats*, February 11, 2015, cuzcoeats.com/frutillada-the-special-drink-of-cuzcos-carnival.

14. Andrew Moore, *Pawpaw: In Search of America's Forgotten Fruit* (White River Junction, VT: Chelsea Green, 2015), 3.

Chapter Ten: Build Your Own Beer

1. Ray Daniels, *Designing Great Beers* (Boulder, CO: Brewers Publications, 1996 and 2000), 29.

2. Brew Your Own, *The Brew Your Own Big Book of Homebrewing* (Minneapolis: Voyageur Press, an imprint of Quarto Publishing Group, 2017), 149.

INDEX

Note: Page numbers in *italics* refer to photographs and figures; page numbers followed by *t* refer to tables.

Index

ABOUT THE AUTHOR

Jenna Zimmerman

Jereme Zimmerman is a writer and fermentation revivalist who lives in Berea, Kentucky, with his wife, Jenna, and daughters Sadie and Maisie. He writes for various sustainability, homesteading, and farming mags, and travels nationwide to present on topics such as fermentation, natural and holistic homebrewing, modern homesteading, and sustainable living. He is an avid fermenter of pretty much everything and researches extensively into traditional fermentation practices in order to revive lost food arts and to educate people on how to preserve food using traditional, natural, and healing ingredients and techniques. His first book, *Make Mead Like a Viking*, was published in 2015, and was translated into German as *Met Brauen wie ein Wikinger* in 2016.

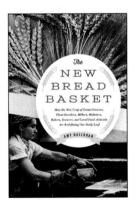
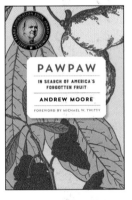